New Property in International Law

OXFORD MONOGRAPHS IN INTERNATIONAL LAW

The aim of this series is to publish important and original pieces of research on all aspects of international law. Topics that are given particular prominence are those which, while of interest to the academic lawyer, also have important bearing on issues which touch the actual conduct of international relations. Nonetheless the series is wide in scope and includes monographs on the history and philosophical foundations of international law.

RECENT TITLES IN THE SERIES

Overlapping Individual and Interstate Claims in International Law
Jessica Howley

Party Status to Armed Conflict in International Law
Alexander Wentker

The Identity of Governments in International Law
Niko Pavlopoulos

Access to Courts for Asylum Seekers and Refugees
State Obligations under the 1951 Refugee Convention
Emma Dunlop

International Law Obligations on Climate Change Mitigation
Benoit Mayer

Coastal State Jurisdiction over Living Resources in the Exclusive Economic Zone
Camille Goodman

International Law and Corporate Actors in Deep Seabed Mining
Joanna Dingwall

The Concept of an International Organization in International Law
Lorenzo Gasbarri

Necessity and Proportionality and the Right of Self-Defence in International Law
Chris O'Meara

Neutrality in Contemporary International Law
James Upcher

Geographical Change and the Law of the Sea
Kate Purcell

New Property in International Law

JEAN HO

Associate Professor of Law, National University of Singapore, Singapore

OXFORD
UNIVERSITY PRESS

OXFORD
UNIVERSITY PRESS

Great Clarendon Street, Oxford, OX2 6DP,
United Kingdom

Oxford University Press is a department of the University of Oxford.
It furthers the University's objective of excellence in research, scholarship,
and education by publishing worldwide. Oxford is a registered trade mark of
Oxford University Press in the UK and in certain other countries

Published in the United States of America by Oxford University Press
198 Madison Avenue, New York, NY 10016, United States of America

British Library Cataloguing in Publication Data

Data available

Library of Congress Control Number: 2024942312

ISBN 9780192873439

DOI: 10.1093/9780191976117.001.0001

Printed and bound by
CPI Group (UK) Ltd, Croydon, CR0 4YY

MIX
Paper | Supporting
responsible forestry
FSC® C013604
FSC
www.fsc.org

For Mom & Pops

toujours

Series Editor Preface

Property is a municipal legal institution *par excellence*, not an institution of international law. Natural or legal persons never own corporeal or incorporeal goods by unmediated operation of international law. Their right of ownership is always a municipal legal right, which is to say a right under the law of some state. For its part, what a state enjoys under international law is not ownership of territory (or of its superjacent airspace or territorial sea) or of the natural resources of the exclusive economic zone or continental shelf but instead sovereignty or sovereign rights over the same, comprehending the right under international law to regulate with respect to the territory and resources, including the right to regulate ownership of land in the territory and of the resources. Nor, for that matter, does international law deem the high seas and their fish the property of all persons or none. Rather, it stipulates that no state may lawfully purport to subject any part of the high seas to its sovereignty and that all states have the right for their nationals to fish on the high seas, the latter right implicitly encompassing the right to regulate ownership of any fish caught by those nationals on the high seas.

Yet while property rights are rights under municipal, not international, law, many rules of international law, both customary and treaty based, refer or otherwise relate to property, some of them to property rights. These rules specify, variously, what states, individuals, or others must, must not, or may do in relation to given property or property rights. In this sense, it can be said that property is an object of international legal regulation.

The main thrust of Jean Ho's *New Property in International Law* is that, as an object of international legal regulation, property lacks 'defining attributes' reflective of coherent principle and that consequently international law is currently 'unfit for the purpose of new property regulation' (ie for the regulation of the use of or interference with 'newer forms of property' that 'def[y] traditional conceptions of property which revolve around the private, individual ownership of tangible things'). In response to what she calls 'an intellectual void', Dr Ho distils from a selection of major legal traditions four 'core attributes' of property to serve as 'criteria for identifying new property in international law'. She then sets about seeking to prove her main thrust and to illustrate the application of her criteria by reference to what she identifies as 'three distinctive and discrete categories of new property', namely 'cultural property'; the so-called 'common property', referring to resources in areas over which states are prohibited under international law from asserting sovereignty; and what she labels 'contingent property', by which she means a corporeal or incorporeal thing the status of which as property 'depend[s] on the context in which its use or interference [with] is being considered'. The final substantive chapter of the book 'addresses the enforcement of property rights in international law across the three different categories of new property'.

New Property in International Law is wide-ranging, original, and provocative. Like most good products of independence of mind, it will elicit agreement and disagreement alike. Either way, it will stimulate. Written with confidence, energy, and style, it will also entertain. Finally, as a monograph on something completely different by a scholar known until now for her work on international investment law, it will hopefully—as the author herself hopes in her preface—inspire other international lawyers to step outside their 'comfort zone'.

RO'K, CR
Milan and Oxford
August 2024

Preface

This monograph is an extended response to a throwaway comment made by Jeremy Sharpe in London in 2017. I was based in London then, working on my first monograph, *State Responsibility for Breaches in Investment Contracts*, as well as my first textbook, *International Investment Law and Arbitration*. Jeremy reached out and invited me to give a short talk on expropriation to his team at the London office of Shearman & Sterling LLP. At the end of the talk, Jeremy looked around the room and asked, 'What is property?'. When no one answered, he threw up his hands and said, 'Well, I don't know why no one has ever written anything to address a question that international lawyers ask all the time!' I did not give too much thought to Jeremy's comment until I was egged on to write a second monograph, almost immediately after my first monograph was published in late 2018. I spent much of 2019 casting around for ideas for my second monograph but kept returning to Jeremy's comment, which I found intriguing but also too unfamiliar and challenging to take on. Then, Covid-19 happened and Singapore went into lockdown mode in April 2020. With nowhere to go and no way of knowing if and when I would live through the pandemic to tell any tale, I decided to stop dithering and take the plunge. I spent the better part of a year reading, thinking, and working out what I wanted to say about property, its definition, and its regulation by international law. I submitted my proposal to Oxford University Press in April 2021 and received formal approval for the project in March 2022. By then, life was slowly returning to normal and I was able to complete the monograph amid relatively few distractions and submit the final manuscript in April 2024. Writing this monograph has been exhilarating. I very much hope it will be of use and interest to the various stakeholders in and students of international law, as well as being written proof that your best self is beckoning from outside your comfort zone.

JH
Duke's Road, Singapore
30 April 2024

Acknowledgements

I am grateful to my mentor, Emeritus Professor M Sornarajah, for encouraging me to write a second monograph that had nothing to do with my first and which fell completely outside my known specialization. I was trained as an international investment law practitioner, then as an international investment law scholar. Subsequent tentative forays into other sub-fields of international law were met with crippling put-downs and never published. However, Sorna was relentlessly optimistic and his unwavering support made me believe that I had the ability to build scholarly expertise beyond international investment law. My former and current Deans, Professors Simon Chesterman and Andrew Simester, and former Vice-Deans for Research, Professors James Penner and Damian Chalmers, were also firmly behind this project, offering me sage advice and steering me through funding opportunities from start to finish. Thanks to their guidance, I was awarded the competitive Singapore Ministry of Education AcRF Tier 1 grant (WBS No R-241-000-169-115), as well as the National University of Singapore Humanities and Social Sciences Research Fellowship (IRMS No 23-0794-A0001), which gave me substantial funding and teaching relief to write my monograph. I also wish to thank my current Vice-Dean for Academic Affairs, Professor Wayne Courtney, for accommodating my requests for additional teaching relief to complete my monograph. My diligent research assistants, NUS Law undergraduates Lee Jia Ying (Class of 2024) and Ng Zhengnan, Ben (Class of 2024), copyedited the submitted manuscript.

This project materialized as a result of Oxford University Press taking a leap of faith. I owe a debt of gratitude to my commissioning editor, Fay Gibbons, for giving my monograph proposal a chance and for always keeping the lines of communication open. I am equally indebted to the editors of Oxford Monographs in International Law (OMIL), Chichele Professor of Public International Law, Catherine Redgwell, and Professor of Public International Law, Roger O'Keefe, for valuing my thesis and for including my monograph in the OMIL series. Their exceptionally kind remarks on why my book earned a spot in the OMIL series kept me going when the writing got tough. The submitted manuscript also benefitted from the salient comments of three anonymous reviewers who endorsed its publication. My project editor, Matthew

Williams, checked in regularly to ensure that the manuscript was on track to completion and timely submission.

It is not my usual practice to float preliminary ideas or work that is very rough around the edges at conferences, large and small. For constructive feedback, I prefer to turn to my network of trustworthy academic friends. I thank Antony Anghie, Eric De Brabandere, Georgios Dimitropoulos, Anna Joubin-Bret, Meg Kinnear, James Penner, Surabhi Ranganathan, Mavluda Sattorova, and Jeremy Sharpe for conversations and comments on my drafts. And last but not least, I thank Sasha Halik, Swati Jhaveri, Hanny Kusnadi, Mark Lim, Gabriel Ong, David Tan, Carol Teo, and Nadezda Vasilyeva for supporting my writing process in a variety of ways.

My Nutrilite® supplements, my legacy business team, and my loved ones soldiered on with me.

Contents

Table of Cases and Awards

ARBITRAL AWARDS

INTERNATIONAL CASES

NATIONAL CASES BY COUNTRY

Singapore

UK

US

Table of Treaties and National Legislation

TREATIES AND OTHER INTERNATIONAL INSTRUMENTS

UNITED NATIONS RESOLUTIONS

OTHER INTERNATIONAL RESOLUTIONS

NATIONAL LEGISLATION BY COUNTRY

Brazil

Canada

China

Germany

List of Abbreviations

Treaties and Other Instruments

1954 Hague Convention	Convention for the Protection of Cultural Property in the Event of Armed Conflict
1970 UNESCO Convention	UNESCO Convention on the Means of Prohibiting and Preventing the Illicit Import, Export and Transfer of Ownership of Cultural Property
1995 UNIDROIT Convention	1995 UNIDROIT Convention on Stolen or Illegally Exported Cultural Objects
ACIA	Association of Southeast Asian Nations (ASEAN) Comprehensive Investment Agreement
ASR	Articles on Responsibility of States for Internationally Wrongful Acts
ATS	Alien Tort Statute
ATS	Antarctic Treaty System
BBNJ Agreement	Agreement on the Conservation and Sustainable Use of Marine Biological Diversity of Areas Beyond National Jurisdiction
BGB	Bürgerliches Gesetzbuch (German Civil Code)
CCAMLR	Convention on the Conservation of Antarctic Marine Living Resources
CCAS	Convention for the Conservation of Antarctic Seals
CETA	Comprehensive and Economic Trade Agreement
CPTPP	Comprehensive and Progressive Agreement for Trans-Pacific Partnership
ECHR	European Convention on Human Rights
FCA	Foreign Claims Act
FTCA	Federal Tort Claims Act
GATT	General Agreement on Tariffs and Trade
Hague Building Blocks	Building Blocks for the Development of an International Framework on Space Resource Activities
ICTY Statute	Statute establishing the ad hoc International Criminal Tribunal for the former Yugoslavia
Moon Treaty	Agreement Governing the Activities of States on the Moon and Other Celestial Bodies

NAFTA	North American Free Trade Agreement
New York Convention	Convention on the Recognition and Enforcement of Foreign Arbitral Awards
Rome Statute	Rome Statute of the International Criminal Court
TRIMs Agreement	Agreement on Trade-Related Investment Measures
TRIPs Agreement	Agreement on Trade-Related Aspects of Intellectual Property Rights
UNCC	United Nations Convention Against Corruption
UNCLOS	United Nations Convention on the Law of the Sea
WHC	Convention Concerning the Protection of the World Cultural and Natural Heritage

Bodies

DSB	Dispute Settlement Body of the World Trade Organization
ICC	International Chamber of Commerce
ICC	International Criminal Court
ICJ	International Court of Justice
ICOMOS	International Council on Monuments and Sites
ICSID	International Centre for Settlement of Investment Disputes
ICTY	International Criminal Tribunal for the former Yugoslavia
ILA	International Law Association
INTERPOL	The International Criminal Police Organization
ISA	International Seabed Authority
ITLOS	International Tribunal for the Law of the Sea
ITU	International Telecommunication Union
PCA	Permanent Court of Arbitration
UN	United Nations
UNCITRAL	United Nations Commission on International Trade Law
UNESCO	United Nations Educational, Scientific, and Cultural Organization
UNHRC	United Nations Human Rights Council
UNIDROIT	International Institute for the Unification of Private Law
WIPO	World Intellectual Property Office
WTO	World Trade Organization

Common Terms

BIT	Bilateral Investment Treaty
CAS	complex adaptive system
FET	fair and equitable treatment
FTA	Free Trade Agreement
ICHL	international cultural heritage law
ICL	international criminal law

IIL	international investment law
ITL	international trade law
PMSC	private military and security company
TCE	traditional cultural expressions
TK	traditional knowledge

Introduction

Reform in the morality of property would mean that property rights widely came to be seen as based not on individual liberty but on the collective good. Even though individual liberty is an important value, and should be protected in the exercise of those property rights that we hold under the collectively valuable property conventions, it should not be seen as the foundation of those rights and should not determine their content. This is an example of how a moral outlook that has considerable intuitive support might be replaced by another that is deemed superior. In my view, even though a conception of property rights based largely on liberty and self-ownership embodies significant values, its replacement by a conventionalist conception that includes some protection of liberty would be a clear example of progress.

Thomas Nagel, 'Types of Intuition—Thomas Nagel on Human Rights and Moral Knowledge' (2021) 43(11) *London Review of Books* 3, 6.

***

Property in international law is an enigma. We are told that international law possesses sufficient content to regulate property, we are shown provisions in international instruments addressing property rights, and we bear witness to the resolution of property disputes in accordance with international law. Yet, when we are asked what the defining attributes of property in international law are, we draw a collective blank. The absence of reformist agitation from the international community towards an international law that brazenly regulates what it cannot or will not even define represents the turning of a collective blind eye to a critical knowledge gap. In the same way that driving a car with closed eyes is a possibly fatal accident in the making, driving the content of international law on property regulation without discerning the object of regulation is a possibly fatal anomaly in the laborious, and supposedly progressive, enterprise of legal development.

New Property in International Law. Jean Ho, Oxford University Press. © Jean Ho 2024.
DOI: 10.1093/9780191976117.003.0001

Suppressed ignorance has a way of resurfacing. Cracks are starting to appear in the façade of an international law that adequately regulates property use and interference with the emergence of newer forms of property. New property is so called because it defies traditional conceptions of property which revolve around the private, individual ownership of tangible things. Without any definitional anchor for property, let alone new property, international law has not developed any principled approaches to the regulation of new property. The current approaches towards new property regulation are best described as reactionary, piecemeal, and deficient. An international law that is buffeted in regulatory content every now and then when new property appears, that attempts but fails to bring newer modes of property interference within its regulatory ambit, and that is constantly on the regulatory back foot, will surely develop in a manner that is more chaotic than coherent. This monograph is essentially a study of how three distinctive and discrete categories of new property—cultural property, common property, and contingent property—reveal an international law that, contrary to prevailing assumptions, is unfit for the purpose of new property regulation. Each category showcases, in its unique way, how international law has fallen short. Together, they present a consolidated outlook on new property and its regulation, informed by realities rather than rhetoric, by deeds rather than declarations, and by outcomes rather than overtures, to replace one where property and its regulation are perched, precariously, on top of an intellectual void.

If it is imperative to accurately capture the object of regulation prior to its regulation, then filling the intellectual void on the defining attributes of new property in international law becomes a priority. This undertaking, which international lawyers have routinely sidestepped or started and subsequently abandoned for a variety of reasons over the course of decades and the lifespans of regulatory projects, is substantiated in Chapter 1. Parsing the proclamation that 'international law has rather a lot to say on property',[1] this chapter embarks on a journey to evaluate what has been said on property, and, more importantly, to exhibit what has *not* been said about property. The former inquiry debunks the misleading claim that property is universally regarded as entailing the absolute right of disposal as well as the right of exclusive use, such attributes reflecting private ownership of property in the capitalist vein. The latter inquiry, which considers and distils common attributes of property across four major juristic traditions (Western, Soviet and post-Soviet, Chinese, and

[1] Rosalyn Higgins, *Problems and Process: International Law and How To Use It* (Clarendon Press 1995) 140.

Islamic), develops more widely acceptable criteria for identifying new property in international law. New property comprises four core attributes, namely, imputable ownership, responsiveness to contextual factors, separability, and conferral of benefit.

Armed with a four-pronged definitional anchor, the journey continues with a thorough assessment and critique of the existing regulatory regimes for cultural property, common property, and contingent property. It becomes increasingly clear that the greatest predicament occasioned by the practice of regulating new property without defining it is severe dissonance between the legal parameters and the penalties surrounding its use and interference. In the case of cultural property, the focus of Chapter 2, regulation without adequate definition has spawned many treaties that make up international cultural heritage law, some of which regulate cultural property, some of which regulate intangible cultural heritage, and some of which regulate underwater cultural heritage. And should the arguably faint, if not invisible, distinction between property and heritage not sow enough seeds of discord, cultural property can simultaneously be regulated as tangible property under international criminal law, as investments under international investment law, and as national treasures under international trade law. The carving up and conversion of cultural property into other objects of regulation generate considerable discrepancies in how international law protects cultural property. Cultural property, both tangible and intangible, is unique, and a discrete category of new property; it symbolizes national history, patrimony, and identity in a way that no other category of property can. A definitional anchor holds the promise of streamlining cultural property regulation, by providing a common conceptual term of reference that welds different fragments from different regimes into an updated international law on cultural property protection.

The current regulation of common property, the focus of Chapter 3, is dissonant because despite a surfeit of treaties and instruments purporting to secure the equitable usage of the Antarctic, the Moon and other celestial objects, and natural resources in the Area and the High Seas, state pledges of sustainable use are simply not borne out in practice. Common property, which is owned by all, has been exploited as though it is owned by one or some. Such self-serving treatment of common property, though often tolerated in international law, veers dangerously close to the misplaced conviction that property in international law refers to privately owned property that can be ring-fenced for exclusive use in pursuit of private gains. Dropping a definitional anchor for common property as new property, one which emphasizes the attributes of imputable collective ownership and the conferral of shared benefit, may not fully reverse the rampant capitalist capture of common property regulation. But it does, at the very least, offer principled, and hopefully in time nurture popular, resistance to further extension of private, capitalist property regulation to common and communal property regulation. A better future for common property regulation is unlikely to lie in more treaties, which have already proven ineffective where cultural property regulation is concerned, but rather in the best practices of common pool resource management.

Dissonance compounds when it comes to the regulation of contingent property, the focus of Chapter 4. Apart from controversy surrounding the legal parameters and penalties of its *use*, there is also controversy associated with its very *being*. This monograph introduces contingent property as a category of new property because, unlike cultural property and common property whose various manifestations endure, contingent property comes or ceases to be depending on the context in which its use or interference is being considered. That said, the definitional anchor, which recognizes contextual factors as only one of four core attributes of new property, strives to ensure that contingent property is an open, yet finite list. The fact that jurisdictional rights and human slaves were once arguably regarded as property but no longer, and that judgments on legal claims and digital assets were not previously regarded as property but now arguably are, point to potentially seismic shifts in the regulatory content of international law. Contingent property is an intriguing category of new property because just as evolving contexts maintain its emergence and extinction in a state of flux, the international law regulating its use and interference is also, seemingly, in a state of flux. Extracting and articulating the content of international law applicable to contingent property regulation is very much an exercise in deduction because the rules governing more established forms of contingent property may change, while the preferred rules for governing emerging forms of contingent property have yet to crystallize.

The dysregulation of new property is exacerbated by the apparent licence afforded by international law to an expanding cast of actors indulging in an expanding collection of actions that interfere with new property. Chapter 5, the final substantive chapter of this monograph, addresses the enforcement of property rights in international law across the three different categories of new property. It explores the paradox of how certain actions can amount to a violation of international law while their protagonists elude sanction by international law. International law at present only admits two configurations of property interference. The first is the destruction of property by an individual during armed conflict, which is prosecuted as a war crime before the International Criminal Court. The second is the uncompensated taking of a foreigner's property by a host state, which founds an expropriation claim before certain international tribunals. Due to this limitation, any prescribed penalties for international law infractions cannot be enforced through existing dispute settlement bodies against individuals and states trafficking cultural property in peacetime, against corporations over-harvesting common property to an unsustainable degree, and against corporations acquiring contingent property through the use of or promise to use force. Reprieve for the struggle that international law appears to be facing when keeping the object and the subjects of regulation in check may lie in the faith held by a considerable number of international lawyers, that international law is a complex adaptive system capable of self-correction and recalibration.

The question that begs, throughout this monograph's unflinching exposé on international law's waning relevance in an era of new property, is whether and how international law can, after decades of habitual spontaneous, expedient, and uncoordinated law-making chiefly through treaties, finally be rendered fit for purpose? While glimpses of solutions are offered in this monograph, the number of stakeholders and the consensus-based mechanisms driving the development and content of international law means there are no easy answers to a difficult question that can no longer be kept under wraps. Hard cases do not necessarily make bad law because the more progressive content of international law, such as the enshrinement of fundamental human rights, has tended to be forged in crisis. While property dysregulation may or may not resemble a global crisis, the disconnect between new property as the regulated and international law as the regulator is sufficiently deep and disconcerting to supply the impetus for change. The road ahead is fraught with challenges. And the only way to know how this journey ends, is to begin.

1

The Struggle and Shape of New Property

1. Introduction*

Newness is a call to action. It draws a line between then and now, between known and unknown, and between continuity and change. International lawyers may be surprised, or even sceptical, to read that property can signal newness, as a result of which property regulation in international law can be hamstrung by reverting to the old ways, by seeking refuge in familiarity, and by resisting change. After all, the verdict that 'international law has rather a lot to say on property'[1] has not been challenged since its publication nearly three decades ago. It appears to be assumed, since any detractors have not made their voices heard, that the current property regulation regime in international law is not broken and does not require fixing.[2] Additionally,

* I am grateful to James Penner for feedback and discussions on earlier drafts. The usual disclaimers apply.

[1] Rosalyn Higgins, *Problems and Process: International Law and How To Use It* (Clarendon Press 1995) 140.

[2] For an extended yet uncritical study of property regulation in international law, see John Sprankling, *The International Law of Property* (OUP 2014).

New Property in International Law. Jean Ho, Oxford University Press. © Jean Ho 2024.
DOI: 10.1093/9780191976117.003.0002

given the currency and frequency of property disputes determined under international law, the absence of complaints from international courts and tribunals hearing property disputes reinforces the impression that the current regime enables the crucial business of adjudication to carry on as usual. Upon closer inspection of the indicators of regime adequacy, regime satisfaction may be misplaced. None of these indicators reveals a sufficiently representative and durable notion of property for international law to regulate. And none of these indicators cater for the reality that, over time, property takes newer forms which may demand newer modes of regulation. Despite operating under the cover of universality, international law at present purports to regulate property use and interference without any widely shared, let alone universal, understanding of property. The anomaly of a regulatory regime that developed in the absence of any principled determination of the object of regulation is evident.

This chapter challenges prevailing complacency in international law's contemporary relevance to property regulation by peeling back a façade spun by treaties that have long obscured international law's content deficiency on the notion of property. The knowledge gap is particularly significant for newer forms of property which are no less susceptible to disputed use and interference but find no expression or equivalence in existing doctrine in the way that basic property does.[3] In depicting the struggle of new property for formal acknowledgement and articulation, and in delineating the shape of new property, this chapter supplies the definitional backbone to the argument made throughout the rest of the book—that an international law unresponsive to the needs and nuances of new property is no longer fit for the purpose of property regulation. Section 2 explains how the fragmentation of international law into specialized subfields governed by different treaties created a knowledge gap on the notion of property. Section 3 explains how this knowledge gap in international law was entrenched by the influence of select Western property theories which espoused private property ownership. It compares and analyses distinctive notions of property from four major juristic traditions for common ground to fill the gap with a more representative and more adaptable notion of property. Section 4 observes the rise of new property and elaborates on the

[3] Every society recognizes basic norms governing tangible things such as access to land and the use of chattels. Some of these norms, such as how the owner of a thing ought to be in control of that thing, are so instinctive that even children are able to grasp them. In *This Moose Belongs To Me* (HarperCollins 2012), multiple award-winning children's author Oliver Jeffers tells the story of a boy who claims a wandering moose as his own, but then fails repeatedly to control it, leaving his young readers to ponder 'whether any of us really own anything.'

core attributes of new property distilled from the comparative analysis conducted in Section 3. Section 5 concludes.

2. Fragmentation, specialization, and the creation of a property knowledge gap

The fragmentation of international law, which denotes its division into multiple discrete subfields, which are then studied, practised, or written about, usually without reference to other subfields, is a well-known phenomenon.[4] The emergence of apparently self-contained specializations,[5] almost all of which are governed by treaties, and many of which involve some measure of property regulation, supplied the façade of intensive international law making on the notion of property. If there are already so many treaties touching on property regulation in one context or another, as the façade would have us believe, then the notion of property must have been so thoroughly explored that reopening the issue for further investigation becomes superfluous. But quantity is no guarantee of quality. Far from generating a coalescing notion of property, the proliferation of governance treaties as by-products of an increasingly fragmented and specialized international law sheds little to no light on the objective attributes of property. Nominal or token definitions may not pose problems in cases involving basic property such as privately owned land or chattels, but they fail to account for new property whose contours have yet to be carved into mass consciousness. When new property has not been factored into the definitional or interpretive discourse, it struggles for acknowledgement and articulation precisely because it has been kept out of sight and consequently out of mind. This section demonstrates how a property knowledge gap was formed by the adoption of various definitional templates in treaty texts that obscure rather than illuminate the notion of property (2.1), and by the reframing of property as the target object of treaty regulation in a given specialized subfield in international law (2.2).

[4] Martti Koskenniemi, 'Fragmentation of International Law: Difficulties Arising from the Diversification and Expansion of International Law' Report of the Study Group of the International Law Commission (13 April 2006) UN Doc A/CN.4/L.682.

[5] The appearance of fairly recent scholarship exploring 'linkages' between different subfields of international law is highly suggestive of, or at least conveys the perception of, self-containment, see for instance Valentina Vadi, 'Culture, Development and International Law: The Linkage Between Investment Rules and the Protection of Cultural Heritage' in Silvia Borelli and Federico Lenzerini (eds), *Cultural Heritage, Cultural Rights, Cultural Diversity—New Developments in International Law* (Brill 2012) 413, 413; also Valentina Vadi, *Cultural Heritage in International Investment Law and Arbitration* (CUP 2014) 13–86.

2.1 Omission through application of treaty definition

Given the number of treaties that touch on property regulation in multiple contexts ranging from armed conflict to foreign investment protection, it is remarkable that the notion of property in international law to date remains vague. This does not mean that no attempts were ever made to define property. Rather, recorded attempts to define property in treaties, where available, offer little or no objective indicia of property, making it almost impossible to ascertain if a thing or right to a thing which is not expressly identified as property in the treaty, if at all, is indeed property. A survey of treaties touching on property regulation reveals the prevalence of three definitional templates, none of which foster a principled and progressive understanding of property that will enable the proper identification of new property. These templates attempt to define property through illustration (2.1.1), through discretion (2.1.2), and, perhaps better construed as a lapse than an attempt, through silence (2.1.3).

2.1.1 Illustrative definition

When property is defined by a list of things that qualify as property, property may be said to be defined through illustration. Whether or not something qualifies as property turns on whether it matches one of the given illustrations of property in the treaty. An illustrative definition may be concise, like Article 2(d) of the United Nations Convention Against Corruption (UNCC):[6]

> 'Property' shall mean assets of every kind, whether corporeal or incorporeal, movable or immovable, tangible or intangible, and legal documents or instruments evidencing title to or interest in such assets[.]

According to UNCC Article 2(d), whatever is an asset is property. Assets can assume any one of six forms (corporeal, incorporeal, movable, immovable, tangible, intangible), and be represented by legal records of title to or interest in such assets. In the context of eradicating corruption, an asset-oriented illustrative definition of property constituting the 'proceeds of crime',[7] which are subject to confiscation by the relevant authorities, may be untroubling because bribes invariably take the form of money, financial instruments, or title to objects of measurable monetary worth such as real estate, automobiles, or artwork. Few will disagree that bribes entail the transfer of assets, so once that

[6] (signed 31 October 2003, entered into force 14 December 2005) 2347 UNTS 41.
[7] UNCC art 2(e).

transfer is ascertained to have taken place and the transferred assets located, proving the existence of property, or the 'proceeds of crime', is straightforward. But an asset-oriented illustrative definition is unable to capture property to which monetary worth cannot be or cannot easily be ascribed. While this limitation may not affect the identification of property in the course of the international fight against corruption, an asset-oriented illustrative definition of property offers no guidance on whether non-assets are property, and therefore bears little instructive value outside the context of corruption.

While it is understandable for treaty definitions of property to be highly context-specific, illustrative definitions eschew the harder option of identifying the attributes of property in a particular context for the softer option of giving examples of the different forms that property can take. This was done in more general terms in UNCC Article 2, and, by way of contrast, in elaborate detail in Article 1 of the UNESCO Convention on the Means of Prohibiting and Preventing the Illicit Import, Export and Transfer of Ownership of Cultural Property (1970 UNESCO Convention).[8] Apart from swapping the articulation of a principled and progressive notion of property with broader and more durable traction for a closed list of examples, an illustrative definition may not even foster a principled understanding of property *within* its designated context. 1970 UNESCO Convention Article 1 illustrates how greater detail does not necessarily engender greater clarity in the notion of property:[9]

> For the purposes of this Convention, the term 'cultural property' means property which, on religious or secular grounds, *is specifically designated by each State* as being of importance for archaeology, prehistory, history, literature, art or science *and* which belongs to the following categories:
> (a) Rare collections and specimens of fauna, flora, minerals and anatomy, and objects of palaeontological interest;
> (b) property relating to history, including the history of science and technology and military and social history, to the life of national leaders, thinkers, scientists and artist and to events of national importance;
> (c) products of archaeological excavations (including regular and clandestine) or of archaeological discoveries;
> (d) elements of artistic or historical monuments or archaeological sites which have been dismembered;

[8] (signed 14 November 1970, entered into force 24 April 1972) 823 UNTS 231.
[9] (emphasis added).

(e) antiquities more than one hundred years old, such as inscriptions, coins and engraved seals;
(f) objects of ethnological interest;
(g) property of artistic interest, such as:
  (i) pictures, paintings and drawings produced entirely by hand on any support and in any material (excluding industrial designs and manufactured articles decorated by hand);
  (ii) original works of statuary art and sculpture in any material;
  (iii) original engravings, prints and lithographs;
  (iv) original artistic assemblages and montages in any material;
(h) rare manuscripts and incunabula, old books, documents and publications of special interest (historical, artistic, scientific, literary, etc.) singly or in collections;
(i) postage, revenue and similar stamps, singly or in collections;
(j) archives, including sound, photographic and cinematographic archives;
(k) articles of furniture more than one hundred years old and old musical instruments.

The presence of eleven categories of cultural property in Article 1, ranging from century-old coins (Article 1(e)), to lithographs (Article 1(g)(iii)), to stamps (Article 1(i)), seemingly exhausts the conceivable forms that cultural property can take. However, relying on illustrations, rather than objective attributes, to define property risks making the list both under- and over-inclusive. For example, it is unclear what criteria 'rare manuscripts' must meet to qualify as cultural property under Article 1(h). It is also unclear whether both tangible and intangible 'property relating to history' or only tangible property as depicted in other categories qualify as cultural property under Article 1(b). When something does not fit squarely into one of the listed categories, its status as cultural property is left to chance. A restrictive reading of an illustration may withhold the label of cultural property on too many occasions, while a relaxed reading may spawn an unexpectedly large category of cultural property. For example, select Philippe Starck furniture created in the 1980s was exhibited at the Musée des Arts Décoratifs (MAD) in Paris from 13 October 2022 to 16 April 2023.[10] Article 1(k) is inapplicable as the articles of Starck furniture are less than one hundred years old. A restrictive reading of Article 1(g) will also disqualify, to the probable surprise of MAD's curators,

[10] MAD Paris, '1980s. Fashion, Design and Graphics in France' <https://madparis.fr/ExpoAnnees80> accessed 30 April 2024.

all Starck furniture as 'property of artistic interest' as furniture is disanalogous to 'pictures, paintings and drawings', 'statuary art and sculpture', 'engravings, prints and lithographs', and 'assemblages and montages'. However, a relaxed reading of Article 1(g), where articles of Starck furniture less than one hundred years old may nonetheless be deemed 'property of artistic interest' potentially renders millions of articles of Starck furniture ever manufactured and sold cultural property.[11]

Moreover, with new discoveries on ancient indigenous culture being made from time to time,[12] and with new ways of illicitly harnessing and exporting such culture and its products being developed from time to time,[13] an illustrative definition which identifies cultural property with the categories devised in 1970 is not equipped to withstand or change with the times. Compounding the superficially comprehensive but substantively inchoate illustrative definition of cultural property in Article 1 is the catch in the chapeau of the provision which, in addition to an applicable category, requires 'specific designation by each State' for qualification as cultural property. In other words, absent 'specific designation by each State', the label of cultural property does not attach. Leaving aside the disproportionate burden this places on states, like war-torn Afghanistan, which are most at risk of cultural property looting and yet are least able to afford and administer the laborious process of designation,[14] asking states to name cultural property approximates an abdication of definition by treaty. If definition by illustration does not promote a principled and progressive understanding of property, definition by state designation on the international plane essentially rejects any conceptual notion of property. This is also why recourse to discretionary definition, to which the discussion now turns, does not advance a principled and progressive understanding of property.

2.1.2 Discretionary definition

Unlike the illustrative definitional template employed in 1970 UNESCO Convention Article 1, the discretionary definitional template does not require

[11] Over three million units of the iconic Louis Ghost chair, which was designed by Philippe Starck for Kartell in 2002, have been sold to date, earning it the accolade of 'the world's best-selling design chair', Carlotta Marelli, 'Louis Ghost, The World's Best Selling Design Chair' *Elle Décor* (16 January 2023).

[12] Will Dunham, 'Oldest and Largest Ancient Maya Structure Found in Mexico' *Reuters* (3 June 2020).

[13] INTERPOL, 'Fighting the Illicit Trafficking of Cultural Property' (2018) 68–75 <www.interpol.int/content/download/8553/file/UNESCO%20Toolkit%20to%20fight%20the%20illicit%20trafficking%20of%20cultural%20property_web....pdf> accessed 30 April 2024.

[14] Matthieu Aikins, 'How One Looted Artifact Tells the Story of Modern Afghanistan' *The New York Times Magazine* (8 March 2021).

potential property to fit an articulated example of property. Discretion to define property lies entirely with the contracting states to the treaty, so that the identification of property as such by a state is the overriding consideration for property to exist. Article 3 of the Convention Concerning the Protection of the World Cultural and Natural Heritage (WHC) sets out a discretionary definition:[15]

> It is for each State Party to this Convention to identify and delineate the different properties situated on its territory mentioned in Articles 1 and 2 above.

Articles 1 and 2 of the WHC set out the traits of 'cultural heritage' and 'natural heritage' respectively, although unlike the illustrative list in 1970 UNESCO Convention Article 1, these traits are more akin to guidelines than binding features. A case in point is the Singapore Botanic Gardens, which was inscribed as a UNESCO World Heritage Site in 2014. While well-loved by residents and a perennial tourist attraction for its vast collection of tropical flora, it is debatable whether the gardens are a site of 'outstanding universal value from the historical, aesthetic, ethnological or anthropological point of view'.[16] Singapore began conducting a feasibility study for inscription in 2010 and submitted an extremely thorough nomination dossier in January 2014. This was swiftly followed by a recommendation for inscription issued by the International Council on Monuments and Sites (ICOMOS) and eventual inscription. The only other botanic gardens to be inscribed as World Heritage Sites are the Orto botanico di Padova in Italy, and the Royal Botanic Gardens in Kew, United Kingdom.

WHC Article 3 and the inscription process for World Heritage Sites outlined above reveal why a discretionary definition cultivates an idiosyncratic rather than a principled understanding of property, or in the case of the WHC, cultural heritage that is used interchangeably with cultural property. If states possess the discretion to 'identify and delineate' cultural property, then whether cultural property can be established depends on the inclination of any given state to launch the inscription process. It is telling that the only three botanic gardens to warrant the label of cultural property are located in highly developed states whose economies receive a significant boost from tourism, and whose governments can spare the resources needed for identification and delineation to make the case for calling a garden cultural property. When a site is declared

[15] (signed 16 November 1972, entered into force 17 December 1975) 1037 UNTS 151.
[16] WHC art 1.

cultural property because a state successfully persuades ICOMOS of the same, the process speaks volumes of the initiative, industry, and perhaps ingenuity of the nominating state. However, this process offers no guidance on how one may go about ascertaining the equivalence of sites that do not obviously exhibit 'outstanding universal value from the historical, aesthetic, ethnological or anthropological point of view', such as botanic gardens, to cultural property.

2.1.3 Non-definition

In addition to illustrative and discretionary definitions, some treaties employ the term 'property' but leave it undefined. Examples of non-definition or silence can be found in the Rome Statute of the International Criminal Court (Rome Statute),[17] the Agreement Governing the Activities of States on the Moon and Other Celestial Bodies (Moon Treaty),[18] and the ASEAN Comprehensive Investment Agreement (ACIA).[19]

Rome Statute Article 8(2)(a)(iv) provides:[20]

> For the purpose of this Statute, 'war crimes' means:
>
> (a) Grave breaches of the Geneva Conventions of 12 August 1949, namely, any of the following acts against persons or property protected under the provisions of the relevant Geneva Convention:
>
> [...]
>
> (iv) Extensive destruction and appropriation of property, not justified by military necessity and carried out unlawfully and wantonly[.]

Moon Treaty Article 11(3) provides:

> Neither the surface nor the subsurface of the moon, nor any part thereof or natural resources in place shall become property of any State, international intergovernmental or non-governmental organization, national organization or non-governmental entity or of any natural person [...]

ACIA Article 4(c)(i) provides:

> '[I]nvestment' means every kind of asset, owned or controlled, by an investor, including but not limited to the following:

[17] (signed 17 July 1998, entered into force 1 July 2002) 217 UNTS 90.
[18] (signed 5 December 1979, entered into force 11 July 1984) 1363 UNTS 3.
[19] (signed 26 February 2009, entered into force 24 February 2012).
[20] See also Rome Statute arts 8(2)(b)(ii), (iii), (v), (ix), (xiii), (xxiv), 8(2)(e)(ii)–(iv), (xii).

(i) movable and immovable property and other property rights such as mortgages, liens or pledges[.]

To be fair, non-definition may not necessarily impair a treaty's mandate to regulate or sanction property use or interference. To the extent that property destroyed and appropriated in times of armed conflict are buildings, dwellings, monuments and artefacts, and other forms of basic property, the object of a war crime may be readily identified pursuant to Rome Statute Article 8(2)(a)(iv). Similarly, to the extent that forms of property on the moon are limited to 'the surface', 'the subsurface', and 'natural resources in place', Moon Treaty Article 11(3) prohibits any claim to such property. The arguably negligible intellectual cost for the non-definition of property in the narrow context of armed conflict, as well as the narrow *and* poorly subscribed context of moon governance, does not sustain non-definition in other contexts or more generally. Investment treaties like the ACIA typically list property as protected investments but do not define property. This has resulted in ambiguity over the qualifying features of the object of an expropriation claim brought under the treaty and raised awareness of the property knowledge gap.[21] To address the ambiguity, a number of investment treaty tribunals and newer generation treaties proclaim the indispensability of proprietary characteristics in an object that is susceptible to expropriation. Yet, most do not articulate what those proprietary characteristics are,[22] leaving property as shapeless as it was before. The non-definition of property in the context of investment protection, which encompasses both basic and new property, is a glaring omission that calls for rectification.

Non-definition may be justified by recourse to domestic law as the default marker of property. This approach has been recommended in international investment law.[23] However, recourse to domestic law carries two significant

[21] Zachary Douglas, 'Property, Investment and the Scope of Investment Protection Obligations' in Zachary Douglas and others (eds), *The Foundations of International Investment Law: Bringing Theory into Practice* (OUP 2014) 363, 391; Zachary Douglas, *The International Law on Investment Claims* (CUP 2012) 213–24; also Jean Ho, *State Responsibility for Breaches of Investment Contracts* (CUP 2018) 140–52.

[22] See eg *Ampal-American Israel Corporation & Ors v Arab Republic of Egypt*, ICSID Case No ARB/12/11, Decision on Jurisdiction (Fortier, McLachlan, Orrego Vicuña) (1 February 2016) para 255, and Decision on Liability and Heads of Loss (Fortier, McLachlan, Orrego Vicuña) (21 February 2017) paras 337 and 347; cf *Accession Mezzanine Capital & Ors v Hungary*, ICSID Case No ARB/12/3, Award (Rovine, Lalonde, Douglas) (17 April 2015) (*AMC v Hungary*) para 154; ACIA Annex 2(1) provides: 'An action or a series of related actions by a Member State cannot constitute an expropriation unless it interferes with a tangible or intangible property right or property interest in a covered investment.'

[23] Monique Sasson, *Substantive Law in Investment Treaty Arbitration—The Unsettled Relationship between International and Municipal Law* (Kluwer 2010) 94–96; *Apotex Holdings Inc. & Anor v United States of America*, ICSID Case No ARB(AF)/12/1, Award (Veeder, Rowley, Crook) (25 August 2014) paras 7.44–7.56.

limitations that may end up hindering the regulation and understanding of property in international law. First, domestic law can be changed at the moment of state succession or at the exercise of sovereign will. Locating the ruling notion of property in domestic law disables any protective shield that international law casts, or purports to cast, over property. Whatever is not recognized as property under domestic law cannot be regulated as property under international law. The dictum that domestic law cannot contravene international law loses purchase when it comes to property use and interference because international law at present lacks sufficient content against which domestic law can be measured.[24] Second, domestic law does not have extraterritorial application, and it is inoperative against forms of property that transcend national boundaries, such as celestial objects and international ventures. Even if new property can be situated within national boundaries, recourse to domestic law may not yield relevant and up-to-date content on the notion of property or may no longer be self-evidently applicable. Therefore, relying on domestic law to fill the property knowledge gap does not truly illuminate what property is or means for the purpose of regulation by international law. When property constantly struggles for definition in treaties purporting to regulate its use, it becomes extremely vulnerable to assimilation to the treaty's principal object of regulation and further obscurity, to which the discussion now turns.

2.2 Omission through alignment with treaty object

Although there are a considerable number of treaties that touch on property regulation, such regulation is often incidental to or a manifestation of the pursuit of the treaty's principal objective. For example, the principal objective of the Rome Statute referred to in the previous section is not the regulation of property *per se*, but the institutionalized prosecution of international crimes committed during armed conflict,[25] which may include the destruction and appropriation of property.[26] Property is regulated by means of sanctions imposed on persons to whom property interference amounting to an international crime as recognized by the Rome Statute can be attributed.[27] That

[24] *Certain Norwegian Loans Case (France v Norway)* (Preliminary Objections) [1957] ICJ Rep 9, 37 (Separate Opinion of Judge Lauterpacht).
[25] Rome Statute Preamble.
[26] Rome Statute arts 8(2)(a)(iv), 8(2)(b)(ii), (iii), (v), (ix), (xiii), (xxiv), 8(2)(e)(ii)–(iv), (xii).
[27] Rome Statute arts 77–80.

said, as property interference is merely one of many forms of misconduct sanctionable as an international crime, the key to conviction does not lie in a thorough understanding, or even precise and consistent use, of the term 'property', when establishing the elements of the crime. The landmark case of *The Prosecutor v Ahmad Al Faqi Al Mahdi*, which is the first to record a war crime conviction under the Rome Statute for property destruction, shows how property interference may be central to the prosecution's factual case, and yet be dispensable during the establishment of the perpetrator's legal liability.[28]

Ahmad Al Faqi Al Mahdi, a member of the Islamic militia group Ansar Dine, was charged at the ICC for intentionally directing attacks against ten religious and historical buildings located in the city of Timbuktu, during the Mali War that began in 2012 and which persists today. After deeming the destroyed buildings cultural property at the start of its judgment,[29] the ICC Trial Chamber VIII declared the importance of cultural property protection,[30] and characterized Mr Al Mahdi's conduct as 'a crime against property'.[31] To be precise, Mr Al Mahdi was neither charged nor convicted for 'a crime against property'. Mr Al Mahdi was charged under Article 8(2)(e)(iv) for '[i]ntentionally directing attacks against *buildings* dedicated to religion, education, art, science or charitable purposes, historic monuments, hospitals and places where the sick and wounded are collected, provided they are not military objectives'[32] and convicted for 'the war crime of attacking protected *objects* as a co-perpetrator under Articles 8(2)(e)(iv) and 25(3)(a) of the [Rome] Statute'.[33] The cursory and unexplained references to cultural property in the judgment have not dampened the enthusiasm of international cultural heritage law scholars who claim *The Prosecutor v Ahmad Al Faqi Al Mahdi* as an important win for cultural property protection under international criminal law.[34] Yet, property scholars ought to be dissatisfied with the judgment because the casual framing and reframing of 'cultural property' as 'buildings' and 'objects' in the judgment hinders the search for a principled notion of property. The incaution may be due in part to the sporadic employment of the term 'property' in the Rome Statute, with some provisions referring to the umbrella term,[35]

[28] ICC-01/12-01/15-171, Trial Chamber VIII, Judgment and Sentence (27 September 2016).
[29] ibid para 14.
[30] ibid paras 14–16.
[31] ibid para 77, see also 42–48, 72.
[32] (emphasis added).
[33] *The Prosecutor v Ahmad Al Faqi Al Mahdi*, Dispositif (emphasis added).
[34] Generally, Philippa Webb and others, 'Culture at the Frontline: Addressing Attacks on Cultural Heritage' (2016) 14 Journal of International Criminal Justice 1139, 1139–220 (symposium).
[35] Rome Statute arts 8(2)(a)(iv), 8(2)(b)(xiii), 8(2)(e)(xii).

while other provisions refer to tangible forms of property such as installations or weapons.[36] It may also be due in part to the perceived negligible impact of an unprincipled notion of property on the establishment of legal liability for a war crime. Since Article 8(2)(e)(iv) criminalizes intentional attacks on buildings dedicated to religion, and since Mr Al Mahdi admitted to intentional attacks on buildings dedicated to religion, the charge of a war crime has been made out. There is no immediate incentive for investing analytical rigour in the notion of property when a conviction can turn specifically and entirely on intentional building destruction, and not generally on intentional property interference.

The reframing of property as the target object of treaty protection, leading to the disappearance of property from the determination of liability, may also be seen in international investment law. Although the earliest investment treaties were conceived as instruments for the protection of foreign-owned property,[37] they have since evolved to stand for investment protection. This has triggered the observation that '[i]nternational investment law does not normally speak of property but of "investments"'.[38] Investment treaties, such as the ACIA referred to in the previous section, typically set out an illustrative list of investments that are eligible for treaty protection. These treaties then outline various substantive standards of protection for qualifying investments, one of the most ubiquitous being protection from uncompensated expropriation. General international law recognizes a cause of action for expropriation when there is state interference resulting in a substantial deprivation of the benefit or enjoyment of property.[39] Under investment treaties though, since protection from uncompensated expropriation extends to all qualifying investments, usually without qualification, the object of expropriation may no longer be limited to

[36] Rome Statute arts 8(2)(b)(iii), 8(2)(e)(iii), 8(2)(b)(xx).

[37] Kenneth J Vandevelde, 'A Brief History of International Investment Agreements' (2005) 12(1) UC Davis Journal of International Law & Policy 157, 158–59, 162–63.

[38] Ursula Kriebaum and Christoph Schreuer, 'The Concept of Property in Human Rights Law and International Investment Law' in Stephan Breitenmoser and others (eds), *Human Rights, Democracy and the Rule of Law: Liber Amicorum Luzius Wildhaber* (Nomos 2007) 1, 2.

[39] Ian Brownlie, 'Causes of Action in the Law of Nations' (1979) 50(1) British Yearbook of International Law 13, 33; also John F Williams, 'International Law and the Property of Aliens' (1928) 9 British Yearbook of International Law 1, 13; Alexander Fachiri, 'International Law and the Property of Aliens' (1929) 10 British Yearbook of International Law 32, 51; Arthur K Kuhn, 'Nationalization of Foreign-Owned Property in Its Impact on International Law' (1951) 45 American Journal of International Law 709, 711; Rudolf L Bindschedler, 'La Protection de la Propriété Privée en Droit International Public' (1959) 90 Recueil des Cours 174, 187; Fritz Münch, 'Les Effets d'Une Nationalisation à l'Etranger' (1959) 89 Recueil des Cours 411, 463, 467; Burns H Weston, '"Constructive Takings" Under International Law: A Modest Foray into the Problem of "Creeping Expropriation"' (1975–1976) 16 Vanderbilt Journal of International Law 103, 129; Thomas Wälde and Abba Kolo, 'Environmental Regulation, Investment Protection and "Regulatory Taking" in International Law' (2001) 50 International and Comparative Law Quarterly 811, 824–25.

property, but may instead be stretched to accommodate all qualifying investments, including property. The critical definition and principal object of regulation in international investment law, therefore, appears to be 'investment', not 'property'. This is evident in repeated attempts by investment treaty tribunals and scholars to calibrate, debate, and refine the attributes of protected investments,[40] as well as the holdings of tribunals that all protected investments, and not just property, can be expropriated.[41]

That said, the diminished status of property as an object of regulation in international investment law is becoming more nuanced than first impressions may suggest. A number of newer generation investment treaties concluded in the late 2000s and beyond, such as the ACIA which entered into force in 2012, expressly limit expropriable investments to those representing a 'property right or a property interest'.[42] Additionally, a number of investment treaty tribunals have held, regardless of the applicable treaty's written stance on expropriable investments, that a claim for expropriation must be founded on property interference. As pointed out in the previous section, these attempts to reposition property as a key object of regulation in international investment law are often unaccompanied by articulated attributes of property, rendering the identification of property from qualifying investments a matter of instinct or guesswork. There are two notable exceptions. The arbitral awards in *Emmis International Holding, B.V. & Ors v The Republic of Hungary*[43] and in *AMC v Hungary* contained efforts to articulate attributes of property. In the former, the tribunal proposed one defining attribute of property—monetary value. According to the *Emmis v Hungary* tribunal, 'the loss of a right conferred by contract may be capable of giving rise to a claim of expropriation but only if it gives rise to an asset owned by the claimant to which a monetary value may be ascribed'.[44] In the latter, the tribunal proposed a different defining attribute of property—alienability, and explained why the absence of this attribute foils any claim for expropriation. According to the *AMC v Hungary* tribunal, '[t]he defining

[40] Ching Leng Lim and others, *International Investment Law and Arbitration—Commentary, Awards and Other Materials* (2nd edn, CUP 2021) 284–97.

[41] See for instance *Caratube International Oil Company LLP & Anor v Republic of Kazakhstan*, ICSID Case No ARB/13/13, Award (Lévy, Aynès, Salès (partially concurring and partially dissenting)) (27 September 2017) paras 822–26.

[42] ACIA Annex 2(1); see also Comprehensive and Economic Trade Agreement (CETA) (signed 30 October 2016, provisional entry into force 21 September 2017) Annex 8-A(1)(b); Treaty Between The Republic of Belarus and The Republic of India (signed 24 September 2018, not yet in force) art 5.3(a)(ii).

[43] ICSID Case No ARB/12/2, Award (McLachlan, Lalonde, Thomas) (16 April 2014) (*Emmis v Hungary*).

[44] ibid para 169.

characteristic of a property right is that it is capable of alienation or assignment... It is precisely because property rights can be alienated or assigned that makes them susceptible to being appropriated or expropriated. What cannot, on the other hand, be appropriated or expropriated are personal rights because the right is not separable in law from the person who has it.'[45]

The recent recognition in some investment treaties and by some investment treaty tribunals of property as a vital object of regulation distinct from other qualifying investments in international investment law cautions against equating property regulation to investment regulation, and underscores property's prominence in international law. Yet, details on this nuance are still lacking. Infrequent, piecemeal, and modest attempts to pinpoint property attributes will not lead to the coherent development of an international law on property regulation, but they invite further reflection and elaboration on the notion of property and urge a return to first principles to impart shape to that notion.

3. Property concepts and the entrenchment of that knowledge gap

When property struggles for definitional footing in treaties setting out the content of international law, the mirage of property as a self-evident notion, one that can be summoned on demand, might discourage investigation into the fundamental characteristics of property. After all, property gap-filling only as and when the occasion calls for it, such as during the adjudication of a property-related dispute, is part and parcel of the practice of international law, whose content is nowhere as extensive as that of domestic law.[46] Complacency among international lawmakers in the consequences of a property knowledge gap appears to breed complicity among international law-writers in the maintenance of that knowledge gap. Quite apart from the dearth of international law scholarship conceptualizing property, it is remarkable that the very few writings on point have managed, for decades, to elude scrutiny and critique for presenting a Western-centric understanding of property as the global norm.

[45] *AMC v Hungary* Award (n 22) para 147; see also *Koch Minerals SARL & Anor. v Bolivarian Republic of Venezuela*, ICSID Case No ARB/11/19, Partial Dissenting Opinion of Arbitrator Zachary Douglas (30 October 2017) paras 3–12.

[46] The observation that many principles in international law are borrowed from or inspired by domestic law attests to the richer, more comprehensive content of domestic law, see Hersch Lauterpacht, *Private Law Sources and Analogies of International Law* (Longmans, Green & Co. 1927) vii-xii.

One of the most influential articulations on the notion of property in international law defines property through the unapologetically capitalist lens of private ownership.[47] Despite choosing Marxist theory, which stands for the abolition of private ownership of property, as a point of comparison with select Western teachings,[48] Higgins' thesis manages to downplay the fundamental disagreement over ownership as a defining attribute of property to insist that 'there is virtual consensus on the *meaning* of property'.[49] And this 'virtual consensus', which was obtained without uncovering what property means in other juristic traditions such as the Chinese and Islamic traditions, says that property entails the absolute right of disposal as well as the right of exclusive use.[50] A reductionist notion of property may encapsulate the key features of basic property such as land or chattels, but it struggles to capture newer forms of property which may or may not be privately owned, and which may or may not be subject to exclusive use. The property knowledge gap is entrenched by a partial depiction of property's nature and attributes and enlarged by the failure to account for new property.

In rejecting the hegemony of select Western property concepts, this section compares and critically analyses how property is viewed in the Western (Section 3.1), Soviet and post-Soviet (Section 3.2), Chinese (Section 3.3), and Islamic (Section 3.4) juristic traditions, to distil commonalities and negotiate compromises that will enable the identification and elaboration of core attributes of new property in Section 4.

3.1 The Western tradition

Higgins' depiction of the notion of property for the purpose of regulation by international law is guided primarily by the second edition of Frederick

[47] Rosalyn Higgins, 'The Taking of Property by the State: Recent Developments in International Law' (1982) 176 Collected Courses of the Hague Academy of International Law 1, 270–78. Definitional entrenchment is evident when a monograph published nearly 40 years later still critiques international dispute settlement solely through the arguably dated lens of privately owned property, see Esmé Shirlow, *Judging at the Interface—Deference to State Decision-Making Authority in International Adjudication* (CUP 2021).

[48] Collective ownership, or ownership by everyone, which epitomizes the Marxist view of property, is anathema to some Western property theorists; see eg James Penner, *The Idea of Property in Law* (OUP 1997) 74.

[49] Higgins, 'The Taking of Property by the State: Recent Developments in International Law' (n 47) 270 (original emphasis).

[50] ibid 270.

H Lawson and Bernard Rudden's *The Law of Property*.[51] And although both authors were Professors of Comparative Law at Oxford University, *The Law of Property* does not purport to be a comparative study and synthesis of how property is understood in different countries or in different juristic traditions. Lawson and Rudden articulate property purely in terms of the rights flowing from ownership, and especially private ownership which John Locke famously legitimized as the natural fruit of one's labour.[52] This encompasses the physical use of things, the entitlement to income derived from things, and the power to alienate.[53] Notably, Lawson and Rudden inform their readers that their approach exemplifies 'the English way of looking at ownership',[54] which Higgins likens to a 'bundle of rights' approach to property.[55] Higgins' attribution of the 'bundle of rights' approach to property to Lawson and Rudden, as well as her elevation of the 'bundle of rights' approach to property to the universal way, is questionable. Unlike Higgins, Western property theorists credit the work of American philosopher Wesley Newcomb Hohfeld 'as a bulwark of the "bundle of rights" picture of property'.[56] And unlike Higgins, Western property theorists, whether through critique and/or their own construction of the notion of

[51] (2nd edn, OUP 1982). Higgins, 'The Taking of Property by the State: Recent Developments in International Law' (n 47) 270–78. While Higgins also refers to the work of American constitutional property scholars such as Bruce Ackerman and Charles Reich during her analysis, the definitional framework for property that she adopts is the one proposed by Lawson and Rudden.

[52] Crawford B McPherson (ed), *Second Treatise of Government* (Hackett Publishing Company, Indianapolis & Cambridge 1980) §§ 27–34.

[53] Lawson and Rudden (n 51) 8–11.

[54] ibid 9. The authors do not appear to have departed from this understanding of ownership in the third and latest edition of *The Law of Property* (3rd edn, OUP 2002), which has been 'entirely rewritten' by Rudden following the death of Lawson, to 'take[] for granted the existence, and legal protection, of private property and does not examine the many philosophical, ethical and political problems to which this gives rise' (viii). Keeping its promise, the third edition greatly simplifies 'what counts as property' to 'the subject matter of dispositions' (4).

[55] Higgins, 'The Taking of Property by the State: Recent Developments in International Law' (n 47) 270.

[56] James E Penner, 'The "Bundle of Rights" Picture of Property' (1996) 43 UCLA Law Review 711, 724; James E Penner, *Property Rights: A Re-Examination* (OUP 2020) 3; Anna di Robilant and Talha Syed, 'Property's Building Blocks: Hohfeld in Europe and Beyond' in Shyamkrishna Balganesh and others (eds), *Wesley Hohfeld A Century Later—Edited Work, Select Personal Papers, and Original Commentaries* (CUP 2022) 223, 223–24; Ted M Sichelman, 'Very Tight "Bundles of Sticks": Hohfeld's Complex Jural Relations' in Shyamkrishna Balganesh and others (eds), *Wesley Hohfeld A Century Later—Edited Work, Select Personal Papers, and Original Commentaries* (CUP 2022) 345, 364. The work of British philosopher, Anthony M Honoré, which specifies eleven standard incidents of property (see 'Ownership' in Anthony G Guest (ed), *Oxford Essays in Jurisprudence—A Collaborative Work* (OUP 1961) 107, 113–26), is often cited as a complement to Hohfeld's 'bundle of rights' and has been abbreviated as '[t]he Hohfeld-Honoré synthesis underpinning BOR', see Penner, *Property Rights—A Re-Examination*, 6. As my objective is simply to demonstrate that Hohfeld's 'bundle of rights' approach to property is not, as Higgins assumes, universal, it is beyond the scope of this chapter to unpack the 'Hohfeld-Honoré synthesis'. For a critique of Hohfeld's and Honoré's views, see Penner, *Property Rights—A Re-Examination*, 6–16; for an extension of those views, see Stephen R Munzer, *A Theory of Property* (CUP 1990) 22–28.

property, do not inspire confidence in the universality of Hohfeld's 'bundle of rights' approach to property. The chequered theoretical landscape begs the question: can the centrality of individual private ownership to the definition of property, packaged in a 'bundle of rights', be regarded as a defining feature of Western property concepts?

Across the Atlantic from Lawson and Rudden, Hohfeld constructed what is perhaps one of the most well-known frameworks to depict property as a relational concept. According to Hohfeld, the notion of property has long been obscured by the focus on rights and duties as the only set of legal relations that property is capable of giving rise to.[57] Instead of merely rights and duties, Hohfeld argues, property relations are better represented by eight sets of relations corresponding to jural opposites (right–no right, privilege–duty, power–disability, immunity–liability) and jural correlatives (right–duty, privilege–no right, power–liability, immunity–disability). While this is not the occasion to delve into Hohfeld's sixteen-part jural framework to agree or disagree with his granular deconstruction of property relations,[58] it suffices to note that Hohfeld deviates from Lawson and Rudden's 'English way' which depicts property neither as a relational concept nor as a 'bundle of rights'. Hohfeld justifies his non-reliance on the right–duty dogma by framing a property relationship in terms of the power–liability correlative, where liability denotes legal sanction for insubordination to the exercise of power until that power is relinquished: 'X, the owner of ordinary personal property "in a tangible object" has the power to extinguish his own legal interest (rights, powers, immunities, etc.) through that totality of operative facts known as abandonment; and—simultaneously and correlatively—to create in other persons privileges and powers relating to the abandoned object, e.g., the power to acquire title to the latter by appropriating it.'[59] While Hohfeld maintains that property relations generate more than rights, he does not contest individual private ownership as an attribute of property, from which rights, privileges, duties, powers, liabilities, immunities, and disabilities flow. This is evident in his power–liability illustration where individual ownership of property is the precursor to individual power over property. Nor does Hohfeld disagree with Lawson and Rudden on how property can be separated (or alienated) from its owner. Turning once again to the power–liability illustration, if property can be abandoned and power

[57] Wesley N Hohfeld, *Fundamental Legal Conceptions as Applied in Judicial Reasoning and Other Legal Essays* (Yale University Press 1919) 35.
[58] For a pithy critique of Hohfeld's framework, see Pavlos Eleftheriadis, 'The Analysis of Property Rights' (1996) 16(1) Oxford Journal of Legal Studies 31, 31–54.
[59] Hohfeld (n 57) 51.

over property transferred to others, then only objects which are separable from their owners are property. Hohfeld's sixteen-part jural framework teases out a 'bundle of rights' approach to property that is difficult to equate with Lawson and Rudden's relatively straightforward 'English way', which combines physical use with entitlement to derived income and with alienability, even if they appear to share some common ground on the criteria of individual private ownership and separability.

More recently, Canadian philosopher James Penner proposes a notion of property that is arguably reminiscent of 'the English way'. Penner perches property on what he calls the 'tripartite structure of ownership', comprising the right to exclusive possession, the power to license, and the power to dispose.[60] This 'tripartite structure of ownership', which bears shades of Lawson and Rudden's depiction of property ownership begetting the physical use of things, the entitlement to income derived from things, and the power to alienate, is a reworking of Penner's earlier conception of property presented in his seminal monograph—*The Idea of Property in Law*.[61] Penner observed that 'property is what the average citizen, free of entanglements of legal philosophy, thinks it is: the right to a thing'.[62] And property rests on two theses, both activated by ownership of property. First, the exclusion thesis posits 'a protected sphere of indefinite and undefined activity, in which an owner may do anything with the things he owns'.[63] The owner's activity in this regard may also be characterized as 'a right to exclude others from things which is grounded in the interest [he/she has] in the use of things'.[64] Second, the separability thesis posits that '[t]o be conceived as an object of property a thing must first be considered as separable and distinct from any person who might hold it, and is for that reason rightly regarded as alienable'.[65] It appears that Penner has since refashioned the exclusion thesis into the right to exclusive possession and the separability thesis into the two powers of licensing and disposition, thus revising his dual-theses structure into a 'tripartite structure of ownership'. Despite repeatedly disavowing Hohfeld's 'bundle of rights' approach,[66] Penner defines property in the language of cumulative rights. In *The*

[60] Penner, *Property Rights: A Re-Examination* (n 56) 14.
[61] *The Idea of Property in Law* began as a doctoral dissertation undertaken at Oxford University. This may explain the subtle influence of 'the English way' on Penner's work.
[62] Penner, *The Idea of Property in Law* (n 48) 2.
[63] ibid 72.
[64] ibid 71.
[65] ibid 113.
[66] See for instance Penner, *The Idea of Property in Law* (n 48) 1–2; Penner, *Property Rights: A Re-Examination* (n 56) 6–10.

Idea of Property in Law, Penner explained that the right of exclusive use is 'the right to determine the use or disposition of a separable thing (i.e. a thing whose contingent association with any particular person is essentially impersonal and so imports nothing of normative consequence), in so far as that can be achieved or aided by others excluding themselves from it, and includes the rights to abandon it, to share it, to license it to others (either exclusively or not), and to give it to others in its entirety'.[67] And in his later work, Penner observes that his tripartite structure reflects 'a sort of "bundle" of jural entities, one right and two powers, which characterize ownership'.[68] Even if Hohfeld's and Penner's notions of property diverge on presentation (jural relations vs exclusion-plus-separability or one-right-plus-two-powers) and in some details (the core rights that constitute property), they appear to converge at least on the centrality of private individual ownership,[69] and on the requirement of separability.[70]

Elsewhere on the Continent, property and the private ownership of property received a rather different and far more politically charged reception than amongst Anglo-American philosophers. Jean-Jacques Rousseau, the Swiss philosopher whose theory of the social contract between man and government was widely credited as the inspiration for the 1789 French Revolution that toppled the French monarchy and paved the way for a French republic, regarded private property ownership as a variable in the pursuit of civil equality amongst men.[71] For Rousseau, property was both a social marker and a political target, whereby the accumulation of too much (property) in too few (people) triggers a redistribution of property, possibly executed through violent means, to restore equality. Rousseau was more concerned with property's function than its attributes and appeared disinclined to detail or strengthen individual private ownership of property, which he believed could be justifiably altered by force. This sets Rousseau's notion of property apart from those presented by Locke, Lawson and Rudden, Hohfeld, and Penner. Private property ownership received an even more hostile reception from the French philosopher Pierre-Joseph Proudhon, whose rejection of privately owned property as

[67] Penner, *The Idea of Property in Law* (n 48) 152.

[68] Penner, *Property Rights: A Re-Examination* (n 56) 14.

[69] James E Penner, 'Property Rights' in Margaret Gilbert and others (eds), *The Palgrave Handbook on the Philosophy of Rights* (Palgrave MacMillan *forthcoming*); Penner, *Property Rights: A Re-Examination* (n 56) 41; Hohfeld (n 57) 51.

[70] Penner, *The Idea of Property in Law* (n 48) 113; Penner, *Property Rights: A Re-Examination* (n 56) 14; Hohfeld (n 57) 51.

[71] Jean-Jacques Rousseau, *Du contrat social; ou Principes du droit politique* (Chez Marc-Michel Rey 1762) 30–34, 39–51.

theft in favour of communally managed property foreshadowed the writings of Karl Marx on the ills of capitalism, one of which was bourgeois private property.[72] As Proudhon did not regard private ownership as an essential feature of property, and was therefore unconcerned with teasing out the rights that accompanied ownership, his notion of property also diverges sharply from that presented by Locke, Lawson and Rudden, Hohfeld, and Penner. The tendency to view property as a social construct vulnerable to the dictates of mobilized social pressure can also be seen in the work of German socio-economic theorist Friedrich Engels. A long-time collaborator of Marx, Engels co-authored with Marx *The Communist Manifesto*, which called for the 'abolition of private property' on the basis that 'modern bourgeois private property is the final and most complete expression of the system of producing and appropriating products, that is based on class antagonisms, on the exploitation of the many by the few'.[73] By advocating the erasure of private bourgeois ownership of property and its replacement with collective proletariat ownership, Engels and Marx, two of the most influential German philosophers of their time, also part company with the Anglo-American philosophers.

The above survey reveals that the landscape on property concepts in the Western tradition is far from homogenous, and is certainly not embodied, as Higgins asserts, in a 'bundle of rights' approach. The attitudes towards individual private ownership as a defining attribute of property range from appreciation (Locke, Lawson and Rudden, Hohfeld, Penner), to agnosticism (Rousseau), to antagonism (Proudhon, Engels, Marx). Additionally, while the Anglo-American philosophers appear to focus more on discerning the attributes of property, such as separability, the Continental philosophers appear to be more concerned with articulating the role and symbolism of property in its broader political, social, and economic contexts. The presence of diverse notions of property in the Western tradition alone recommends circumspection and flexibility when distilling the core attributes of new property. Placing a premium on individual private ownership may reflect the chosen focus of select philosophers, but it does not reflect the aggregate of property concepts in the Western, let alone other, traditions.

[72] Pierre-Joseph Proudhon, *Qu'est-ce que la propriété? Recherche sur le principe du droit et du gouvernement* (La Librarie de Prévot 1841) 2–6, 29–54, 60–68, 80–84.

[73] Karl Marx and Frederick Engels, *The Communist Manifesto* (Samuel Moore tr, Penguin 2015, first published 1888) 22–23.

3.2 The Soviet tradition and beyond

The notion of property in the Soviet tradition and beyond evolved over three distinct periods. The first period began in 1917 with the Russian Revolution that led to the establishment of the Soviet Union, and it lasted until the early 1990s with the collapse of the Soviet Union and the creation of the Commonwealth of Independent States. The second post-Soviet period from 1994 to 2006 saw the promulgation of a new Russian Civil Code and the rise of privatization which marked the transition of previously socialist to market economies. Despite the switch from a collective-oriented to an individual-oriented notion of property, the understanding and approach to property in the Soviet tradition would endure in a post-Soviet setting. The third post-Soviet period from 2006 to the present witnesses residual tensions over the private ownership of property that the wave of privatizations in the 1990s brought about, and serves as a reminder that the recognition of private rights in post-Soviet states, far from being sacrosanct, is still influenced by the Soviet tradition of collectivism and may fluctuate in accordance with the prevailing ideal of social ordering.

With Marxism as the driving ideology for the 1917 Russian Revolution, the notion of property in the first period under consideration underwent a reset. The call to arms for the Russian proletariat to 'become masters of the productive forces of society... by abolishing [the upper classes'] previous mode of appropriation... [and] to destroy all previous securities for, and insurances of, individual property'[74] brought an end to the reign of the Russian monarchy as well as the wealth grip of the Russian bourgeoisie. Property in post-Revolution Russia thus began on a clean slate and is divided into two categories, namely (i) the means of production such as machinery and farming instruments, which must be subject to 'socialist ownership', and (ii) consumer goods such as clothing and household appliances, which can be subject to 'private ownership'.[75] 'Socialist ownership' of property denotes 'state ownership' or 'collective or co-operative ownership' or 'ownership by trade unions and other organisations',[76] and ownership manifests itself by possession, use, and disposition.[77]

[74] ibid 18; Karl Marx, *Capital*, vol 1 (Pelican Books 1976) 929.

[75] Vladimir Gsovski, *Soviet Civil Law* (University of Michigan Law School 1949) 566–67.

[76] According to Olimpiad S Ioffe in *Soviet Civil Law* (Martinus Nijhoff 1988) 111, 'the three forms of socialist ownership are actually nothing more than different types of state ownership. This means that in the USSR the state owns the entire economy of the country, becoming as a result not only politically unlimited but also economically monopolistic'.

[77] Oleg N Sadikov, *Soviet Civil Law* (ME Sharpe 1988) 122–23.

'Ownerless' property such as 'wild beasts, birds, fishes' automatically falls under state ownership.[78] Conspicuously absent from the variants of 'socialist ownership' is individual private ownership of property, since, with the very limited exception of consumer goods, all other forms of private ownership are considered opposed to 'socialist ownership'. Soviet allegiance to Marxism, which regards law as a tool for advancing revolutionary ideals and purposes and whose content is always subject to change, tempers positivistic reliance on periodic attempts to codify the Soviet property regime as the last word on the notion of property. Therefore, while the 1924 and 1964 Civil Codes expressly recognize the private or personal ownership of property, the scope and importance of individual ownership are far eclipsed by the scope and importance of socialist or collective ownership.[79] This is particularly evident in the regulation of intellectual property where inventors are incentivized by monetary rewards from the government rather than the formal recognition of individual ownership over their creations. Moreover, major categories of non-patentable products such as medicines and chemicals give the Soviet state a de facto monopoly over inventions.[80] Unlike some property concepts in the Western tradition, individual private ownership is not historically central to the understanding and regulation of property in the Soviet tradition.

The collapse of the Soviet Union in the early 1990s was accompanied by a transition from a socialist economy to a capitalist one in post-Soviet states. Private ownership of property, previously anathema to socialism, was now enshrined as a fundamental right in the 1993 Russian Constitution and governed by nearly 200 provisions in the heavily revised 1994 Russian Civil Code.[81] Similar legislative overhauls can be seen in ex-Soviet states such as Uzbekistan,[82] and in post-socialist states such as Romania.[83] However, apart from the character of ownership as a key demarcation of property, property in the Soviet tradition was defined through enumeration, rather than conceptually or through the identification of other attributes.[84] Conceptualizing

[78] ibid 114; Gsovski (n 75) 588–89.

[79] Asya Ostroukh, 'Russian Society and its Civil Codes: A Long Way to Civilian Civil Law' (2013) 6(1) Journal of Civil Law Studies 374, 386, 390–93.

[80] Gsovski (n 75) 594–95.

[81] Ostroukh (n 79) 394, 398.

[82] The Civil Code of the Republic of Uzbekistan, eg arts 18, 25 (unofficial English translation from the original Russian on file with author); also K Rakhmanqulov and S Asyanov (eds), *Commentaries to the Civil Code of the Republic of Uzbekistan*, vol 1 (Ministry of Justice of the Republic of Uzbekistan 2010) 7 (unofficial English translation from the original Russian on file with author).

[83] Katherine Verdery, *What Was Socialism, And What Comes Next?* (Princeton University Press 1996) 83–103.

[84] Gsovski (n 75) 560, 572.

property may have been thought unnecessary by contemporary Soviet scholars since the means of production, which mattered the most, were to vest in the state. So long as the state and those who ran it had the first and last word on what amounted to means of production, any abstract notion of property was superfluous and highly susceptible to constant modification. The legacy of largely collectively owned and largely shapeless property from the Soviet tradition does not disappear with the acceptance of privately owned property in the post-Soviet period. Instead, and particularly in ex-Soviet states, the engineered collision between the collective and the individual fostered a systemic bias for state or collective over individual ownership of property that new legislation alone could not immediately overcome.[85] In some post-socialist regions like Transylvania, private land owners may not acquire full rights of possession, use, and disposal if such rights also vest either by law or by practice in the state or in collective associations. The absence of clear edges of the notion of property in the Soviet tradition and the absence of clear edges of the notion of private ownership and exclusive use in the post-Soviet period result in what Katherine Verdery calls 'fuzzy property'.[86] The notion of property that emerges from the post-Soviet period is both complex and acutely contextual because it comprises 'overlapping use and revenue rights lodged in external conditions that give the holders of those rights incomplete powers for exercising them' and 'is also more than just the surrounding political economy; it entails complex meanings, often revolving around ideas about labour, persons, community, and kinship'.[87]

Today, Russia's active participation in the global economy and open support for economic liberalization through the conclusion of free trade agreements and investment treaties seemingly cements its transition to capitalism and the replacement of Marxist ideology with neoliberalism in the post-2006 property landscape. At the very least, individual ownership of property has come a long way from the days when authorization had to be sought and given for the purchase of pricier consumer goods such as cars. However, this depiction arguably oversimplifies the notion of property and the nature of property ownership in the contemporary post-Soviet world. The tension between the

[85] Scott Newton, *The Constitutional Systems of the Independent Central Asian States—A Contextual Analysis* (Hart 2017) 107–09.

[86] Katherine Verdery, 'Fuzzy Property: Rights, Power, and Identity in Transylvania's Decollectivization' in Michael Burawoy and Katherine Verdery (eds), *Uncertain Transition—Ethnographies of Change in the Postsocialist World* (Rowman & Littlehead Publishers 1999) 53, 55, also 65, 75.

[87] ibid 65.

Marxist ideal of collective ownership of the means of production and the capitalist expectation of private ownership of the same lingers in the bankruptcy of Russian oil giant Yukos. Yukos was acquired by Russian businessman Mikhail Khodorkovsky during the privatization wave of the mid-1990s where shares in state-owned companies were being sold by the government to well-connected individuals in a 'loans for shares' scheme. This arrangement minted a generation of oligarchs, such as Khodorkovsky and Roman Abramovich, and was the antithesis of Marxism, which deplored the accumulation of property in the hands of a few. The forcible divestment of the most lucrative holdings of oil barons by President Vladimir Putin signals a potential retreat of private ownership. Yukos' bankruptcy, which followed from the Russian government's demand for billions of dollars of unpaid taxes, was considered a cover as 'the primary objective of the Russian Federation was not to collect taxes but rather to bankrupt Yukos and appropriate its valuable assets' for state-owned oil companies Gazprom and Rosneft.[88] Around the time of Yukos' bankruptcy, Gazprom also acquired the majority shareholding in Sibneft, another oil competitor, which was owned by Abramovich.[89] While the reversal of the 'loans for shares' arrangement probably had more to do with the consolidation of political power through state control of energy resources, the strategic chipping away at private property ownership despite assurances to the contrary in the Russian Civil Code and in the Russian Constitution parks property in a place that is neither wholly Marxist nor capitalist. The evolved notion of property in modern day Russia appears to be a shifting political construct that purports to adjust and optimize social ordering, and whose shape and ownership may be individualized when it suits one occasion, and collectivized when it suits another occasion.

As the 'fuzziness' of property in the Soviet tradition and beyond has no parallel in the Western tradition, Higgins' claim to consensus on the meaning of property between the two traditions is both surprising and misleading. Higgins rests her claim on Konstantin Katzarov's celebrated *The Theory of Nationalisation* which was published in 1964 and which she calls a 'leading Marxist study'.[90] Katzarov posited that property entails '(a) a right of disposal which is both absolute and also unlimited in point of time; this is the positive aspect; [and] (b) it is exclusive, which means that it confers upon its holder

[88] *Yukos Universal Limited (Isle of Man) v The Russian Federation*, PCA Case No AA227, Final Award (Fortier, Poncet, Schwebel) (18 July 2014) para 756.

[89] ibid para 848.

[90] Higgins, 'The Taking of Property by the State: Recent Developments in International Law' (n 47) 270.

the power to forbid any other person to perform an act of disposal; this is the negative aspect'.[91] Katzarov was a Swiss-educated Bulgarian scholar who was imprisoned by the Bulgarian government for his *anti*-Marxist views, and who published *The Theory of Nationalisation* after he was released from jail.[92] Even if we leave aside Katzarov's personal convictions and circumstances, his choice of private property ownership as the centre of gravity of his work simply does not reflect the marginalization of private property ownership in a Marxist regime. Katzarov's attempt to align Marxist and certain Western notions of property is an isolated one because not even contemporary Russian scholars who were critical of the post-Revolution regime, such as Olimpiad Ioffe, went that far.[93] Moreover, apart from consumer goods, private property ownership in the Soviet Union was practically non-existent in 1964. As such, there would have been little to no occasion to apply Katzarov's theory of nationalization. That said, there is some common ground on the notion of property between the Soviet, post-Soviet, and Western ways of thinking about property. First, ownership, be it individual or collective, is essential to property.[94] A more comprehensive survey of Western property concepts, the Soviet tradition, and the post-Soviet period reveals that property ownership is not, and therefore ought not to be, limited to private ownership. Second, property is defined by the context in which it is viewed and used. Property's susceptibility to shaping and re-shaping by social, economic, and political pressures is explored in the works of Western philosophers such as Marx, Engels, and Penner,[95] and is evident in property's evolution in the Soviet tradition and beyond.[96]

[91] Konstantin Katzarov, *The Theory of Nationalisation* (Anthony W Bradley tr, Martinus Nijhoff 1964) 103.

[92] Venelin Tsachevsky, 'Konstatin Katzarov: A Life Devoted to the Sciences and Bulgaria' (17 April 2016) <http://philosophyclub.bg/konstantin-katzarov-a-life-devoted-to-the-science-and-bulgaria/> accessed 30 April 2024.

[93] Ioffe (n 76) 14, 111.

[94] It is often said that English law does not recognize the concept of ownership because being in exclusive possession of a thing does not create positive rights in that thing which the possessor can claim from the world at large, and because the right to possession of a thing implies the power to transfer possession of that thing, thereby obviating the need to mention ownership. However, ownership is how people conceptualize their relationship to things, see David Lametti, 'The Concept of Property: Relations *Through* Objects of Social Wealth' (2003) 53(4) The University of Toronto Law Journal 325, 327–30, 333. Moreover, in Lawson and Rudden, *The Law of Property* (n 51) 9, the authors already proffered 'the English way of looking at ownership'. For a recent book-length elaboration on how English law recognizes the concept of ownership in property, see Luke Rostill, *Possession, Relative Title, and Ownership in Property* (OUP 2021).

[95] Marx and Engels (n 73) 22–23; Penner, *The Idea of Property in Law* (n 48) 164–68; see also Jatin Dua, 'A Sea of Profit—Making Property in the Western Indian Ocean' in Georgy Kantor and others (eds), *Legalism—Property and Ownership* (OUP 2017) 175, 179.

[96] Verdery, 'Fuzzy Property: Rights, Power, and Identity in Transylvania's Decollectivization' (n 86) 65.

3.3 The Chinese tradition

Like the Soviet and post-Soviet notions of property, the Chinese notion of property evolved over time and in conjunction with major political events. But unlike the post-Soviet property landscape that was shaped by the break with communism and the move to capitalism, China embraced communism in 1949 and remains communist. The turning point for China came in 1979, when then Chinese Premier Deng Xiaoping's announcement of China's 'Open Door Policy' nudged China's command economy towards a mixed market economy and precipitated the development of a property framework that accommodated private property rights.[97]

Before communism, China was an absolute monarchy for thousands of years. Imperial China was ruled by an absolute sovereign while government, society, family, and personal lives were organized in accordance with the teachings of Confucianism and Legalism. Confucianism, which was articulated by Confucius and later by Mencius, urges the conformity of individual behaviour and social interaction with moral rules and rites (礼 or *Li*).[98] *Li* is akin to a code of conduct which, when duly internalized and implemented by every person, begets a harmonious, cultured, and prosperous society where every man, woman, and child knows his or her place within the family unit and on the broader social stratum, and acts in a manner that befits that status. Legalism, on the other hand, which was propounded by Han Feizi, envisages the creation or maintenance of social order through the punitive sanction of law (法 or *Fa*).[99] Law in the eyes of Legalists neither refers nor is it comparable to the rule of law that informs much of Western legal thought. Instead, *Fa* refers exclusively to the imperial law on crimes which punishes violators for criminal offences.[100] *Fa* is not regarded as a means for the enforcement or vindication of infringed civil rights or interests. When *Fa* is considered alongside *Li*, the law in Imperial China plays little to no role in regulating individual behaviour because if every person comports himself or herself in accordance with the Confucian ideal, there will be no crimes to sanction, let alone civil disputes to resolve. The cult of Confucianism and the subordinate role of Legalism relied on self-regulation as the principal method of social ordering. As a result, the notion of property, which was likened

[97] Lan Cao, 'Chinese Privatization: Between Plan and Market' (2000) 63(4) Law & Contemporary Problems 13, 14, also 18–28.

[98] Junwu Pan, 'Chinese Philosophy and International Law' (2011) 1(2) Asian Journal of International Law 233, 233–34.

[99] ibid 234.

[100] ibid.

to personal holdings and belongings, fell within the purview of self-regulation, and received little attention from scholars of Confucianism and Legalism.

Imperial rule in China came to an end in 1912 with the abdication of the boy emperor Puyi. The revolutionaries then established a democratic Chinese Republic with Sun Yat-sen as its first President. Factionalism crippled the fledgling republican government, and the long civil war that ensued only ended with the establishment of the People's Republic of China by the Chinese Communist Party in 1949.[101] The notion of property in the early stages of communist rule in China greatly resembled that in the post-Revolution Soviet Union outlined in the previous section, where private property ownership was replaced by state and collective property ownership.[102] Chinese scholars appeared unconcerned with property theorizing probably because, like their Soviet counterparts, so long as the state and those who ran it had the first and last word on what amounted to property, mapping the contours of property became unnecessary. Vagueness was gradually supplemented by precision with the adoption of Deng's 'Open Door Policy' in 1979, which sought to liberalize China's trading relations with the rest of the world and welcome foreign investment. The shift from a command to a mixed market economy prompted the Chinese government to decentralize, though not privatize, property tenure rights in land.[103] The result was a complex system of overlapping individual, collective, and state rights pertaining to the use of property in land,[104] analogous to the 'fuzzy property' regime in post-socialist Transylvania discussed in the previous section. China's receptivity to foreign investment was complemented by its willingness to borrow from foreign laws when drafting the Chinese Civil Code. And some of the fuzziness in China's decentralized property regime was trimmed in the 1986 Civil Code, which was modelled after the German Bürgerliches Gesetzbuch (BGB), whose notion of property was in turn grounded in Roman law.[105] Article 71 of the 1986 Civil Code defines property through ownership, which entails possession, use, right to benefit, and disposition.[106] Article 71's approach to defining property is also reminiscent of

[101] Hui Wang, *China from Empire to Nation-State* (Michael G Hill tr, Harvard University Press 2014) 136–43.

[102] Weitseng Chen, 'Arbitrage for Property Rights: How Foreign Investors Create Substitutes for Property Institutions in China' (2015) 24(1) Washington International Law Journal 47, 78.

[103] ibid 54.

[104] ibid 78.

[105] Liming Wang, 'The Modernization of Chinese Civil Law Over Four Decades' (2019) 14(1) Frontiers of Law in China 39, 55.

[106] Art 71 provides: '"Property ownership" means the owner's rights to lawfully possess, utilize, profit from and dispose of his property' <http://www.asianlii.org/cn/legis/cen/laws/gpotclotproc555/> accessed 5 August 2024.

'the English way' as described by Lawson and Rudden and outlined at the start of Section 3.1.

Given the very distinct historical exegesis and cultivated political economies of states belonging to the Western, Soviet, post-Soviet, and Chinese traditions, property conceptualization is not accorded the same attention and level of detail across traditions. And where attempts are made to define property through its attributes, the notions of property are also unlikely to be identical. However, as in the case of the heterogenous notions of property in the Western tradition and the evolving nature of property in the Soviet and post-Soviet regimes, where ownership and sensitivity to contextual factors appear to be the key shared attributes of property, it is also possible to identify shared attributes between the Western, Soviet, post-Soviet, and Chinese notions of property. First, like in the Soviet and post-Soviet setting, property ownership in the Chinese tradition may be held by an individual or collectively, and is not limited to private ownership. Second, like its Soviet, post-Soviet, and Western analogues, the character of property in China is shaped by the context property finds itself in at a given point in time. From omission at the height of Confucianism, to fuzziness in the wake of post-communist market liberalization, to approximation to the German codified and English notions of property in the current age of China Inc,[107] property in the Chinese tradition has evolved in response to internal policies and external pressures. Third, the ability to dispose of property, expressly recorded as a manifestation of ownership in Article 71 of the 1986 Civil Code, is implied under imperial rule for individual property owners as well as the sovereign, and under communist rule for the state. And for property to be disposed of, it must be separable from its owner. The attribute of separability, which has endured throughout the evolving notion of property in the Chinese tradition, is also explicitly recognized in the Western tradition,[108] in the socialist depiction of property ownership,[109] and in post-socialist legislation.[110]

[107] Mark Wu, 'The "China, Inc." Challenge to Global Trade Governance' (2016) 57(2) Harvard International Law Journal 261, 264–65 where the Chinese economy is said to be unlike any other because it is fraught with contradictions: 'While one might think of the economy as state-dominated, private enterprises drive much of China's dynamic growth. In addition, economic intervention does not always flow through the state. Alongside the state is the Chinese Communist Party, a separate political actor that plays an active role in the management of state-owned enterprises. The economy embraces market-oriented dynamics, yet it is not strictly a free-market capitalist system. Networked hierarchies and embedded relationships exist among businesses, but not necessarily in the way they operate elsewhere in the world' (footnotes and acronyms omitted).

[108] Lawson and Rudden, *The Law of Property* (n 51) 8–11; Hohfeld (n 57) 51; Penner, *Property Rights: A Re-Examination* (n 56) 14.

[109] Sadikov (n 77) 122–23.

[110] See eg Civil Code of the Russian Federation arts 18, 209(1).

3.4 The Islamic tradition

In comparison to the rather shapeless notion of property that emerged from Imperial China and in early post-socialist regimes, property or *mal* in the Islamic tradition has been subject to scholarly reflection and debate and, as a result, has clearer contours. Property and its regulation are addressed in the Quran, which records the commandments of Allah conveyed by the Prophet Muhammad. Together with the Sunnah, which sets out the teachings of the Prophet Muhammad, the Quran is regarded as the supreme authoritative text on Islamic law.[111] As Islamic scholars believe that the Quran and the Sunnah direct the pursuit of social good and the overall betterment of mankind,[112] and since property ownership and rights enable human flourishing,[113] the notion of property is prominent in the Islamic tradition. That said, there is, to date, no unified view on the notion of property among Islamic scholars. The need for the Quran and Sunnah, which date back to the seventh century, to be interpreted to suit modern times has given rise to different schools of Islamic thought. Sunni Islam, which is practised by the preponderance of Muslims worldwide, comprises four schools of thought, namely the Hanafi school, the Maliki school, the Shafi`i school, and the Hanbali school. The notion of property has received two divergent interpretations, one from the Hanafi school and one from the other three Sunni schools, with the latter representing the majority view.

According to the Hanafi school, property has two fundamental attributes.[114] The first is tangibility, which can be owned or protected. The second is beneficial use in accordance with prevailing customs. The Hanafi limitation of ownership to tangible things denies the label of property to intangibles such as 'knowledge, health, dignity, intelligence; all usufructs, debts, mere rights such as the right to development, the right of pre-emption, [and] the right to water'.[115] It also denies the label of property to anything which, arguably, eludes human control, such as 'free air, heat of the sun and moonlight'.[116] The Hanafi understanding of beneficial use further limits the scope of property. Not only are objects of sustenance such as wheat (stalk) or water (drop) in small units

[111] Ezieddin Elmahjub, *An Islamic Vision of Intellectual Property—Theory and Practice* (CUP 2018) 19.
[112] ibid 31.
[113] ibid 40.
[114] Muhammad W Islam, 'Al-Mal: The Concept of Property in Islamic Legal Thought' (1999) 14 Arab Law Quarterly 361, 363–64.
[115] ibid 363.
[116] ibid.

deemed to be of no benefit and therefore not property, objects of beneficial use in times of necessity such as carrion to combat severe hunger are also not considered property.[117] The Hanafi notion of property, which represents the minority view in Sunni Islam, is the most restrictive of the variety of notions emanating from the various juristic traditions considered thus far. Although the Hanafi school does not purport to limit property ownership to private ownership, the cumulative requirements of tangibility *and* unexceptional beneficial use in sufficient quantities would rule out many established forms of property, such as intellectual property and perishable consumer goods, that will easily pass the property threshold in the Western, Soviet, post-Soviet, and Chinese traditions.

In contrast, the consolidated notion of property according to the Maliki, Shafi`i, and Hanbali schools is more accommodating. The Maliki school focused on the conferral of ownership and the owner's ability to exclude others from interference as integral features of property.[118] This is similar to Lawson and Rudden's notion of property, reflects the Hohfeldian power–liability correlative, and recalls Penner's exclusion thesis, later refashioned as the right to exclusive possession. The Shafi`i school posited that property, which can be tangible or intangible, has beneficial value and is exchangeable.[119] Unlike the minority Hanafi school which seems to regard intrinsic value, such as the quenching of thirst by drinking enough water, as beneficial, the Shafi`i school equates beneficial value to quantifiable financial value. Additionally, defining property in terms of its capacity to be exchanged or transferred indicates that the Shafi`i school endorses the attribute of separability which also features in the Western, socialist, post-socialist, and Chinese notions of property. The Hanbali school, like the minority Hanafi school, also defines property in terms of its capacity for beneficial use. Although the Hanbali school does not limit property to corporeal things, the benefit derived from property must be lawfully permissible and derived in unexceptional circumstances, which would rule out carrion and wine (since they cannot be lawfully consumed in unexceptional circumstances) as property.[120] The consolidated notion of property according to the Maliki, Shafi`i, and Hanbali schools exhibits the following attributes: (i) assignable and transferable ownership; (ii) capacity for being

[117] ibid 364.
[118] ibid 365.
[119] ibid 364.
[120] ibid 365.

possessed and stored; and (iii) conferring a lawful benefit such as commercial value or gain in the relevant context.[121]

One shared attribute of property between the otherwise divergent Hanafi and majority schools is the benefit, be it intrinsic or commercial, that property confers on its owner. Besides ownership which appears to be the principal common denominator in the different notions of property within and without the Islamic tradition, it may therefore be said a distinctive attribute of property in the Islamic tradition is its capacity for beneficial use. Beneficial use is alluded to in the Lawson and Rudden (income) and Lockean (fruits of labour) notions of property and implied in terms of privileges and powers owners exercise over property in the Hohfeldian framework. Beneficial use also underscores the case for collective over private ownership of property advocated by Rousseau, Proudhon, Engels, and Marx, which was implemented in the Soviet tradition and in early communist rule in China, since any benefit derived from means of production should be shared by the proletarian many instead being enjoyed by the bourgeois few. The right to benefit from property is also paraphrased in the Russian Civil Code[122] and characterized as an attribute of property ownership in the Chinese Civil Code.[123] Upon comparing the notions of property in the Western, Soviet, post-Soviet, Chinese, and Islamic traditions, the four attributes of property which appear to be shared, to varying degrees, across traditions are ownership, separability, sensitivity to contextual dictates and factors, and the conferral of benefit.

4. The rise and attributes of new property

The creation of a property knowledge gap through deficient treaty definitions, and the entrenchment of that knowledge gap by Higgins' venerated but defective claim that the 'bundle of rights' approach to property is representative, obscure the existence and emergence of new property whose contours

[121] ibid.

[122] Art 18 of the 2006 Russian Civil Code provides in relevant part: 'The citizens may possess the property by the right of ownership... may *enjoy* the rights of the authors of the works of science, literature and art, of inventions and of other law-protected results of the intellectual activity; and may also *enjoy* other property and personal non-property rights' (emphasis added).

[123] Art 71 of the 1986 Chinese Civil Code provides: '"Property ownership" means the owner's rights to lawfully possess, utilize, *profit from* and dispose of his property' (emphasis added); art 114 of the 2020 Chinese Civil Code provides: 'Real rights are the rights to directly and exclusively control a specific thing by the right holder in accordance with law, which consists of the ownership, *right to usufruct*, and security interests in the property' (emphasis added).

do not match Hohfeldian conceptual parameters. The dominant, if not exclusive, focus on private ownership in Locke's, Lawson and Rudden's, Hohfeld's, and Penner's concepts of property is not designed to accommodate, and consequently is unlikely to contemplate, the regulation of property which is not privately owned.[124] And yet, various forms of non-privately owned things are already attracting recognition as property in international law. One example is intangible cultural heritage, such as indigenous languages and customs, which is not normally owned by any individual but has nonetheless been regarded as property in international cultural heritage law scholarship.[125] Another example is places and objects that are neither privately owned nor subject to the sovereignty of any state, such as the High Seas, the moon, and resources in outer space, but which may nonetheless qualify as property by virtue of collective ownership and use in the socialist vein.[126] A third example is rights which may defy typical manifestations of private ownership like exclusive use and disposal, such as contractual rights, but which have been characterized as property by those seeking more familiar, more concrete, or more generous redress for interference.[127] Anglo-American concepts of property will struggle to explain why cultural heritage, collectively owned natural resources, and contracts are property, and perhaps even deny that new property is property. So, when biased concepts are actively relied on, or acquiesced in, to determine the shape of property, international law will always lag behind new and newer forms of property that it purports to regulate. The continued suppression of new property through the maintenance of the property knowledge gap will result in an international law that fails to develop the acumen, the blueprint, and the finesse for regulating new property.

The previous section demonstrated that concepts of property vary considerably across the Western, Soviet, post-Soviet, Chinese, and Islamic juristic traditions. Therefore, a more representative shape of new property cannot be drawn with reference to a single juristic tradition, let alone a specific sector

[124] To be fair, Anglo-American philosophers acknowledge that property can be owned by, for instance, a state, see Penner, 'Property Rights' (n 69); Lawson and Rudden, *The Law of Property*, 3rd edn (n 54) 7–9. But any acknowledgement is made in passing and the discourse invariably revolves around the private, individual ownership of property.

[125] Andrzej Jakubowski, *State Succession in Cultural Property* (OUP 2015) 3; cf Janet Blake, 'On Defining Cultural Heritage' (2000) 61 International and Comparative Law Quarterly 61, 62–66, but Blake does not address the assimilation of intangible cultural heritage to intellectual property; for this see Mira Burri, 'Cultural Heritage and Intellectual Property' in Francesco Francioni and Ana Filipa Vrdoljak (eds), *International Cultural Heritage Law* (OUP 2020) 459, 471.

[126] See eg United Nations Convention on the Law of the Sea (signed 10 December 1982, entered into force 16 November 1994) 1833 UNTS 397 arts 136–55; also Moon Treaty arts 11(1) and 11(3).

[127] Ho (n 21) 153–57, 162–71.

within a single juristic tradition. Instead, the shape of new property in international law should be drawn with reference to attributes which are common or very similar to the four major juristic traditions surveyed. Relying on more widely shared attributes of property, rather than the Anglo-American attributes of property, sketches a notion of property that is more inclusive and, in all likelihood, better able to adapt to and capture the rise of new property. The rest of this section elaborates on the core attributes of new property which were distilled from the analytical survey and comparison of property concepts across the four major juristic traditions in the previous section. They are: imputable ownership (Section 4.1), responsiveness to contextual factors (Section 4.2), separability (Section 4.3), and conferral of benefit (Section 4.4).

4.1 Imputable ownership

Ownership is recognized as a core attribute of property in all the major juristic traditions surveyed because only ownership confers an enforceable legal and moral right on the owner to use a thing. When ownership is the base right from which all other rights to property flow, it follows that whatever cannot be owned cannot give rise to any right to property and, as such, cannot be property. One example of a thing that cannot be owned is the air that we breathe. The Hanafi school in the Islamic tradition denies that air is property because air is not subject to human control. However, as control, or at least lawful control, is an extension of ownership, the incapacity for ownership lays down the more fundamental disagreement over air as property. Airspace, on the other hand, is property because it can be owned (by the state above whose territory it is found) and, by extension, controlled (by the owner state, through its representatives, that determines when and whether foreign aircraft have permission to enter).

Ownership comprises two principal dimensions. The first dimension is putative, while the second dimension is qualitative. The putative dimension of ownership concerns the conferral and recognition of ownership over a thing, such that the owner's right to property can be exercised without interference from non-owners and can be enforced against non-owners. Ownership is normally conferred by law, be it domestic law or treaty law, the former stemming from the legislative process in each state, while the latter represents an agreement between states. However, ownership may also be established by unilateral conquest or by forcible acquisition, and acquiescence by non-owners in a claim to ownership. When ownership is contested, the putative owner's right to property is validated by the recognition of the putative owner as the rightful owner.[128] Recognition can mean legal recognition, which is obtained by recourse to judicial processes, or political or social recognition, which is obtained through the approbation of the community in which the claim to ownership is embedded. A good illustration of how putative ownership is not necessarily rightful ownership can be found in Russia's annexation and absorption of Crimea into Russian territory in 2014. Russia's forcible acquisition of ownership over Crimea, which is part of Ukrainian territory, met with international disapprobation and sanctions. Absent external recognition of its claim to ownership, Russia's sovereignty over Crimea remains putative and sharply contested. The putative dimension of ownership calls for the verification of a claim to ownership in a thing that can give rise to a right to property. Verification may reveal that the putative owner is not the rightful owner, or that the thing is incapable of being owned (such as illusory contractual rights) and therefore not new property.

The qualitative dimension of ownership concerns the manner of ownership. While Anglo-American concepts of property seem to focus on private, individual ownership, this emphasis neither dominates the Western juristic tradition, nor defines the Soviet, post-Soviet, Chinese, and Islamic juristic traditions. In the context of new property, ownership can mean private, individual ownership, privately led collective ownership, state-led collective ownership, state ownership, and multi-state ownership. Accommodating variety in the manner of ownership as a core attribute of new property serves two objectives. The first is to reiterate the inappositeness of aligning property ownership in international law, which often caters to different issues and interests than domestic law, with property ownership according to Anglo-American terms. The second is to reinforce the direct link between ownership and property, because unduly limiting the manner of ownership to private, individual ownership dulls awareness and appreciation of property that is not or cannot be subject to private, individual ownership. Accepting variety in the manner of ownership is an important first step in enabling new property to come to light.

Regardless of whether property can be owned individually, collectively, or by the state, ownership requires the identification of the owner/s. And in this regard, ownership can be either asserted or attributed. Therefore, ownership as a core attribute of new property refers to imputable ownership, which begets

[128] Putative ownership is similar to the relativity of titles to land in common law legal systems, where 'the title to possess [is] generated by a person[] being in adverse possession of unregistered land', see David Fox, 'Relativity of Title at Law and in Equity' (2006) 65(2) Cambridge Law Journal 330, 330–32.

identified or identifiable owners with a recognized right to use the thing owned without interference from non-owners.

4.2 Responsiveness to contextual factors

As property is always identified, used, disputed, and regulated in a specific context and never in the abstract, its shape is necessarily determined in part by context-specific factors. As a result, what qualifies as property in one context may not be regarded as property in a different context. Penner will certainly regard the existence of a market for buying, selling, and consuming wine as enabling the identification of a bottle of wine as property, but the Hanbali school will disagree because the Quran forbids alcohol consumption. The prohibition disables a bottle of wine from conferring a lawful benefit on anyone and from qualifying as property. Context-specific factors were also integral to the shape of property in post-socialist agricultural societies and in post-communist China. In the former, Verdery's study on 'fuzzy property' in Transylvania described a complex web of overlapping ownership and user rights over agricultural land and tools that may breach the limits of property concepts elsewhere, but which merely responded to the transition from socialism to capitalism and the changing ideals of 'labour, persons, kinship, and community' that the transition triggered. In the latter, property assumed a more distinct shape on the heels of economic liberalization and political choice which led to the incorporation of the attributes of property found in the German BGB within the Chinese Civil Code. As new property will also be identified and regulated in specific contexts and not in the abstract, it is therefore imperative that new property is responsive to contextual factors, such as but not limited to social, economic, and political pressures, to the extent that such factors, alone or in tandem, are present. This attribute of new property calls for the identification and evaluation of factors in the relevant context that will either facilitate or frustrate a thing from taking shape as property.

Responsiveness to contextual factors is what imparts fluidity to the shape of new property because factors can vary across contexts, and applicable factors in a given context can change over time. This does not mean that new property is nebulous or the product of speculation, because other core attributes (such as imputable ownership, separability, and conferral of benefit) must still be present for the label of new property to attach. However, it does mean that the list of new property is not closed. Newer forms of new property, forged in part by changing or previously absent contextual factors, can and will appear. The three categories of new property discussed in this monograph, namely, cultural, common, and contingent property, represent a starting point for enriching the existing discourse on property regulation in international law. It is likely that these three categories may, in time to come, be supplemented by additional categories of new property.

4.3 Separability

For property to be sold, transferred, assigned, exchanged, or otherwise disposed of, it must be separable from its imputed owner. It has been said that whatever is intrinsic to a person, such as medical skills, is not separable from the person and cannot be considered property.[129] It follows, so the argument goes, that a medical doctor's licence to practice is also intrinsic to the holder of the licence, cannot be transferred to anyone else, and therefore cannot be considered property. In contrast, a medical doctor's car is not intrinsic to the doctor; it can be owned by the doctor or by anyone else the doctor chooses to sell or transfer the car to; or it can be melted down into scrap metal at the doctor's choice as a result of which there will be no new car owner. While these textbook illustrations offer seemingly straightforward markers of separability, separability may be a more nuanced property attribute than these illustrations suggest.

The quality of disposability that property possesses in the major juristic traditions surveyed does not necessarily entail the transfer of ownership. While some Western theorists and the Shafi`i school in the Islamic tradition envisage disposability largely in terms of an actual or potential transfer of ownership,[130] the more common view neither restricts disposability to the transfer of ownership nor rules out simple abandonment or relinquishment as a mode of disposal. The medical doctor can abandon or relinquish his licence to practice by, for instance, failing to renew it in compliance with the legal requirements for renewal. While the doctor cannot abandon or relinquish his medical skills, he can dispose of his licence which attests to his professional qualifications. Disposal of a licence to practice, in this case, does not entail a new owner for the disposed licence; the doctor simply ceases to be the owner of a valid licence

[129] Douglas, 'Property, Investment and the Scope of Investment Protection Obligations' (n 21) 375.
[130] Hohfeld (n 57) 51; Penner, *The Idea of Property in Law* (n 48) 152; Islam (n 114) 364.

to practice without there being a new owner for the lapsed licence. This is analogous to the doctor choosing to melt his car down into scrap metal, which is another instance of disposal without there being a new owner for the disposed thing waiting in the wings. To insist that separability must manifest itself through an actual or potential transfer of ownership might distort the shape of new property in international law because it readily disqualifies cultural property, whose ownership many believe can only ever be imputed to the state of origin[131] and cannot be legitimately transferred or altered by any means, not even by conquest, as property.

When property is separable from its imputed owner, it can also be taken away from its imputed owner. Appropriation is the other side of the coin to disposability since both processes bring about the divestment of property.[132] To return to the illustration of the medical doctor, while his medical skills cannot be appropriated by another (barring maiming), his licence to practice can be taken away from him either temporarily (suspension) or permanently (disbarment) by his local medical association for, say, malpractice. The inability of the medical association to transfer the revoked licence to a different doctor does not change the fact that the revocation divests the first doctor of his privilege to practice and separates the doctor from his licence. Therefore, while the transfer of ownership may follow in some cases of disposal or appropriation, it is not critical to a determination of whether a thing is separable from its imputed owner. When separability is understood in terms of the capacity to be divested, rather than the prospect of ownership transfer, this opens a field of new possibilities for what may constitute new property. On the more conservative end of the new property spectrum is cultural property mentioned above, and on the more controversial end is human rights which can be voluntarily surrendered by the rights-holders as well as forcibly divested from the rights-holders. Someone who is falsely imprisoned can surely claim that he or she has a human right to liberty and freedom of movement, but it remains a fact that he or she has, at least until the day of release, been divested of that right.

[131] 1970 UNESCO Convention, Preamble arts 2(1), 4(a), 4(b). To date, the 1970 UNESCO Convention has been ratified by 140 states, see UNESCO, 'Fight Illicit Trafficking (1970 Convention)' <https://en.unesco.org/fighttrafficking/1970> accessed 30 April 2024.

[132] Appropriation is broadly defined in international law. State interference with or dispossession of alien property, even if that property is not subsequently put to beneficial use by the state, may be regarded as an appropriation, see Muthucumaraswamy Sornarajah, *The International Law on Foreign Investment* (4th edn, CUP 2017) 453, also 432–33.

4.4 Conferral of benefit

Property's ability to confer a benefit on its imputed owner is a shared attribute in the major juristic traditions surveyed. Although acknowledgement of this attribute is not always explicit, the derivation of benefit is an important incentive for demarcating a thing as property and for asserting ownership over it. The proven or prospective benefit that property confers on its imputed owner is a principal reason for the divestment of bourgeois ownership of the means of production during the 1917 Russian Revolution and its replacement with collective ownership. History repeated itself during China's transition from republican to communist rule in the 1940s and 1950s, where private property ownership was replaced with state or collective ownership. If there were nothing to gain from owning property, the forcible reassignment of property ownership from private into state or collective hands would not have achieved the redistribution of wealth that Marx and his adherents advocated. The conferral of benefit as an attribute of property is most pronounced in the Islamic tradition, where both the minority and majority schools acknowledge this feature. To shape a more inclusive notion of new property, it is preferable to admit that even within the Islamic tradition, the benefit can refer to either financial (Shafi`i school) or non-financial benefit (Hanafi and Hanbali schools). As few will disagree that personal items of purely sentimental value to no one but their owner are property, there is no compelling reason to limit the type of benefit property can confer on its imputed owner to financial benefit when speaking of property on a larger scale. The moon, for instance, may not confer a financial benefit on its imputed owners of 'all mankind', because there is no market for the moon to be bought and sold like a regular commodity. However, it does not preclude moon exploration from yielding non-financial benefits such as educational insights into outer space and scientific discoveries that contribute to the betterment of 'all countries'.[133] Therefore, that which can be situated in a cognizable regulatory context, which is separable from and which confers a financial or non-financial benefit on its imputed owner/s, is new property.

[133] Moon Treaty art 4(1) provides: 'The exploration and use of the moon shall be the province of *all mankind* and shall be carried out for the *benefit* and in the interest of *all countries*, irrespective of their degree of economic or scientific development. Due regard shall be paid to the interests of present and future generations as well as to the need to promote higher standards of living and conditions of economic and social progress and development in accordance with the Charter of the United Nations' (emphasis added).

5. Conclusion

This chapter has attempted to dispel the myth that 'international law has rather a lot to say on property'. While the regulation of property use and interference has arisen for consideration and codification in multiple subfields of international law, this did not lead to greater clarity or precision in articulating the notion of property. Beneath the façade of comprehensiveness maintained by treaties and by scholarly disinclination to challenge the perception of a content-rich international law on property regulation, there lurk newer forms of property that struggle for recognition and for definition. Given the frequency of property or property-related disputes potentially subject to regulation by international law, it is necessary to understand how a knowledge gap on property, especially new property, was created, and how it may be closed.

The property knowledge gap was created by greater specialization in international law and the proliferation of treaties as governance manuals for the various specialized subfields of international law. These treaties often adopt an illustrative or discretionary definition of property or employ the term property but leave it undefined. Illustrative definitions tend to freeze property in time because illustrations cannot capture newer forms of property that have yet to emerge, while discretionary definitions by treaty signatories tend to cultivate obscurity in the notion of property, because they do not converge towards a common threshold or shared set of attributes. Moreover, as property is usually incidental to or a variant of the principal object of regulation by these governance treaties, ranging from war crimes to foreign investment, property is often framed in terms of the principal object of regulation. New property naturally struggles to take shape if property is constantly underdefined in treaties that supply much of the content of international law and constantly aligned with the treaties' principal object of regulation by treaty interpreters.

The property knowledge gap may be closed by discerning the shape of property imparted by property attributes that are shared, to varying degrees, in property concepts found in the major juristic traditions. This ensures that the resulting notion of property that is destined for regulation by international law is a reasonably representative snapshot of how property is conceptualized in different parts of the world. A comparative survey and analysis of the Western, Soviet, post-Soviet, Chinese, and Islamic juristic traditions reveal that there are plausibly four core attributes of property that merit general applicability. They are: (i) imputable ownership, (ii) responsiveness to contextual factors, (iii) separability, and (iv) conferral of benefit. These attributes undoubtedly capture basic property such as land, and, more importantly, they *also* capture newer forms of property such as cultural heritage, collectively owned natural resources, and contracts. Now that new property has finally taken shape, it is appropriate to consider, in the following chapters, what international law can and ought to say on new property regulation. I start with cultural property.

2

Cultural Property

1. Introduction

Profiling and regulating cultural property as new property is a potentially hazardous exercise. As briefly explained in the preceding chapter, cultural property to date has been defined through illustrative lists in international conventions, through discretionary labelling by states, or not at all. There is little controversy when property, usually tangible, is captured by an illustration or explicitly labelled by a state as cultural property. But there is great uncertainty about whether previously unarticulated, unlabelled, or even intangible property can also be recognized and regulated as cultural property. A possible workaround is to limit property talk when there are variables, and instead employ the terms 'cultural objects', 'cultural expressions', and the seemingly all-encompassing 'cultural heritage' to accommodate all the variables.[1]

[1] See eg 1995 UNIDROIT Convention on Stolen or Illegally Exported *Cultural Objects* (emphasis added) (signed 24 June 1995, entered into force 1 July 1998) 2421 UNTS 457 (1995 UNIDROIT Convention); 2005 Convention on the Protection and Promotion of the Diversity of *Cultural Expressions* (emphasis added) (signed 20 October 2005, entered into force 18 March 2007) 2440 UNTS 311 (2005 Cultural Expressions Convention); 2001 Convention on the Protection of Underwater *Cultural Heritage* (emphasis added) (signed 2 November 2001, entered into force 2 January 2009) 2562

New Property in International Law. Jean Ho, Oxford University Press. © Jean Ho 2024.
DOI: 10.1093/9780191976117.003.0003

Yet, designating culture over property as the common denominator results in multiple regulatory regimes, over and above the existing ones for cultural property. Moreover, eschewing property for 'objects', 'expressions', and 'heritage' requires developing autonomous definitions for 'objects',[2] 'expressions', and 'heritage', when they are already, respectively, tangible, intellectual, and intangible property. Far from providing needed clarity, limiting property talk leads to unnecessary, though probably unintended, complication. Therefore, and ironically so, cultural property regulation and all its subsets make up one of the most prescriptive but unprincipled fields of study in international law.

This chapter argues that cultural property is poorly regulated and understood in international law due to uncoordinated overlapping regulatory regimes and a persistent failure to develop and adopt a functional and progressive definition of cultural property. It further explains how transposing the attributes of new property identified in Chapter 1, namely, imputable ownership, responsiveness to contextual factors, separability, and conferral of a benefit to cultural property, imparts credibility and coherence to an umbrella notion of cultural property that lends itself to more predictable regulation. To this end, Section 2 examines how cultural property is concurrently regulated by four distinct bodies of international law, none of which appear to absorb newer forms of cultural property. Section 3 critiques the tendency of international lawmakers to favour piecemeal regulatory regimes specific to cultural property when a common regulatory regime could have sufficed. The outcome of this piecemeal approach is a series of bifurcations, where cultural property is distinguished from cultural heritage, and regulated differently depending on whether it is tangible or intangible, and on whether it lies above water or underwater. These divisions have a distortive effect, cultivating the erroneous impression that cultural property is merely one of several discrete objects of regulation when it is, in fact, the principal object of regulation. Section 4 advocates the assimilation of cultural property to new property to

UNTS 1 (2001 Underwater Cultural Heritage Convention); 2003 Convention on the Safeguarding of the Intangible *Cultural Heritage* (emphasis added) (signed 17 October 2003, entered into force 20 April 2006) 2368 UNTS 3 (2003 Intangible Cultural Heritage Convention).

[2] According to Carsten Stahn, *Confronting Colonial Objects—Histories, Legalities, and Access to Culture* (OUP 2023) 5, cultural objects 'have a dual nature' and 'are part of material culture (["]cultural property["]) and become part of heritage, in the sense that they carry historical and symbolic meaning that transcends their origins and evolves over time'. By this definition, to understand cultural objects, we must first define cultural property.

mitigate the definitional chaos brought about by uncoordinated and piecemeal regulation outlined in Sections 2 and 3, and discusses the implications of regulating cultural property as new property in international law. Section 5 concludes.

2. Diffuse and deficient regulation of cultural property

Cultural property is governed by four distinct regimes in international law. The first, and some might say main, regime is international cultural heritage law, which developed in response to the need for cultural property protection in times of armed conflict (Section 2.1). The second regime is international criminal law as codified in the Rome Statute of the International Criminal Court,[3] which has been invoked to sanction the destruction of cultural property (Section 2.2). The third regime is international investment law, where thousands of investment treaties potentially constrain states from prioritizing cultural property protection over foreign investment protection (Section 2.3). The fourth and final regime is international trade law, which expressly allows states to impose non-discriminatory measures to protect 'national treasures of artistic, historic or archaeological value' without being in violation of their obligations towards free trade as set out in Article XX(f) of the General Agreement on Tariffs and Trade (Section 2.4).[4] These four regimes overlap because international cultural heritage law lacks concrete means of cultural property protection, while cultural property is not the target object of regulation in international criminal law (international crimes), international investment law (foreign investment), and international trade law (trade-related measures). The latter three regimes thus draw on international cultural heritage law when cultural property protection arises for consideration. The existence of four regulatory regimes, which presumably complement each other, suggests comprehensive cultural property regulation under international law. This section challenges the presumption by showcasing how the spread of cultural property regulation across international cultural heritage law, international criminal law, international investment law, and international trade law has led to diffuse and deficient regulation.

[3] (signed 17 July 1998, entered into force 1 July 2002) 217 UNTS 90 (Rome Statute).
[4] (signed 30 October 1947, entry into force 1 January 1948) 55 UNTS 194 (GATT) art XX(f).

2.1 International cultural heritage law (ICHL)

ICHL is articulated in an impressive number of international conventions, of which six are binding on ratifying states.[5] The six binding conventions are the 1954 Convention for the Protection of Cultural Property in the Event of Armed Conflict and its two Protocols (1954, 1999),[6] the 1970 Convention on the Means of Prohibiting and Preventing the Illicit Import, Export and Transfer of Ownership of Cultural Property,[7] the 1972 World Heritage Convention,[8] the 2001 Underwater Cultural Heritage Convention, the 2003 Intangible Cultural Heritage Convention, and the 2005 Cultural Expressions Convention. Despite the formal breadth of coverage for cultural property protection offered by various conventions, substantive ICHL has barely evolved from the 1950s (Section 2.1.1). The failure to modernize is compounded by the absence of adjudicatory mechanisms for dealing with ICHL violations, compelling ICHL to feed on other regulatory regimes for concrete means of cultural property protection (Section 2.1.2).

2.1.1 Stagnant ICHL

ICHL grew from a specific objective, namely, 'the protection of cultural property in time of war'.[9] The first source treaty of ICHL, which was concluded in the wake of wanton cultural property destruction during the First and Second World Wars, is the 1954 Hague Convention.[10] The 1954 Hague Convention defines cultural property as 'movable or immovable property of great importance to the cultural heritage of every people', 'buildings whose main and effective purpose is to preserve or exhibit . . . movable cultural property', and 'centers containing a large amount of cultural property'.[11] It then directs contracting

[5] The three non-binding conventions are: (i) the 1995 UNIDROIT Convention; (ii) the World Intellectual Property Office (WIPO) Draft Articles on the Protection of Traditional Knowledge, <www.wipo.int/edocs/mdocs/tk/en/wipo_grtkf_ic_40/facilitators_text_on_tk.pdf> accessed 30 April 2024 (WIPO Draft Articles on TK); (iii) the WIPO Draft Articles on the Protection of Traditional Cultural Expressions, <www.wipo.int/edocs/mdocs/tk/en/wipo_grtkf_ic_40/facilitators_text_on_tces.pdf> accessed 30 April 2024 (WIPO Draft Articles on TCE).

[6] (signed 14 May 1954, entered into force 7 August 1956) 249 UNTS 215 (1954 Hague Convention); First Protocol to the 1954 Hague Convention (signed 14 May 1954, entered into force 7 August 1956) 249 UNTS 358; Second Protocol to the 1954 Hague Convention (signed 26 March 1999, entered into force 9 March 2004) 2253 UNTS 172.

[7] (signed 14 November 1970, entered into force 24 April 1972) 823 UNTS 231 (1970 UNESCO Convention).

[8] (signed 16 November 1972, entered into force 17 December 1975) 1037 UNTS 151.

[9] Janet Blake, 'On Defining the Cultural Heritage' (2000) 49 International & Comparative Law Quarterly 61, 61.

[10] Roger O'Keefe, *The Protection of Cultural Property in Armed Conflict* (CUP 2006) 36–91.

[11] 1954 Hague Convention art 1.

states to mark cultural property under special protection with a 'distinctive emblem',[12] and to refrain from 'any act of hostility directed against such property and . . . from any use of such property or its surroundings for military purposes'.[13] The 1954 Hague Convention is supplemented by its First and Second Protocols, which respectively address the illicit removal of cultural property from zones of armed conflict and reinforce the implementation of the provisions in the main convention.[14] Together, these conventions regulate cultural property protection in armed conflict settings.[15]

The logic of prevention behind the recognize-and-refrain approach to cultural property protection that underscores the 1954 Hague Convention and its two Protocols is straightforward. This approach presupposes the methodical affixing of emblems by states onto cultural property and the voluntary, honourable restraint of invading or occupying forces towards emblematized cultural property, all before fighting commences.[16] Such a salutary version of warfare exists in the imagination but not in practice. The recognize-and-refrain approach of 1954 is demonstrably futile against spontaneous, iconoclastic attacks, which are a hallmark of modern, and especially terrorist, warfare.[17] No heed was paid to the 1954 Hague Convention and its Protocols by the terrorist organization, Islamic State in Iraq and Levant (ISIL), when desecrating and looting cultural property over an extended period of time in Iraq and Syria.[18] And despite acknowledging that ISIL was deliberately desecrating cultural

[12] ibid arts 6, 10, 16, 17.

[13] ibid arts 4, 9.

[14] For a detailed analysis of the role of and relationship between the First and Second Protocols and the 1954 Hague Convention, see O'Keefe, *The Protection of Cultural Property in Armed Conflict* (n 10) 195–201, 236–45.

[15] Cultural property protection in international and non-international armed conflict is briefly addressed in Additional Protocols I (arts 53, 85(4)(d)) and II (art 16) to the Geneva Conventions of 1949 (Protocol Additional to the Geneva Conventions of 12 August 1949, and Relating to the Protection of Victims of International Armed Conflicts (signed 8 June 1977, entered into force 7 December 1978) 1125 UNTS 3 (Protocol I); Protocol Additional to the Geneva Conventions of 12 August 1949, and Relating to the Protection of Victims of Non-International Armed Conflicts (signed 8 June 1977, entered into force 7 December 1978) 1125 UNTS 609 (Protocol II). Since the relevant provisions in Protocols I and II defer to and merely reiterate art 4(1) of the 1954 Hague Convention, they will not be discussed as part of ICHL in this chapter. That said, art 85(4)(d) read with art 85(5) of Protocol I pegs cultural property destruction as a war crime; it will be discussed as part of international criminal law in Section 2.2 below.

[16] The Second Protocol to the 1954 Hague Convention contains a 'comprehensive and weighty regime of penal sanctions for breach' (arts 15–21), see O'Keefe, *The Protection of Cultural Property in Armed Conflict* (n 10) 241, but it is for individual contracting states to enact the relevant punitive legislation.

[17] See eg the well-documented targeted and collateral destruction of cultural property during drawn-out conflicts in Libya (2011–2020), Mali (2008–present), and Afghanistan (early 1990s–present), Marina Lotsal, *International Cultural Heritage Law in Armed Conflict* (CUP 2017) 122–31, 157–60.

[18] Adnan Almohamad, 'The Destruction and Looting of Cultural Heritage Sites by ISIS in Syria: The Case of Manbji and its Countryside' (2021) 28(2) International Journal of Cultural Property 221, 228–33.

property 'to deny historical roots and cultural diversity' and 'generating income from engaging directly or indirectly in the illegal excavation and the looting and smuggling of cultural property', the United Nations Security Council doggedly recommended ratification of the 1954 Hague Convention as the way forward and out in Resolution 2347 of 2017.[19] Another case in point is the Russian invasion of Ukraine in February 2022. To date, the Ukrainian Ministry of Culture and Information Policy claims that more than 350 cultural sites have been destroyed by Russian forces, fuelling suspicion that Russia is deliberately desecrating cultural property in Ukraine as part of its occupational strategy.[20] Ironically, Iraq, Syria, Russia, and Ukraine have all ratified the 1954 Hague Convention and its First Protocol, which boast 135 and 112 signatories respectively.[21] Widely adopted conventions that are specifically designed to but repeatedly fail to prevent or minimize cultural property destruction in armed conflict are clearly unfit for purpose. Widely adopted conventions that repeatedly fail to evolve with modern circumstances, and yet continue to be approved as the blueprint for 'the protection of cultural property in time of war', reflect stagnation in ICHL.

The failure of ICHL to resolve dilemmas in cultural property regulation is also apparent in non-armed conflict settings. Two of the more prominent concerns are the illicit trade in and repatriation of stolen cultural property, and the potential regulation of traditional knowledge (TK) and traditional cultural expressions (TCE) as intellectual property. The 1970 UNESCO Convention purports to combat trafficking in cultural property. Many culture-rich countries like Syria and Yemen are parties to the 1970 UNESCO Convention.[22] That said, countries with significant art markets like the United Kingdom, Japan, and Switzerland are not.[23] The 1970 UNESCO Convention places the onus of curbing cultural property trafficking squarely on individual countries.[24] But strong and unfettered demand from art and antiquities collectors in non-participating wealthy destination countries promises steady profits for

[19] UNSC Res 2347 (24 March 2017) UN Doc S/RES/2347.

[20] Tom Seymour, 'Is Ukrainian Cultural Heritage under Coordinated Attack?' *The Art Newspaper* (10 June 2022).

[21] UNESCO, 'Convention for the Protection of Cultural Property in the Event of Armed Conflict with Regulations for the Execution of the Convention' <https://www.unesco.org/en/heritage-armed-conflicts/convention-and-protocols/states-parties> accessed 5 August 2024.

[22] UNESCO, 'Convention on the Means of Prohibiting and Preventing the Illicit Import, Export and Transfer of Ownership of Cultural Property' <https://en.unesco.org/about-us/legal-affairs/convention-means-prohibiting-and-preventing-illicit-import-export-and> accessed 30 April 2024.

[23] One possible exception is the United States, which signed the 1970 UNESCO Convention in 1983 and passed the Convention on Cultural Property Implementation Act 19 USC §2601 in the same year to further its commitment to combat cultural property trafficking.

[24] Arts 2(2), 5–8, 10, 13–14.

excavators, dealers, and assorted suppliers. It is therefore participating impoverished source countries who bear the heaviest burden of combating cultural property trafficking to their best endeavours. It is unsurprising that this burden has not been discharged. ICHL's conspicuous inability to dampen demand or staunch supply sustains a growing black market that incentivizes the illicit procurement, supply, and purchase of cultural property.[25] ICHL is equally helpless when it comes to the repatriation of cultural property pillaged and preserved by former imperial powers and invading forces from former colonies and conquest zones.[26] Absent any rules to determine rightful ownership of cultural property[27] or any mechanism to ensure that repatriation actually takes place,[28] whether or not cultural property, taken from its place of origin and rehoused on foreign soil, like the Benin Bronzes in the British Museum, gets returned depends almost entirely on the goodwill of the possessor museum or state.[29] ICHL offers no recourse and no remedy if promised repatriation does not materialize.[30]

ICHL is also largely silent on how TK and TCE should be regulated. The 2003 Intangible Cultural Heritage Convention and the 2005 Cultural Expressions Convention are highly abstract and aspirational instruments which merely direct states to 'safeguard' TK (such as medicinal uses for indigenous plants) and TCE (such as folklore and folk songs).[31] This gap raises the

[25] Helen Stoilas, 'Ten Most Wanted Antiquities: Have You Seen These Missing Artefacts?' *The Art Newspaper* (30 October 2020).

[26] Stahn takes a more optimistic view on the role of law in the context of repatriating cultural property, asserting that 'the criteria for return proposed in new frameworks on cultural colonial objects, such as contexts of acquisition or the cultural significance of objects to countries or communities of origin, are not only grounded in morality or ethics, i.e. the inclination to "do the right thing", but have a basis in law', (n 2) 417.

[27] John Henry Merryman, 'Thinking About the Elgin Marbles' (1985) 83(8) Michigan Law Review 1880, 1895–1902. Merryman's account of the title acquired by Lord Elgin in the Parthenon Marbles, which were removed from Greece and subsequently housed in the British Museum where they remain till today, is vigorously contested by Catharine Titi who disagrees with Merryman that the evidence pointed to the retroactive ratification of Lord Elgin's actions by the Ottoman authorities, *The Parthenon Marbles and International Law* (Springer 2023) 79–82, also 110–22. The fact that rightful ownership over the Parthenon Marbles is still disputed after nearly four decades discourages reliance on ICHL to determine the rightful owner of and to secure the return of cultural property to that rightful owner.

[28] Even Titi who is adamant that the UK should return the Parthenon Marbles to Greece concedes that ICHL does not offer Greece 'access to adjudicative dispute settlement means, with an advisory proceeding before the International Court of Justice (ICJ) appearing as the most viable option' and therefore 'suggests that soft means of dispute settlement (notably negotiations and mediation, in that order) are the most appropriate for the Parthenon marbles case', ibid 190.

[29] Gareth Harris, 'What Happened to France's Grand Plans to Return African Heritage?' *The Art Newspaper* (1 June 2022).

[30] For an engaging account of why repatriation may be less than straightforward, and is in fact a process fraught with many considerations including the optimal resting site for a piece of cultural property and the possibility of shared stewardship between states, see Stahn (n 2) 478–536.

[31] 2003 Intangible Cultural Heritage Convention arts 1(a), 19(1); 2005 Cultural Expressions Convention arts 4(7), 8(1). While the 2003 Intangible Cultural Heritage Convention is accompanied by

possibility of regulating TK and TCE as intellectual property.[32] As patent law protects ideas and inventions, which bear some alignment to TK, and copyright law protects artistic and original expressions, which loosely capture TCE, the regulation of TK and TCE as intellectual property seems, at first glance, unobjectionable. However, the prevailing approach to intellectual property regulation is a Western-centric one, which focuses on ownership determination to ascertain who has the right to control the use and dissemination of an idea or an expression.[33] The objective of intellectual property regulation is to encourage innovation by protecting the owner of an intellectual property right from infringement of that right by non-owners, and to compensate the owner accordingly should infringement occur. Moreover, ownership typically refers to private ownership since ideas and expressions can usually be attributed to an individual or select individuals. Yet, as TK and TCE are often passed down from generation to generation, or even from one community to another, a piece of TK or TCE may not be readily attributable to a specific individual or a specific community.[34] For example, the folklore of Cinderella as TCE has known so many different iterations across so many different communities that it is impossible to pinpoint its owner or originating community.[35] Any ownership in TK and TCE is thus more akin to communal or shared ownership, which Western-centric intellectual property regimes do not recognize because patents and copyrights cannot be held communally.[36] In 2019, the World Intellectual Property Office (WIPO) supplied frameworks to 'safeguard' TK and TCE, in the form of the WIPO Draft Articles on TK and the WIPO Draft Articles on TCE. These Draft Articles temper the Western-centric notion of intellectual property regulation by incorporating notions of communal

detailed Operational Principles, these recommend extra-legal means such as inscription, information gathering, community engagement and education to 'safeguard' TCE.

[32] Mira Burri, 'Cultural Heritage and Intellectual Property' in Francesco Francioni and Ana Filipa Vrdoljak (eds), *International Cultural Heritage Law* (OUP 2020) 459, 470–74, 478–81.

[33] Olufunmilayo Arewa, 'Culture As Property: Intellectual Property, Local Norms and Global Rights' (2007) Northwestern Public Law Research Paper No 07-13, 7–8.

[34] Additionally, TK which is passed down from one generation to the next, and often documented in some form, may not be considered sufficiently novel to warrant the grant of a patent, see Burri (n 32) 471.

[35] Arewa (n 33) 52–33.

[36] For how patents in TK cannot be held communally, see Stephen R Munzer and Kal Raustiala, 'The Uneasy Case for Intellectual Property Rights in Traditional Knowledge' (2009) 27 Cardozo Arts and Entertainment Law Journal 37, 51–52 and Madhavi Sunder, 'The Invention of Traditional Knowledge' (2007) 70 Law and Contemporary Problems 97, 98; for how copyrights in TCE cannot be held communally, see Burri (n 32) 480–81; also *Bulan Bulan & Anor v R & T Textiles (Pty) Ltd* (1998) 157 ALR 193, 194 where the Federal Court of Australia held that while the copyright holder of aboriginal artwork owed a fiduciary obligation to the Ganalbingu People, no communal title to copyright could be asserted by the Ganalbingu People.

ownership, use, dissemination, and benefit from TK and TCE,[37] and represent a step in the right direction. Uptake for the WIPO Draft Articles, and whether indigenous interests will permanently displace the foundational tenets of intellectual property regulation where TK and TCE are concerned, remains to be seen. As I will explain in Section 4 below, the regulatory gap left by a stagnant ICHL in relation to TK and TCE may be better filled by identifying TK and TCE as cultural property, redefined as a category of new property, and regulated as such.

2.1.2 Parasitic ICHL

Apart from being stagnant, ICHL lacks concrete means of cultural property protection. This may be because ICHL's importance is arguably more symbolic than real, with states simultaneously proclaiming the need to protect cultural property while declining to assume stronger obligations towards cultural property protection. An ICHL that commends and yet consistently fails to ensure cultural property protection has prompted the biting observation that 'governments do not want to commit themselves to expend significant resources to protect foreign cultural property during wartime or peacetime'.[38] The reason for this duplicity is twofold. First, ICHL's wartime impotence stems from the deliberate policy of some states or invading forces to target and destroy enemy cultural property to demoralize local troops and populations.[39] This was seen in the Yugoslav civil war, in ISIL's terror campaign in Iraq and Syria, in the Taliban's blowing up of the Buddhas of Bamiyan in Afghanistan, and in the ongoing Russo-Ukraine war. An assembly of states is unlikely to propose, let alone accede to, obligations that will constrain intended or future wartime strategies and measures. Second, ICHL's peacetime impotence stems from the mismatch between impoverished source countries' desire for stronger cultural property export restrictions and wealthy destination countries' desire to maintain a flourishing antiquities trading market.[40] Without the collective buy-in and support of destination countries to shut down international trade in antiquities, illegal supply will continue to exist to meet unsated demand. When states are unwilling or unable to commit fully to cultural property protection, they

[37] WIPO, 'Traditional Knowledge and Intellectual Property—Background Brief' <www.wipo.int/pressroom/en/briefs/tk_ip.html> accessed 30 April 2024.
[38] Eric Posner, 'The International Protection of Cultural Property: Some Skeptical Observations' (2007) 8 Chicago Journal of International Law 213, 220.
[39] ibid.
[40] ibid.

will not create a regime for cultural property regulation that imposes sanctions on a failure to protect.

To secure concrete means of cultural property protection, ICHL needs to latch onto another regime with an existing adjudicatory mechanism. ICHL already exhibits parasitic behaviour elsewhere. As discussed in Section 2.1.1 above, ICHL has latched onto intellectual property law to fill the regulatory gap on TK and TCE, to criticism and controversy. Additionally, ICHL offers no guidance when states contest ownership of cultural property, requiring it to latch onto principles of general international law, such as ratification and prescription, to determine which state can lay claim to a stronger legal title to that piece of cultural property.[41] When it comes to concrete protection, one regime that ICHL has latched onto is international criminal law. The Rome Statute criminalizes the destruction of property for non-military purposes in both international and non-international armed conflict settings as war crimes.[42] The reference to property in the Rome Statute has been deemed to encompass cultural property.[43] Any individual charged with and convicted of a war crime under the Rome Statute may be subject to imprisonment (including life imprisonment), a fine, or a forfeiture of proceeds, property, and assets derived from that crime, as determined by the International Criminal Court.[44] As compared to ICHL that contains no sanctions, the punitive powers of a judicial body set out in the Rome Statute potentially render international criminal law a greater deterrence against cultural property destruction.[45] However, it would be hasty to regard international criminal law as the panacea to all of ICHL's shortcomings. As the next section explains, despite the existence of a concrete protective mechanism, which ICHL conspicuously lacks, international criminal law is nonetheless deficient when it comes to cultural property regulation.

2.2 International criminal law (ICL)

The Rome Statute stipulates penalties that can be imposed by the International Criminal Court (ICC) on natural persons falling within its jurisdiction and who are charged with, tried for, and subsequently convicted

[41] Merryman (n 27) 1897–902.
[42] Rome Statute arts 8(2)(a)(iv), 8(2)(b)(xiii), 8(2)(e)(iv), 8(2)(e)(xii).
[43] *The Prosecutor v Ahmad Al Faqi Al Mahdi*, ICC-01/12-01/15-171, Trial Chamber VIII, Judgment and Sentence (27 September 2016) paras 14–16, 42–48, 72, 77.
[44] Rome Statute art 77.
[45] Lotsal (n 17) 104.

of the crime of genocide, crimes against humanity, war crimes, and/or the crime of aggression.[46] The ICC has the power to issue a warrant of arrest or a summons to appear,[47] and to request the assistance of a custodial state in arresting an accused.[48] The ICC also has the power to order reparations to victims, which are either satisfied by the convicted person or made through a Trust Fund established and managed by the Assembly of States Parties to the Rome Statute.[49] Accused persons are held in the United Nations Detention Unit, which is located within the Scheveningen Prison in The Hague, while convicted persons will serve their prison sentences in a state designated by the ICC from a list of states willing to accept sentenced persons.[50] In theory, to the extent that cultural property destruction can be construed as a crime within the jurisdiction of the ICC, the person or persons responsible for that destruction can be sanctioned by ICL, in accordance with the provisions of the Rome Statute.

The Rome Statute makes no express mention of cultural property.[51] Nor is there an express reference to cultural property in the Statute establishing the ad hoc International Criminal Tribunal for the former Yugoslavia (ICTY Statute), which pre-dates the Rome Statute.[52] Protocols I and II to the Geneva Conventions of 12 August 1949,[53] the latter of which is specifically incorporated into the Rome Statute and the ICTY Statute,[54] prohibit the destruction of 'cultural objects' in international and non-international armed conflicts respectively.[55] Neither Protocol defines 'cultural objects', and the commentaries

[46] Rome Statute arts 1, 4(2), 5–8, 13, 25, 63–65, 76–78, 106, 109.

[47] ibid art 58.

[48] ibid art 59.

[49] ibid arts 75 and 79.

[50] ibid art 103.

[51] Art 8(2)(b)(ix) of the Rome Statute provides: 'Other serious violations of the laws and customs applicable in international armed conflict, within the established framework of international law, namely, any of the following acts: Intentionally directing attacks against buildings dedicated to religion, education, arty, science or charitable purposes, historic monuments, hospitals and places where the sick and wounded are collected, provided they are not military objectives.'

[52] Art 3(d) of the ICTY Statute (adopted 25 May 1993 by UN Security Resolution 827) provides: 'The International Tribunal shall have the power to prosecute persons violating the laws or customs of war. Such violations include, but not be limited to: seizure of, destruction or wilful damage done to institutions dedicated to religion, charity and education, the arts and sciences, historic monuments and works of art and science.'

[53] Geneva Convention for the Amelioration of the Condition of the Wounded and Sick in Armed Forces in the Field 75 UNTS 31; Geneva Convention for the Amelioration of the Condition of Wounded, Sick and Shipwrecked Members of Armed Forces at Sea 75 UNTS 85; Geneva Convention Relative to the Treatment of Prisoners of War 75 UNTS 135; Geneva Convention Relative to the Protection of Civilian Persons in Times of War 75 UNTS 287.

[54] Rome Statute art 8(2)(a); ICTY Statute art 2.

[55] Protocol I art 53, see also arts 85(4)(d) and 85(5); Protocol II art 16.

to both Protocols simply refer back to the 1954 Hague Convention while reiterating concern for the 'heritage of mankind'.[56] As explained in Sections 2.1.1 and 2.1.2 above, the 1954 Hague Convention marked the birth of an ICHL that turned out to be stagnant in substance and parasitic in operation. Relying on ICL to enforce ICHL is therefore hardly self-evident. One must be prepared to read cultural property protection into the ICTY Statute or the Rome Statute via the reference to 'cultural objects' in Protocols I and II of the 1949 Geneva Conventions.

The arguably tenuous connection between ICL and cultural property regulation appears to have gone unnoticed. ICL was first invoked to sanction cultural property destruction in *Prosecutor v Pavle Strugar*. Both the Trial Chamber and the Appeals Chamber of the ICTY held that the 1991 shelling of the Old Town in Dubrovnik, a UNESCO World Heritage Site, ordered by Mr Strugar, who was then Lieutenant-General of the Yugoslav Peoples' Army, amounted to the destruction of cultural property prohibited by Article 3(d) of the ICTY Statute.[57] To recap, Article 3(d) considers the 'destruction or wilful damage done to institutions dedicated to religion, charity and education, the arts and sciences, historic monuments and works of art and science' as a violation of the laws or customs of war. It is unclear, and neither the Trial Chamber nor the Appeals Chamber attempted to clarify, which (or all) of the items listed in Article 3(d) are cultural property. It is also unclear why both Chambers felt the need to reframe the shelling of Dubrovnik as the destruction of cultural property, when Mr Strugar's violation of Article 3(d) would already be made out on the basis of Strugar's intentional destruction of historic monuments. Similarly, in *The Prosecutor v Ahmad Al Faqi Al Mahdi*, which has been hailed as a historic win for cultural property protection under the

[56] Commentary to Protocol 1, art 53, para 2040 <https://ihl-databases.icrc.org/en/ihl-treaties/api-1977/article-53/commentary/1987?activeTab=undefined> accessed 5 August 2024; Commentary to Protocol II, art 16, paras 4826–27 <https://ihl-databases.icrc.org/en/ihl-treaties/apii-1977/article-16/commentary/1987?activeTab=undefined> accessed 5 August 2024.

[57] Judgment of Trial Chamber II, 31 January 2005, Case No IT-01-42-T paras 229–33; Judgment of the Appeals Chamber, 17 July 2008, Case No IT-01-42-A paras 277–80. This chapter regards ICL as encompassing international humanitarian law for the simple reason that international crimes as defined in arts 7 and 8 of the Rome Statute include violations of international humanitarian law as set out in the 1949 Geneva Conventions. While it is beyond the scope of the present discussion to detail the relationship between ICL and international humanitarian law, it suffices to note at this juncture that international humanitarian law has previously been subsumed under ICL, see Ivan Simanovic, 'The Role of the ICTY in the Development of International Criminal Adjudication' (1999) 23(2) Fordham International Law Journal 440, 444 where the author, a former Minister for Justice and Croatia's Permanent Representative to the United Nations, wrote that 'the establishment of the ICTY' whose mandate, according to the Preamble of the ICTY Statute, is to prosecute 'persons responsible for serious violations of international humanitarian law', 'represented a breakthrough in the development of *international criminal law*' (emphasis added).

Rome Statute,[58] the unexplained references to cultural property by ICC Trial Chamber VIII seemed superfluous to Mr Al Mahdi's Article 8(2)(e)(iv) charge of '[i]ntentionally directing attacks against buildings dedicated to religion' in Timbuktu.[59] It remains unclear why ICC Trial Chamber VIII saw the need to deem religious buildings cultural property when Mr Al Mahdi was neither charged with nor ultimately convicted of cultural property destruction.[60] More recently, a team led by Alison Macdonald QC of Essex Court Chambers published a lengthy opinion detailing the criminal responsibility of the Chinese government for its treatment of the Uyghur population in Xinjiang (the Uyghur Opinion). Specifically, the Uyghur Opinion contends that the large-scale destruction of mosques and confiscation of religious items and artefacts amount to a destruction of cultural property and a 'form of persecution falling within Art. 7(1)(h)' of the Rome Statute.[61] Persecution under Article 7(1)(h) is defined in the Rome Statute as 'the intentional and severe deprivation of fundamental rights contrary to international law by reason of the identity of the group or collectivity'.[62] In the absence of any reference to property destruction, let alone cultural property destruction, as an indicator of persecution, it is unclear why evidence of religious persecution had to be recharacterized as evidence of cultural property destruction in the Uyghur Opinion.

A possible explanation for the unexpected references to cultural property in *Prosecutor v Pavle Strugar*, *The Prosecutor v Ahmad Al Faqi Al Mahdi*, and the Uyghur Opinion, is the desire to convey the greater reprehensibility of destroying cultural property, as opposed to other species of property. So, while property destruction suffices for criminal responsibility to attach, *cultural* property destruction is an aggravating factor, rendering the wrongful act/s of destruction much more grievous. Cultural property's hallowed status arguably stems from the perception, whether instinctive or cultivated, that such property is worthy of protection given its perceived ability to represent collective identities in semiotic interactions.[63] A perception-based appreciation of cultural property can change depending on who the perceiver is and becomes

[58] See generally Philippa Webb and others, 'Culture at the Frontline: Addressing Attacks on Cultural Heritage' (2016) 14 Journal of International Criminal Justice 1139, 1139–220 (symposium).

[59] See *Prosecutor v Ahmad Al Faqi Al Mahdi* (n 43) paras 14–16, 42–48, 72, 77.

[60] For a more detailed discussion of this decision, see Chapter 1, Section 2.2.

[61] Uyghur Opinion paras 60, 74, 107. In the wake of sanctions imposed by the Chinese government on the authors of the Uyghur Opinion, the document is no longer available from the website of Essex Court Chambers, but is on file with the author, see Primrose Riordan and Jane Croft, 'UK Chambers Removes Xinjiang Genocide Opinion Reference After China Sanctions' *Financial Times* (28 March 2021).

[62] Rome Statute art 7(2)(g).

[63] Richard Handler, 'Cultural Property and Culture Theory' (2003) 3(3) Journal of Social Archaeology 353, 356–57.

extremely unpredictable. It also exempts the perceiver from exercising analytical or definitional rigour when employing the term 'cultural property', since what is or is not cultural property is surely self-explanatory. So, while the sporadic references to cultural property in *Prosecutor v Pavle Strugar*, *The Prosecutor v Ahmad Al Faqi Al Mahdi*, and the Uyghur Opinion may establish precedent in applying ICL to cultural property regulation, we are no closer to a principled and progressive notion of cultural property under ICL than we were under ICHL. Moreover, the supposed benefit of concrete cultural property protection that ICHL derives from latching onto ICL's adjudicatory mechanism may be overstated. While prosecutorial discretion at ICC is not unfettered and has to be exercised in 'the interests of justice',[64] the fact remains that despite numerous well-documented instances of wilful cultural property destruction during armed conflicts,[65] none of the perpetrators have ever been specifically prosecuted for cultural property destruction before the ICC. When cultural property regulation is at best ancillary or tangential to a charge or conviction under ICL, it is very unlikely for ICL or the ICC to develop bespoke provisions for cultural property regulation, therefore greatly discounting ICL's hoped-for deterrent effect on cultural property destruction. In the search for effective cultural property regulation that ICHL and ICL are unable to offer, the discussion now turns to two other regulatory regimes with adjudicatory mechanisms, namely, international investment law and international trade law.

2.3 International investment law (IIL)

IIL developed through the proliferation of bilateral investment treaties establishing standards of treatment that contracting host states are obliged to confer on investments and investors from the other contracting state. These treaties typically contain a clause stipulating that in the event of a dispute between a foreign investor and a host state, that dispute will be submitted to arbitration. IIL is articulated, applied, and developed by arbitral tribunals constituted to hear investor–state disputes, as these tribunals issue awards scrutinizing the compatibility of challenged respondent host state conduct with its treaty obligations. Awards in investor–state arbitration are binding on the parties to the dispute.

[64] Rome Statute arts 53(1) and 53(2).
[65] For a selection of these instances, see Lotsal (n 17) chs 4–6.

In the course of admitting foreign capital and its accompanying activities, a number of host states have faced the dilemma where a foreign investment project poses actual or potential harm to cultural property, compelling them to choose between foreign investment protection and cultural property protection. Host state measures prioritizing cultural property protection, such as the cancellation of a concession or a licence previously awarded to the foreign investor, can form the basis of a treaty claim that the affected investor submits to arbitration. In determining the merits of such a claim, the arbitral tribunal is confronted by a clash between economic and cultural interests,[66] and thus presented with an opportunity to regulate this clash. However, a survey of the relevant arbitral awards reveals that investment arbitration tribunals approach cultural property protection and its place in IIL in a haphazard and cursory manner, almost erasing the cultural property dimension in an investor–state dispute.

An early claim involving cultural property protection was presented in *SPP (Middle East) Limited and Anor v Arab Republic of Egypt & Anor.*[67] The claimant investors concluded an agreement with the second respondent, an Egyptian state entity, to develop two tourist complexes, one of which was to be situated on the Pyramids plateau in Giza.[68] Due to the suspected presence of buried antiquities in the development sites, there was intense local opposition to the project, and it was eventually cancelled by the Egyptian Parliament.[69] The claimant investors sought compensation of USD 42.5 million for their expropriated investment and were awarded USD 12.5 million by a majority of the tribunal.[70] Although the majority held that Egypt's cancellation of the project was 'not capricious' since it was 'giving recognition to the cultural, social and political instances emerging within the community of citizens',[71] it stopped short of saying that a deep discount was applied to the compensation claim because Egypt only cancelled the project to protect its cultural property. Instead, the majority based the reduction almost entirely on its choice of a different quantification method than that proposed by the claimants,[72]

[66] Muthucumaraswamy Sornarajah, *Resistance and Change in the International Law on Foreign Investment* (CUP 2015) 340–41.

[67] ICC Arbitration No YD/AS NO 3493, Award (Bernini, Elghatit (dissenting), Littman) (11 March 1983). Although the claim here was not a treaty claim, the investors sought 'just compensation for expropriatory measures' in accordance with 'the general principles of international law', see Award para 49, making their claim akin to an investment treaty claim for uncompensated expropriation.

[68] ibid paras 4–7.

[69] ibid paras 27–28.

[70] ibid paras 64, 68(1).

[71] ibid para 62.

[72] ibid paras 63–65.

relegating the central clash between foreign investment protection and cultural property protection to the sidelines. Another claim involving the expropriation of a site previously earmarked for touristic development was presented in *Compañía del Desarrollo de Santa Elena S.A. v The Republic of Costa Rica*.[73] Here, Costa Rica expropriated the claimant's lands for the purpose of protecting indigenous 'flora and fauna of great scientific, recreational, educational, and tourism value',[74] thereby prioritizing TK protection over foreign investment protection. In assessing the appropriate amount of compensation to be paid by Costa Rica to the claimant investor, the tribunal deemed cultural property protection irrelevant to the assessment, holding that such measures are, 'no matter how laudable and beneficial to society as a whole[,] ... similar to any other expropriatory measures that a state may take in order to implement its policies ... [and] the state's obligation to pay compensation remains'.[75] To drive home the point that compensation trumps culture, the tribunal fixed the amount of compensation at USD 4.15 million, which was derived by simply, and somewhat cavalierly, adding the claimant's valuation at USD 6.4 million to the respondent's valuation at USD 1.9 million and dividing the sum of USD 8.3 million by two.[76] The later claims of uncompensated expropriation and denial of the international minimum standard of treatment, brought under the North American Free Trade Agreement in *Glamis Gold, Ltd. v United States of America*,[77] stemmed from the US imposing strict rules on mining methods so as to protect Native American cultural sites where mining would take place. In a 300-page award dismissing the investor's claims, the tribunal acknowledged the importance of preserving Native American cultural property,[78] but avoided addressing the clash between cultural property protection and foreign investment protection by holding that 'it is not for an international tribunal to delve into the details of and justifications for domestic law'.[79] Therefore, while cultural property protection lay at the heart of the contested mining regulations giving rise to the present dispute, it became peripheral to an assessment of the compatibility of a host state's conduct with its treaty obligations.

[73] ICSID Case No ARB/96/1, Final Award (Fortier, Lauterpacht, Weil) (17 February 2000).
[74] ibid para 18.
[75] ibid para 71.
[76] ibid paras 93–95.
[77] NAFTA-UNCITRAL, Award (Young, Caron, Hubbard) (8 June 2009). North American Free Trade Agreement (signed 17 December 1992, entered into force 1 January 1994, terminated 1 July 2020) arts 1110 and 1105, replaced by the Agreement between the United States of America, the United Mexican States and Canada (signed 30 November 2018, entered into force 1 July 2020).
[78] ibid paras 105–08.
[79] ibid para 762.

The absence of a clear or coherent approach in IIL when an investor–state dispute features cultural property protection[80] may be attributed to several factors. First, the original target object of regulation in IIL, and particularly in investment treaties, is foreign investment. There have been recent attempts to insert additional objects of regulation such as investor conduct and sustainability commitments into IIL,[81] but the regime and its sovereign stakeholders appear largely resistant to substantive change.[82] When there is no express or implied directive to embed cultural property regulation into IIL, treaty drafters and tribunals are conditioned by habit to retain their focus on foreign investment regulation. Second, the traditional focus in IIL on foreign investment protection facilitates the viewing of a cultural property dimension as being merely incidental to the investment claim. This was seen in the cultural property protection cases of *SPP v Egypt*, *Santa Elena v Costa Rica* and *Glamis Gold v USA* where cultural property protection, ironically, had no apparent bearing on the outcome of each dispute.[83] In other cases, the cultural property dimension is incidental to the investment claim originating in a contractual dispute.[84] When cultural property considerations are routinely deemed incidental to an investment claim, regardless of whether these considerations are truly incidental, few will bother to develop IIL-derived analytical approaches and frameworks to address a perennially incidental concern. Third, investor–state arbitration has long been mired in a legitimacy crisis. Critics maintain that party-appointed arbitrators, who are mostly practising lawyers and academics with no governing experience, are unqualified to scrutinize and sanction state measures for treaty non-compliance.[85] Wary of overreach

[80] Valentina Vadi, *Cultural Heritage in International Investment Law and Arbitration* (CUP 2014) 133.

[81] Jean Ho and others, 'Investor Responsibility: The Next Frontier in International Investment Law' (2019) 117 American Journal of International Law Unbound 1, 1–37; Barnali Choudhury, 'The Role of Soft Law Corporate Responsibilities in Defining Investor Obligations in International Investment Agreements' in Jean Ho and Mavluda Sattorova (eds), *Investors' International Law* (Hart 2021) 151, 152–64.

[82] The ongoing negotiations on investor–state dispute settlement reform at UNCITRAL Working Group III are concerned with procedural reforms, see agenda in UNCITRAL, 'Working Group III: Investor-State Dispute Settlement Reform' <https://uncitral.un.org/en/working_groups/3/investor-state> accessed 30 April 2024. An earlier call to discuss the substantive reform of IIL and hold investors accountable for misconduct, see Erasmus Institute for Public Knowledge, 'Open Letter on the Asymmetry of ISDS' (13 February 2019) <www.eur.nl/en/news/erasmus-institute-public-knowledge> accessed 30 April 2024, was ignored by the member states of Working Group III.

[83] It remains to be seen if the pending case of *Elitech B.V. & Anor v Republic of Croatia*, ICSID Case No ARB/17/32, which involves the stalled construction of a golf resort near UNESCO World Heritage site, Dubrovnik, will buck this trend.

[84] See for instance *Malaysian Historical Salvors Sdn, Bhd v The Government of Malaysia*, ICSID Case No ARB/05/10, Award on Jurisdiction (Hwang) (17 May 2007) paras 7–14.

[85] Muthucumaraswamy Sornarajah, 'Evolution or Revolution in International Investment Arbitration? The Descent into Normlessness' in Chester Brown and Kate Miles (eds), *Evolution in Investment Treaty Law and Arbitration* (CUP 2011) 631, 641–42, 648–49.

or backlash, tribunals are usually reluctant to openly balance competing state interests and investor interests when deciding on a prevailing interest. Therefore, even if cultural property protection played a part in the outcome of a dispute, its precise role and significance is unlikely to be articulated in the award. Fourth and finally, when later tribunals obtain no guidance on cultural property protection from earlier tribunals, path dependency suggests that the non-treatment of cultural property regulation in IIL remains the norm, while the breakthrough test case becomes the far-off exception. Occasional mentions of cultural property and allusions to cultural property protection in IIL offer the flimsiest of foundations for relying on IIL to plug the gaps in ICHL when it comes to cultural property regulation. IIL, at present, is barely able to regulate foreign investment to overall satisfaction; the utility of harnessing IIL for cultural property regulation is questionable.

2.4 International trade law (ITL)

The principal adjudicatory mechanism in ITL is located in the Dispute Settlement Understanding of the World Trade Organisation (WTO). The WTO was established in 1995, and with it came the creation of a Dispute Settlement Body (DSB) to adjudicate disputes between WTO member states for alleged infringement of the GATT. When member states are unable to reach a mutually agreeable solution, they may refer their dispute to the DSB. A panel will be constituted to hear the dispute and issue a report. Findings and recommendations in panel reports are binding on the member states parties to the dispute.[86] The GATT was concluded to bring about 'the substantial reduction of tariffs and other barriers to trade and . . . the elimination of discriminatory treatment in international commerce'.[87] There are, however, exceptions to the rule. Article XX(f) of the GATT permits WTO member states to adopt any measures 'imposed for the protection of national treasures of artistic, historic or archaeological value', so long as these measures are non-arbitrary, non-discriminatory, and not a disguised restriction on international trade. Article XX(f) of the GATT has been reiterated in some bilateral and multilateral free trade agreements post-dating the GATT,[88] and these iterations of Article XX(f)

[86] WTO, 'Legal Effect of Panel and Appellate Body Reports and DSB Recommendations and Rulings' <www.wto.org/english/tratop_e/dispu_e/disp_settlement_cbt_e/c7_s2p1_e.htm> accessed 30 April 2024.

[87] GATT, Preamble.

[88] See for instance Free Trade Agreement between the Government of Australia and the Government of the People's Republic of China (signed 17 June 2015, entered into force 12 December

can be enforced via the dispute settlement mechanism established in each agreement.[89]

At first glance, 'national treasures of artistic, historic or archaeological value' in Article XX(f) of the GATT are akin to 'cultural property... specifically designated by each State as being of importance for archaeological, prehistory, history, literature, art or science' in Article 1 of the 1970 UNESCO Convention,[90] suggesting that cultural property is already protected in ITL. Article XX(f) of the GATT has also been regarded as 'crucial to the implementation of the 1970 UNESCO Convention'.[91] On closer examination, however, it is highly uncertain if 'national treasures' in the GATT is synonymous with 'cultural property' in the 1970 UNESCO Convention. The definition of cultural property in Article 1 of the 1970 UNESCO Convention comprises an illustrative list that names fixed forms of tangible property. It is unclear if tangible property not matching an item on the illustrative list counts as cultural property. It is also unclear if intangible property, such as TK and TCE, can be construed as cultural property when the illustrative list covers only tangible property. When 'national treasures' in the GATT 'might include items of intangible cultural heritage or cultural expressions',[92] the ITL and ICHL regimes on cultural property regulation may not be as complementary as previously thought.

Moreover, the only trade-related measures for cultural property regulation are export and import controls in domestic legislation designed to stifle illicit trade in cultural property. These controls are usually absent or perfunctory in domestic legislation, both in source countries like Iraq, Syria, and Egypt trying to staunch the illicit export of cultural property,[93] and in destination countries like the UK that are ostensibly committed to stopping the illicit

2015) (Australia-China FTA) art 9.8(1)(c): 'For the purposes of this Chapter and subject to the requirement that such measures are not applied in a manner which would constitute arbitrary or unjustifiable discrimination between investments or between investors, or a disguised restriction on international trade or investment, nothing in this Agreement shall be construed to prevent a Party from adopting or enforcing measures *imposed for the protection of national treasures of artistic, historic or archaeological value*' (emphasis added).

[89] ibid arts 9.10–9.25, 15.1–15.17.

[90] Tania Voon, 'National Treasures at the Intersection Between Cultural Heritage and International Trade Law' in Francesco Francioni and Ana Filipa Vrdoljak (eds), *International Cultural Heritage Law* (OUP 2020) 507, 516.

[91] ibid 526.

[92] ibid 516.

[93] Of the nineteen-country chapter-studies on relevant domestic legislation or regulations in James AR Nafziger and Robert K Paterson (eds), *Handbook on the Law of Cultural Heritage and International Trade* (Edward Elgar 2014), none is devoted a source country known for plundered cultural property. This strongly suggests that countries that need export controls the most are, ironically, the ones without it.

import of cultural property for an insatiable art market.[94] To make matters worse, applications for export and import licences, where required, are usually approved. WTO member states are also extremely unlikely to challenge a fellow member state's export or import restrictions on cultural property as an impediment to free trade before the DSB, dimming hopes of a future test case on Article XX(f) to clarify the parameters of cultural property regulation in ITL.[95] The marginalization of Article XX(f) and the meagreness of available trade-related measures for cultural property protection, plus their poor uptake among states, explains why ITL, despite having an adjudicatory mechanism in the form of the DSB, holds little promise for cultural property regulation. To make matters worse, the DSB in ITL, like investment arbitration in IIL, is currently facing an existential crisis. As of 30 November 2020, the Appellate Body of the DSB was no longer able to hear appeals because the terms of two of the three members needed for a quorum expired, and the Trump administration in the US blocked the appointment of replacement members. The fate of the DSB now hangs in limbo,[96] injecting precarity into international trade regulation, and further discouraging the extension of ITL to cultural property regulation.

From the foregoing, it is apparent that cultural property regulation is not optimized within ICHL or by pairing ICHL with ICL, IIL, or ITL. The adjudicatory mechanisms present in ICL, IIL, and ITL, but absent in ICHL, may offer concrete cultural property protection, but are not designed or invoked to confer such protection in a principled way. Whether or not cultural property ends up being protected, and whether or not cultural property destruction ends up being sanctioned, becomes a lottery. This is due in part to how regimes with punitive options are not and are unlikely ever to be oriented towards cultural property regulation, and in part to how cultural property has thus far been defined in a manner that is spontaneous rather than conceptual. The result is considerable definitional chaos, which the next section discusses.

[94] The three-pronged Waverley Criteria (1. Is it so closely connected with our history and national life that its departure would be a misfortune? 2. Is it of outstanding aesthetic importance? 3. Is it of outstanding significance for the study of some particular branch of art, learning, or history?) are applied to determine the propriety of *exporting* cultural property from the UK, not *importing* cultural property into the UK, Arts Council England, 'Export of Objects of Cultural Interest 2021–22' <www.artscouncil.org.uk/supporting-collections-and-cultural-property/reviewing-committee#section-2> accessed 30 April 2024.

[95] Voon (n 90) 518–19.

[96] Simon Lester, 'Ending the WTO Dispute Settlement Crisis: Where to from Here?' *International Institute For Sustainable Development* (2 March 2022) <www.iisd.org/articles/united-states-must-propose-solutions-end-wto-dispute-settlement-crisis> accessed 30 April 2024.

3. Definitional dilemmas and false dichotomies

Earlier attempts to define cultural property in international conventions have been either illustrative, where an object matching an entry in a list of illustrations of cultural property is cultural property,[97] or discretionary, where states have full autonomy to pronounce what cultural property is.[98] An illustrative definition of cultural property risks being both over- and under-inclusive because non-alignment with an illustration may disqualify an object as cultural property if one adopts a restrictive reading of the treaty, but not if one adopts a liberal reading of the same treaty. The general rule of treaty interpretation enshrined in Article 31 of the Vienna Convention on the Law of Treaties calls for treaties to be 'interpreted in good faith in accordance with the ordinary meaning to be given to the terms of the treaty in their context and in the light of its object and purpose',[99] but there is insufficient indication whether a treaty interpreter should err on the side of constraint or generosity when applying an illustrative definition. A discretionary definition offers even less guidance than an illustrative definition of cultural property. States are not known to periodically and systematically review, classify, and update all objects within their territorial boundaries as cultural property or non-cultural property, leaving a potentially vast number of objects, both old and new, in definitional limbo.

The upshot of cultural property being subject to illustrative and discretionary definitions is the emergence of piecemeal regulatory frameworks for different *types* of cultural property. In the absence of a generally applicable and acceptable definition of cultural property, states gravitated towards negotiating expedient conventions addressing a prevailing concern without regard for whether that concern can and should be considered and regulated as a type of cultural property. This led to a series of possibly unintended bifurcations where cultural non-property regulation is carved out from cultural property regulation, and created the impression that cultural property is merely one of several target objects of regulation in ICHL. This section unpacks any expressed or inferred rationale for bifurcation to argue that the dichotomies between cultural property and cultural heritage (Section 3.1), between tangible cultural property and intangible cultural heritage (Section 3.2), and between above-water cultural property and underwater cultural heritage (Section 3.3)

[97] See eg 1970 UNESCO Convention art 1; see also Chapter 1, Section 2.1.1.
[98] See eg 1972 World Heritage Convention art 1; see also Chapter 1, Section 2.1.2.
[99] (signed 23 May 1969, entered into force 27 January 1980) 1155 UNTS 331.

are false. It advocates the recognition of cultural property as the overarching and principal object of regulation in ICHL.

3.1 Cultural property vs cultural heritage

The distinction between cultural property and cultural heritage merits explanation. Some conventions seem to regard the two as interchangeable terms.[100] According to the Preamble of the 1954 Hague Convention:[101]

> [D]amage to cultural property belonging to any people whatsoever means damage to the cultural heritage of all mankind, since each people makes its contribution to the culture of the world.

And according to Section II(A) the 2021 Operational Guidelines for the Implementation of the 1972 World Heritage Convention:[102]

> States Parties are invited to submit nominations of properties of cultural . . . value considered to be of 'Outstanding Universal Value' for inscription on the World Heritage List.

Other conventions or international instruments seem to regard cultural property as a subset of cultural heritage. According to Article 4 of the 1970 UNESCO Convention:

> [Cultural] property which belongs to the following categories forms part of the cultural heritage of each State . . .

And according to Resolution 2347 of 2017, the United Nations Security Council:

> Deplores and condemns the unlawful destruction of cultural heritage, *inter alia* destruction of religious sites and artefacts, as well as the looting and smuggling of cultural property from archaeological sites, museums, libraries,

[100] Titi, in *The Parthenon Marbles and International Law* (n 27) 26–27, 112, 167, 175, 194, 225, 246–49, also uses the terms cultural property and cultural heritage interchangeably; see also Stahn (n 2) 306.
[101] cf Vadi (n 80) 28.
[102] UNESCO, 'The Operational Guidelines for the Implementation of the World Heritage Convention' para 50 <https://whc.unesco.org/en/guidelines/> accessed 30 April 2024.

archives, and other sites, in the context of armed conflicts, notably by terrorist groups ...

Notably, none of the conventions above record any drafting insight into the choice of presenting one relationship between cultural property and cultural heritage over another, leaving the onus of explanation to legal scholars. And legal scholars have tended to view cultural property as a subset of cultural heritage for reasons that are not entirely compelling. Cultural property has been distinguished from cultural heritage, with the latter emerging as the favoured umbrella concept,[103] on the basis that cultural heritage is the more inclusive notion as it encompasses both tangibles and intangibles that represent the 'manifestations of human life'.[104] In contrast, cultural property is the more problematic notion as '"property" has acquired a wide range of emotive and value-laden nuances, from the arguments of John Locke to the challenge of Communism in the first two-thirds of this century'.[105] However, as its proponents candidly admit, the real reason for cultural heritage being crowned the more inclusive and therefore superior notion is because '"cultural heritage" is a relatively new term' that can be presumably moulded and stretched to fit new demands.[106] And the real reason for cultural property being sidelined as a principal object of regulation is the presumption that property can only be viewed through the lens of private ownership as select Western property theorists propound.[107] Favouring cultural heritage talk over cultural property talk, and insisting on a distinction between the two, becomes little more than personal preference to avoid the hard task of deconstructing property theories to look for common denominators.[108] It is easier to start anew.

[103] Lotsal in *International Cultural Heritage Law in Armed Conflict* (n 17) 61 considers that the conventions purporting to safeguard cultural heritage 'denote a higher relative interest on the part of the international community' while 'conventions on "cultural property" seem to highlight a higher national concern'.

[104] Lyndel V Prott and Patrick J O'Keefe, '"Cultural Heritage" or "Cultural Property"?' (1992) 1(2) International Journal of Cultural Property 307, 307–08; this was endorsed by Blake, 'On Defining the Cultural Heritage' (n 9) 67, which was in turn cited with approval by Vadi (n 80) 28.

[105] Prott and O'Keefe, ibid 308; Blake, 'On Defining the Cultural Heritage' (n 9) 65–66; Vadi (n 80) 28.

[106] Prott and O'Keefe (n 104) 309.

[107] ibid 309–12; Blake, 'On Defining the Cultural Heritage' (n 9) 65–66; Stahn (n 2) 381–82. For a comparative critique of property theories from the Western, Soviet and post-Soviet, Chinese, and Islamic juristic traditions, see Chapter 1, Section 3.

[108] In Vadi's words, 'without delving into the complexities of property theory, this book adopts the concept of cultural heritage rather than that of cultural property, following current treaty practice', (n 80) 29. As set out in the opening paragraphs to this section, treaty practice is neither uniform nor unequivocal in recognizing cultural heritage as the genus, and cultural property as the species. Therefore, Vadi's brief treatment of the distinction between cultural heritage and cultural property points to personal preference.

Yet, as shown in Section 2.1 above, ICHL has not evolved to offer robust protection for either cultural heritage or cultural property. It is a feeble regime marked by persistent failure to adapt and modernize. Moreover, it is impossible to avoid property talk when the target object of regulation in a given convention, such as the 1954 Hague Convention or the 1970 UNESCO Convention, is cultural property. To the extent that property refers to tangibles and intangibles, conviction in the notion that cultural heritage is more inclusive is misplaced. And to the extent that property regulation in international law is not limited to the defence of private capital and private ownership, the turn to cultural heritage to simplify matters is misguided. The dichotomy between cultural property and cultural heritage is false because it was borne from a misunderstanding of property and retained by those who, perhaps unknowingly, perpetuate that misunderstanding of property. The dichotomy should be discarded because it enables avoidance of the notion of cultural property and its replacement with cultural heritage. Neither outcome has advanced cultural property understanding or regulation in international law.

3.2 Tangible cultural property vs intangible cultural heritage

As touched on in the preceding section, another bifurcation in ICHL is that between tangible and intangible culture. Tangible culture, which is manifested by 'physical remains' that one can see or touch, can be labelled cultural property, but not intangible culture, which may be manifested 'only in terms of knowledge or ideas'.[109] The latter, so the argument goes, is better labelled cultural heritage, since cultural property 'is a purely Western legal category which is far too narrow and . . . it has been global influences that have allowed the broadening of the concept of cultural heritage'.[110] This characterization of 'Western legal' thought on property is highly questionable. To the best of my knowledge, only the Hanafi school, which represents the minority view in Sunni Islamic legal thought, explicitly denies the label of property to intangibles;[111] the same cannot be said for or inferred from property theories emanating from the Western, Soviet, post-Soviet, and Chinese juristic traditions.[112] In fact, the

[109] Blake, 'On Defining the Cultural Heritage' (n 9) 66; also Andrzej Jakubowski, *State Succession in Cultural Property* (OUP 2015) 5.
[110] Blake, 'On Defining the Cultural Heritage' (n 9) 66 paraphrasing Lyndel V Prott, 'International Standards for Cultural Heritage' in *UNESCO World Culture Report* (UNESCO 1998) 222, 227–28.
[111] See Chapter 1, Section 3.4.
[112] See Chapter 1, Sections 3.1, 3.2, 3.3.

official stance of most states is that property refers to both tangible and intangible property. According to Article 2(d) of the United Nations Convention on Corruption, which has been ratified by more than 150 states, '"[p]roperty" shall mean assets of every kind, whether . . . tangible or intangible'.[113]

Additionally, the protection of cultural 'knowledge and ideas', namely TK and TCE, is reminiscent of the protection of artistic creations and innovations as intellectual property. Objections to the use of intellectual property law tools, such as patent and copyright infringements, to regulate TK and TCE stem from the inability of these tools to accommodate the communal ownership dimension of TK and TCE.[114] Further support for not regulating intangible culture as intellectual property can be found in the WIPO Draft Articles on TK and the WIPO Draft Articles on TCE. The WIPO Draft Articles are regulatory regimes specifically designed to co-exist with, but are not subservient to, intellectual property regimes.[115] These objections and observations caution against regulating intangible culture as intellectual property, but they do not stand between regulating intangible culture as cultural property. Nothing in the scholarly or WIPO approaches to intangible culture regulation turns on its classification as intangible cultural heritage. And nothing in the existing scholarly definition of cultural property conclusively disallows the inclusion of intangible culture, or convincingly discredits its regulation as cultural property. Therefore, the dichotomy between tangible cultural property and intangible cultural heritage is also false and should be discarded.

3.3 Above-water cultural property vs underwater cultural heritage

A third bifurcation of dubious validity in ICHL is between tangible culture on land and tangible culture underwater. An example of tangible culture on land is the Elgin Marbles, housed in the British Museum and termed cultural property. An example of tangible culture underwater is RMS *Titanic*, which in 1912 struck an iceberg and sank to the bottom of the Atlantic Ocean, and which is termed underwater cultural heritage. Unlike the second bifurcation in

[113] (signed 31 October 2003, entered into force 14 December 2005); United Nations Office on Drugs and Crime, 'Signature and Ratification Status' <www.unodc.org/unodc/en/corruption/ratification-status.html> accessed 30 April 2024.
[114] Arewa (n 33) 58–59; Burri (n 32) 470–81.
[115] See for instance WIPO Draft Articles on TK arts 2, 4–5; WIPO Draft Articles on TCE arts 4, 8, 15.

Section 3.2, which turned on the tangibility of culture to determine what constitutes cultural property (tangibles) and what constitutes cultural heritage (intangibles), the current bifurcation turns on whether an item of tangible culture is located above water or underwater for it to be considered cultural property or cultural heritage.

The source of the bifurcation between above-water cultural property and underwater cultural heritage is the 2001 Underwater Cultural Heritage Convention, which defines 'underwater cultural heritage' to include:[116]

> [A]ll traces of human existence having a cultural, historical or archaeological character which have been *partially or totally under water*, periodically or continuously, for at least 100 years such as:
> (i) sites, structures, buildings, artefacts and human remains, together with their archaeological and natural context;
> (ii) vessels, aircraft, other vehicles or any part thereof, their cargo or other contents, together with their archaeological and natural context; and
> (iii) objects of prehistoric character.

The definition of cultural heritage in the 2001 Underwater Cultural Heritage Convention is similar to the general definition of cultural property in the 1970 UNESCO Convention, which includes 'property . . . of importance for archaeology, prehistory, history, literature, art or science',[117] since both Conventions aim to preserve tangible culture of historical or archaeological value. Yet, cultural property is neither a term of reference nor of comparison with cultural heritage in the 2001 Underwater Cultural Heritage Convention because 'it was decided early in the negotiations that property issues lay outside its scope'.[118] Some scholars have simply linked (but not defended) the choice of cultural heritage over cultural property in the context of underwater tangible culture to a conceptual shift from regulating cultural property in the earlier 1954 and 1970 UNESCO Conventions to regulating cultural heritage in the later UNESCO Conventions.[119] Others have simply recorded a change from the regulation of 'underwater cultural property' in the 1985 Draft European

[116] Art 1(a) (emphasis added).
[117] Art 1.
[118] Patrick J O'Keefe, *Shipwrecked Heritage—A Commentary on the UNESCO Convention on Underwater Cultural Heritage* (2nd edn, Institute of Art and Law 2014) 86.
[119] 1972 World Heritage Convention; 2001 Underwater Cultural Heritage Convention; 2003 Intangible Cultural Heritage Convention; see for instance Sarah Dromgoole, *Underwater Cultural Heritage and International Law* (CUP 2013) 80–94.

Convention on the Protection of the Underwater Cultural Heritage,[120] to the regulation of 'underwater cultural heritage' in the 1994 International Law Association (ILA) Draft Convention on the Protection of the Underwater Cultural Heritage,[121] both draft instruments informing the 2001 Underwater Cultural Heritage Convention, without investigating the reasons underlying the change.[122] And yet others, whether or not cognisant of the possibly momentous turn from cultural property to cultural heritage to denote underwater tangible culture, nonchalantly unturn to equate underwater cultural heritage to 'marine cultural property'.[123] As existing scholarship appears unconcerned with why underwater tangible culture has to be regulated as underwater cultural heritage but not underwater cultural property, the bifurcation between above-water cultural property and underwater cultural heritage must either be self-evident or self-serving.

It may be preferable to regulate underwater cultural heritage over underwater cultural property on the basis that ascertaining a salvaged object's ownership is challenging.[124] The bulk of underwater tangible culture comprises ancient, shipwrecked vessels, sunken cities, and their accompaniments. The end of colonization ushered in a new era of self-determination and state succession, which led to the reinstatement or redrawing of national land and maritime boundaries. A shipwrecked military vessel may fly the flag of state A subsequently succeeded by state B, and may be previously located within the territorial waters of state C subsequently ceded to a newly independent state D. If property ownership is limited to individual ownership, be it private or sovereign, and if a shipwrecked vessel's true owner cannot be ascertained

[120] Draft European Underwater Cultural Heritage Convention art 1(1) provides: 'For the purposes of this Convention all remains and objects and any other traces of human existence located entirely or in part in the sea, lakes, rivers, canals, artificial reservoirs or other bodies of water, or in the tidal or other periodically flooded areas, or recovered from any such environment, or washed ashore, shall be considered as being part of the underwater cultural heritage, and are hereinafter referred to as "underwater cultural property".'

[121] ILA Draft Convention on Underwater Cultural Heritage art 1(1) provides: 'For the purposes of this Convention: "Underwater cultural heritage" means all underwater traces of human existence including: (a) sites, structures, buildings, artifacts and human remains, together with their archaeological and natural contexts; and (b) wreck such as a vessel, aircraft, other vehicle or any part thereof, its cargo or other contents, together with its archaeological and natural context.'

[122] Janet Blake, 'The Protection of the Underwater Cultural Heritage' (1996) 45(4) International and Comparative Law Quarterly 819, 824–27, 831–38.

[123] Patrick J O'Keefe and James A R Nafziger, 'The Draft Convention on the Protection of the Underwater Cultural Heritage' (1994) 25(4) Ocean Development and International Law 391, 401; see also Carla J Shapreau, 'Extension of Express Abandonment Standard for Sovereign Shipwrecks in Sea Hunt, Inc. et al., Raises Troublesome Issues Regarding Protection of Underwater Cultural Property' (2001) 10(2) International Journal of Cultural Property 276, 303–04 where the terms 'underwater cultural property' and 'underwater cultural heritage' are used interchangeably.

[124] O'Keefe, *Shipwrecked Heritage* (n 118) 19, 37.

with confidence or certainty,[125] then there is no owner, no enforceable legal or moral right of the owner to use a thing, and no underwater cultural property to regulate. In contrast, cultural heritage is typically expressed as belonging to humanity and all mankind,[126] and not to an individual person, entity, or state. So, it does not matter if a shipwrecked vessel's individual owner cannot be ascertained with confidence or certainty; it can nonetheless be regulated as cultural heritage, which does not require any individual ownership determination. However, as shown in Chapter 1 and will be further fleshed out in Section 4.1 below, ownership in new property refers to imputable ownership and not individual ownership.[127] Contrary to prevailing views, the Anglo-American exaltation of and emphasis on individual property ownership is not universal. So long as ownership can be imputed to an individual, a collective, a state, or multiple states, ownership as a core attribute of new property is satisfied. By updating the ownership attribute of basic property to fit cultural property, the bifurcation between above-water cultural property and underwater cultural heritage is no longer, if it ever was, self-evident.

Finally, there can be little doubt that a self-serving bifurcation between above-water cultural property and underwater cultural heritage will stand up to neither scrutiny nor the test of time. Whether its proponents instinctively believed that avoiding property talk shed all the ideological baggage that property carried or that cultural heritage was a more encompassing object of regulation than cultural property, neither impression is borne out in Sections 3.1 and 3.2 above. A more profound understanding of property, and a more critical look at heritage, renders cultural property no less facilitative and encompassing an object of regulation than cultural heritage. And just like how the dichotomies between cultural property and cultural heritage, and tangible cultural property and intangible cultural heritage, are false, the dichotomy between above-water cultural property and underwater cultural heritage is also false. The way forward is to recognize cultural property as the overarching and principal object of regulation in ICHL, and to regulate it as new property.

[125] For an overview of the proper exercise of sovereignty over sunken state vessels under general international law, see Dromgoole (n 119) 136–53.

[126] The Preamble to the 2001 UNESCO Underwater Cultural Heritage Convention acknowledges 'the importance of underwater cultural heritage as an integral part of *the cultural heritage of humanity* and a particularly important element in *the history of peoples, nations, and their relations with each other concerning their common heritage*...' (emphasis added).

[127] See Chapter 1, Section 4.1.

4. Cultural property as new property

To date, cultural property regulation in international law has been beset by multiple deficiencies in ICHL, ICL, IIL, and ITL which end up undermining cultural property protection. It has also been saddled with the mistaken distinction between cultural property and cultural heritage, which generates confusion over the proper object of regulation. Not only is cultural property potentially subject to regulation under several idiosyncratic regimes, it is also, by dint of conventional prescription, regulated separately from cultural heritage under ICHL. The surfeit of applicable treaty provisions, regime-specific analytical approaches, and the identification of different forms of cultural heritage (intangible, underwater) for discrete regulation from cultural property breed unnecessary complexity. This section strives to mitigate the current chaos afflicting cultural property regulation in international law by first explaining why cultural property is better defined as a category of new property (Section 4.1), before suggesting how cultural property as new property portends more streamlined and predictable regulation (Section 4.2).

4.1 Towards a principled understanding of cultural property

Cultural property has thus far been defined by illustrations in conventions or by discretionary state designation. Neither approach promotes a principled understanding of cultural property because illustrations cannot capture then unknown forms of cultural property, while discretionary state designation cannot capture all forms of cultural property. Relying on these approaches to identify what is or is not cultural property is highly unsatisfactory because there remains a large category of unillustrated and undesignated items whose status as cultural property will always be ambiguous. This ambiguity can be minimized by adopting a conceptual definition of cultural property that proffers attributes rather than outcomes, so that an item bearing the requisite attributes will qualify as cultural property. And it appears that cultural items, including the intangible and those located underwater, bear all four attributes of new property.

Imputable ownership: The ownership of new property comports a putative dimension which refers to attributed or asserted ownership over a thing, as well as a qualitative dimension which refers to the manner of ownership over a thing.[128] That which is incapable of being owned, such as the air that we

[128] See Chapter 1, Section 4.1.

breathe or illusory contractual rights, is not new property. And that which is capable of being owned can be owned in a variety of ways, including private, individual ownership, privately led collective ownership, state-led collective ownership, state ownership, and multi-state ownership. When cultural items have identified or identifiable owners with a recognized right to use the items they own without interference from non-owners, they satisfy the imputable ownership criterion of new property.

The imputation of ownership to cultural monuments or artefacts such as the Benin Bronzes (located in various European museums and owned by Benin) poses little difficulty, and such monuments and artefacts are readily acknowledged as cultural property. The imputation of ownership to TK and TCE, and to underwater cultural items may, in contrast, be less straightforward. When TK in the form of therapeutic uses of indigenous herbs for instance, or TCE in the form of indigenous burial practices for instance, are passed down from one generation to the next within a given community, it may be difficult to impute rightful ownership over a specific piece of TK or TCE to a single individual or a single community who controls its use and dissemination. This is because the birth and evolution of TK or TCE may not be rigorously documented, resulting in breaks and uncertainties in the chain of ownership over an extended period of time. However, the attribute of ownership in new property is not limited to ownership by a specific individual or specific group of individuals. New property can be collectively or communally owned.[129] So when TK or TCE as new property is misappropriated, any person or group of persons with a verified claim to such collective or communal ownership must be entitled to seek legal redress. Fear of a floodgate of hypothetical owners contesting the use and dissemination of TK and TCE by hypothetical non-owners is symptomatic of the extended neglect of TK and TCE regulation in international law. It echoes the disregard of non-owners who previously commodified TK and TCE for profit for their indigenous owners,[130] and reveals how much more TK and TCE protection needs to be enhanced.[131] A high imputable ownership count may discomfit those with a limited view of ownership in property, but it certainly enables TK and TCE to satisfy the ownership criterion of new property.

[129] Sita Reddy, 'Making Heritage Legible: Who Owns Traditional Medical Knowledge?' (2006) 13(2) International Journal of Cultural Property 161, 162–64.

[130] Karin Timmermans, 'Intellectual Property Rights and Traditional Medicine: Policy Dilemmas at the Interface' (2003) 57(4) Social Science & Medicine 745, 746–47.

[131] As indicated in Section 2.1.1 above, the WIPO Draft Articles are a step in the right direction.

With respect to underwater cultural items, it is opportune to revisit the example of a shipwrecked military vessel having four potential state owners given in Section 3.3 above. If ownership in property is restricted to a single state, then determining which one of the four states is the military vessel's owner in accordance with the guidelines on state succession in relation to state property may be so daunting or complex as to discourage the classification of that shipwrecked military vessel as property. That said, perceived difficulty in identifying the rightful owner of the shipwrecked military vessel does not mean impossibility of identification. In the case of a military vessel flying the flag of state A subsequently succeeded by state B, and which sank in the territorial waters of state C subsequently ceded to a newly independent state D, the rightful owner of the vessel is, unless otherwise agreed by states A and B, most likely state B.[132] This deduction is reinforced if state B's ownership is recognized by the internal law of state C as the predecessor state in whose territory state B's military vessel is located.[133] Therefore, even on a limited reading of ownership in property, ownership in a shipwrecked vessel, regardless of factual permutations, is ascertainable. If, however, ownership in property accommodates state-led collective ownership or multi-state ownership, as it does in new property, then ownership determination ceases to be an obstacle in the classification of underwater cultural items as new property. Ownership in the shipwrecked military vessel can either be imputed solely to state B, or jointly to states B and D. When the ownership of underwater cultural items can be imputed to a state or states, then underwater cultural items undoubtedly satisfy the ownership criterion of new property.

Responsiveness to contextual factors: Tangible, intangible, and underwater cultural items are all highly responsive to contextual factors. The global movement to protect and preserve culture in its various forms stems from the widespread conviction, borne from extended and extensive political and social conditioning, that certain items which record or reflect a piece of history or a practice or an identity of a segment of mankind should be 'canonized' to merit exaltation and bespoke conservation.[134] What has been or should be deemed worthy of preservation 'always depend[s] on contemporary ideological concerns',[135] and this can be seen in how states' attention to cultural protection was first focused on tangible cultural items in the 1950s, before

[132] Vienna Convention on Succession of States in respect of State Property, Archives and Debts (signed 8 April 1983, not yet in force) arts 8–11.
[133] ibid art 12.
[134] Handler (n 63) 359.
[135] ibid.

shifting to underwater cultural items in the 2000s, and then onto intangible cultural items in more recent times. Contemporary objectification of culture is complemented by the establishment of numerous museums to house tangible cultural items, guided museum tours to inform the masses of the history and significance of the assembled collections, and UNESCO initiatives and the rise of responsible eco-tourism to raise awareness and concern for underwater cultural sites and items. It also includes prominent efforts to recognize the rights of indigenous peoples over their lands and resources and,[136] by extension, over their traditional customs, practices, knowledge, and expressions. All these complementary indicators not only reinforce what the objects of protection are, they also convey their historical, educational, aesthetic, or scientific value, their irreplaceability, or even their pricelessness, implying that strong moral approbation will attach to their destruction or disrespect. When the genres of preservation-worthy cultural items increase in the wake of evolving political will and social awareness and pressures, tangible, intangible, and underwater culture clearly satisfy the criterion of responsiveness of new property.

Separability: The attribute of separability in new property refers to the capacity of a thing to be divested from its imputed owner/s, without any need for the transfer of ownership. In addition to having identifiable owners and being responsive to contextual factors, tangible, intangible, and underwater cultural items are all separable from their imputed owner/s. An example of a separable tangible cultural item is the Elgin Marbles from Greece, currently housed in the British Museum. Crafted in the fifth century BCE as part of the temple of Parthenon situated on the Acropolis of Athens, the Elgin Marbles and its surrounding ceremonial structures are regarded as enduring symbols of Ancient Greece, Western democracy, and civilization. The high visibility of the Elgin Marbles as a sacred cultural artefact and persistent calls for its return to Greece mark a long-standing campaign mounted by successive Greek governments to defend and restore the Greek patrimony. And although Greece and the UK continue to dispute ownership over the Elgin Marbles,[137] the fact remains that Greece was divested of the Marbles had it been the rightful owner, and that the UK, even if it is the rightful owner, will be divested of the Marbles if they are transported back to Greece.

[136] UN General Assembly, 'Declaration on the Rights of Indigenous Peoples' (13 September 2007) A/Res/61/295.

[137] Merryman in 'Thinking About the Elgin Marbles' (n 27) 1895–1902 contends that the acquisition of the Elgin Marbles from the Ottoman rulers by Lord Elgin, who later transferred ownership in the Marbles to the British government, was legitimate; cf Titi (n 27) 79–82, also 110–22.

An example of a separable intangible cultural item is the practice of traditional Mayan medicine. Its ownership can be imputed to the Mayan indigenous communities mostly found in Guatemala and southern Mexico, while its cultural value as TK has been established through considerable scholarly and scientific interest in how the ancient Mayan civilization used native plants to treat various physiological disorders. Although the knowledge and skills of traditional Mayan medicine cannot be removed from any individual or community in possession of that knowledge and those skills, the practice of traditional Mayan medicine can nonetheless be divested from its imputed owners through a simple refusal or failure to utilize that knowledge and those skills, or to instil them in later generations.

An iconic example of a separable underwater cultural item is RMS *Titanic.* Ultimately owned by a US national, and whose disastrous maiden voyage in 1912 has been memorialized in books, films, and documentaries, the Titanic's sinking and wreckage lying at the bottom of the Atlantic Ocean have been propelled by mass media to cult historical and cultural significance. Since its sinking, many expeditions have been launched to explore or salvage objects for exhibition from the Titanic's wreckage. The fact that salvors, whether or not authorized by the Titanic's rightful owner/s, managed to remove parts of the wreckage for display elsewhere is proof that the owner/s of underwater cultural items can be divested of these items. When tangible, intangible, and underwater cultural items have imputable owners, are responsive to contextual factors, and are separable from their owners, they bear three of the four core attributes of new property, rendering the assimilation of cultural property to new property almost complete. The fourth and final attribute, to which the discussion now turns, is the conferral of a benefit.

Conferral of a benefit: New property is that which confers a benefit, financial or otherwise, on its imputed owner/s. The type of benefit that cultural property confers on its imputed owner/s will differ depending on who its owner is. When cultural property is owned by an individual, that individual may derive benefit in the form of personal satisfaction in possession or observation of its aesthetic form, or in the form of financial gain by trading it (legally) or exhibiting it for a fee. When cultural property is owned by a community, that community may derive benefit in the form of identity reinforcement and conservation through its use and dissemination, or in the form of financial gain by licensing the use and dissemination of its cultural property by other communities or entities. When cultural property is owned by a state, that state may derive benefit in its role as a provider of public goods by being equipped to offer its people access to a source and symbol of national identity, unity, and pride. The state may also derive financial benefit by exhibiting its cultural property, both locally and abroad (where applicable), to visitors for a fee. At the very least, all cultural property, be it tangible, intangible, or underwater, offers an insight into life in the past or a consolidation of accumulated wisdom, practices, and beliefs. This strongly suggests that imputable owners of cultural property will usually, if not always, derive some educational benefit from this category of new property.

4.2 Towards predictable regulation of cultural property

Treating cultural property as new property addresses the intra-regime fragmentation currently seen in ICHL, where cultural items are subject to different governing frameworks depending on whether they are tangible, intangible, or lie underwater. Treating cultural property as new property also addresses the haphazard regulation of cultural property in other regimes such as ICL, IIL, and ITL. The status quo is untenable because greater sub-specialization in ICHL, and the crossover to ICL, IIL, and ITL, have not provided strong and principled protection for cultural property. The former has generated more confusion than precision in cultural property protection with the introduction and subsequent entrenchment of the unnecessary distinction between cultural property and cultural heritage, while the latter invariably subordinates cultural property protection to the main regulatory target of an international crime, a foreign investment, or a trade measure. All this makes cultural property regulation in international law both complex and unpredictable.

Regulating cultural property as new property fosters three potential developments. First, the acknowledgement that international law is deficient when it comes to new property may jumpstart the development, refinement, and consolidation of cultural property-oriented regulations into a body of international cultural property law. If and when cultural property-oriented regulations, based on a more representative and progressive understanding of cultural property, appear, they can be applied uniformly to all instances of cultural property protection. The more inclusive notion of cultural property as new property does away with the need for multiple regulatory sub-regimes in ICHL and enables undivided focus on cultural property regulation. Second, a body of cultural property-oriented regulations serves as a common point of reference when cultural property regulation arises for consideration under ICL, IIL, or ITL. Rather than disregarding, paying lip service to, or simply declaring cultural property protection, international crime, investment, and trade tribunals can obtain guidance from these existing or emerging regulations to make reasoned decisions on cultural property protection. Third, regulating cultural property as new property replaces the provocative proposal to protect cultural property by commodifying and de-regulating it.[138] According to this view, greater regulation will only encourage irresponsible looting and illegal trade since '[i]f it were legal to remove cultural property and sell it, then professionals would take over and use care because antiquities are worth more when their provenance is known and when they are undamaged'.[139] If trade in cultural property is no different from trade in artworks, the latter being mostly unregulated, then there is no reason to treat cultural property differently from any other kind of property to which monetary value can be attached.[140] This proposal is provocative because it does not account for the nature of state ownership of cultural property, nor the nature of benefit that cultural property confers on its sovereign owner. States have made it abundantly clear through a series of international conventions and resolutions that cultural property is to be preserved and protected, *not* traded. This is because state ownership of cultural property, inherited from earlier generations and preserved for future generations, is predominantly custodial. Moreover, the benefit conferred by cultural property on its sovereign owner is the public interest act of constructing and maintaining a national identity, which cannot be measured in monetary terms. State-owned cultural property is thus unlike privately owned artwork, which is voluntarily traded for financial gain. States may, of course, choose to sell their cultural property, but few would be willing to do so in the absence of exceptional circumstances, and none should be compelled to consider trading cultural property in order to sidestep current regulatory problems. The better solution to deficient regulation is not to de-regulate, but to find a different approach to regulation. In this regard, regulating cultural property as new property respects the distinctive nature of cultural property while presenting a unified alternative to the current diffuse modes of regulation.

While there is little prospect of starting on a clean slate for cultural property regulation in international law, it is nonetheless possible to gradually steer it in the direction of new property regulation. The combined effect of the possible developments outlined above normalizes the treatment of cultural property as new property with a common point of reference in the form of progressive

138 Posner (n 38) 218–19, 222, 225, 229.
139 ibid 225.
140 ibid 222, 229.

cultural property-oriented regulations, thereby streamlining cultural property regulation and helping to make it more predictable across different regimes.

5. Conclusion

This chapter has attempted to showcase the current deficient regulation of cultural property in international law and forecast the possible improvements should cultural property be regarded and regulated as new property. Ironically, cultural property regulation remains unsatisfactory despite a surfeit of regulations found in six binding conventions in ICHL. A closer examination of these conventions, and their ratifying states, reveals that while states appear united on the idea of cultural property protection, they are less committed to the reality of what concrete protection entails. This half-heartedness explains why these conventions establish formalistic guidelines that do not sit comfortably with actual, anarchic conditions on the ground or with the actual capacity of culture-rich but cash-poor states to comply. It also explains why these conventions do not establish an adjudicatory mechanism to determine when their provisions are breached. States wish to be seen making a pledge regarding cultural property protection, but do not wish to be called out when that pledge, for one reason or another, cannot be kept.

The failure of the ICHL treaty regime with respect to cultural property regulation is the status quo, which reflects dysfunctional complexity on two levels. The first level is intra-regime complexity, where cultural heritage, intangible cultural heritage, and underwater cultural heritage regulation are seemingly carved out from cultural property regulation and subject to different provisions, without a proper and profound consideration of whether such fragmentation is truly necessary or beneficial. As it turns out, the move from property to heritage was triggered by the perceived, but unproven and ultimately false, unsuitability of retaining property as the target object of regulation. The second level is inter-regime complexity, where cultural property protection is recognized in ICHL but potentially secured through the different adjudicatory mechanisms in ICL, IIL, and ITL. As cultural property protection is typically relegated to a peripheral consideration in the application of ICL in the institutional prosecution of international crimes, of IIL to the arbitral resolution of investor–state disputes, and of ITL to inter-state trade disputes, none of these regimes have developed rules or doctrines specific to cultural property protection. Having to assess cultural property protection through the different lens of international crimes, foreign investment, and international trade pulls cultural property protection in three different directions, none of which have yielded optimal or principled results.

Regarding and regulating cultural property as new property is my response to the dysfunctional complexity that cultural property protection in international law currently attracts. This is because new property possesses core attributes that do not limit its manifestations to tangible things or things with one identifiable owner or things to which a financial value attaches. New property thus captures the spectrum of representations of culture, ranging from priceless historical monuments, to shipwrecks, to undocumented traditional knowledge, rituals, and expressions. The treatment and regulation of cultural property as new property mitigates intra-regime complexity by doing away with unnecessary and unhelpful bifurcations between property and heritage and recentring attention on cultural property as the target object of regulation in ICHL. The prevailing tendency to craft a new convention for every new concern should be replaced by efforts to develop a coherent body of cultural property-oriented regulations that is better attuned to the notion and regulation of cultural property as new property. The treatment and regulation of cultural property as new property also mitigates inter-regime complexity by offering a common point of reference that permeates distinct governing regimes. The inquiry can then evolve from the present, fruitless one which asks abstractly where cultural property protection is situated within ICL, IIL, and ITL (nowhere), to a more incisive and rewarding one which asks how and to what extent specific cultural property-oriented regulations intersect and interact with ICL, IIL, and ITL. Having reached streamlined coherence as the end-game for cultural property regulation, I now turn to the next category of new property—common property.

3

Common Property

1. Introduction

The story of common property and its regulation by international law is one of unfinished compromise. It is a compromise because property belonging to either no one or to everyone naturally attracts competing objectives and interests in its definition and use. And this compromise is unfinished because power and profit tend to derail or hijack attempts at principled communal regulation, resulting in thwarted or fragile deals that suppress some voices to appease others, and paving the way for future backlash by the marginalized. Unfinished compromises can be observed in the three key examples of common property, namely, the Antarctic, the Moon and other celestial objects in outer space, and the seabed lying beyond the limits of national jurisdiction (the Area).[1] The unfinished compromise in the Antarctic is manifested by a very limited regulatory framework designed to preserve, or at the very least not disrupt, the overlapping territorial claims of Norway, Chile, Argentina, the UK, France, Australia, and New Zealand over parts of Antarctica. Descent into

[1] Oscar Schachter, 'Who Owns the Universe?' *Collier's Weekly* (22 March 1952) 71.

New Property in International Law. Jean Ho, Oxford University Press. © Jean Ho 2024.
DOI: 10.1093/9780191976117.003.0004

disorder is impeded only by difficulties of access to the South Pole, which may change over time with advancements in travel technology. Over and above in outer space, the unfinished compromise appears in the existence of distinct regimes addressing the use of the Moon and other celestial objects. One regime is represented in the main by the 1967 Outer Space Treaty and the 1979 Moon Treaty;[2] the other regime is represented by the non-binding Artemis Accords concluded in 2020.[3] The paradox of these parallel regimes is a largely, if not entirely, unregulated space race. The most arresting study of unfinished compromise in common property is probably the role and mandate of the International Seabed Authority (ISA) in regulating the use of the Area. The ISA was established by the 1982 United Nations Convention on the Law of the Sea,[4] and remodelled in 1994 to supposedly reconcile diametrically opposed developed and developing state interests regarding deep seabed mining.[5] The ISA regulates the Area via a discretionary licensing scheme and has recently come under intense scrutiny for allegedly prioritizing commercial profit over ocean health,[6] suggesting that while conflicting aspirations for the Area were recognized in 1982, they were not necessarily resolved in 1994.

This chapter contends that international law thus far offers no compelling framework for common property regulation because its makers have either advanced or acquiesced in the extension of private, capitalist property regulation to common, communal property regulation. By paying lip service to the multi-state ownership attribute of common property as new property, while crafting regimes that optimize benefit-sharing from common property use only among select states and stakeholders, international lawmakers afford an opportunity to review and rectify the misalignments in common property regulation. Section 2 explains how the current regulatory arrangements for the

[2] Treaty on Principles Governing the Activities of States in the Exploration and Use of Outer Space, including the Moon and Other Celestial Bodies (signed 27 January 1967, entered into force 10 October 1967) 610 UNTS 205 (1967 Outer Space Treaty); Agreement governing the Activities of States on the Moon and Other Celestial Bodies (signed 5 December 1979, entered into force 11 July 1984) 1363 UNTS 3 (1979 Moon Treaty). As of 30 April 2024, the 1967 Outer Space Treaty has 113 states parties, while the 1979 Moon Treaty has 18 states parties.

[3] National Aeronautics and Space Administration (NASA), 'Artemis Accords' <www.nasa.gov/wp-content/uploads/2022/11/Artemis-Accords-signed-13Oct2020.pdf> accessed 30 April 2024. To date, the Artemis Accords has twenty-five signatories.

[4] (signed 10 December 1982, entered into force 16 November 1994) 1833 UNTS 397 (UNCLOS) art 156.

[5] Agreement relating to the Implementation of Part XI of the United Nations Convention on the Law of the Sea of 10 December 1982 (signed 28 July 1994, entered into force 28 July 1996) 1836 UNTS 3 (1994 UNCLOS Agreement) Annex.

[6] Eric Lipton, 'Leader of International Seabed Mining Agency Admonished by Diplomats' *The New York Times* (19 March 2023); Eric Lipton, 'Secret Data, Tiny Islands and a Quest for Treasure on the Ocean Floor' *The New York Times* (29 August 2022).

Antarctic, the Moon and other celestial objects, and the Area reveal a capitalist orientation where commercial, not communal, interests hold sway. Section 3 then elaborates on how these existing arrangements fail to cope with present and projected uses of common property, thereby jeopardizing the prospect of sustainable natural resource consumption. Section 4 recommends turning to common pool resource management principles for guidance on common property regulation, and considers the outlook for stakeholder commitment to a modified regulatory blueprint. Section 5 concludes.

2. Capitalist capture and the compromised regulation of common property

Common property has often been referred to as 'global commons' and, more controversially, as 'common heritage of mankind'.[7] While I do not aim to standardize terminology in this monograph, my choice of 'common property' over more prominent alternative labels in the ensuing analysis warrants explanation. First, 'global commons' is a generally accepted umbrella term for spaces and natural resources 'beyond national jurisdictions'.[8] That said, while 'global commons' accommodates discourse on the regulation of common spaces and natural resources, it does not anchor the discussion on the regulation of these common spaces and natural resources in new property. 'Common property' is thus the more appropriate term of reference for this monograph and this chapter. Second, 'common heritage of mankind', in addition to lacking property content signalling effects like 'global commons', has been explicitly rejected by powerful states as a label for the Moon and for the Area.[9] In comparison to 'common property', 'common heritage of mankind' seems the more divisive, more distracting label.[10] Moreover, it has been suggested that little

[7] Modern property forms derived from Roman property forms do not accommodate common ownership because Celsus the Younger advocated that property can only be owned by one individual at any one time. As a result, Roman jurists and scholars interpreting the work of Roman jurists did not readily embrace common property, see Anna di Robilant, *The Making of Modern Property* (CUP 2023) 228–33. However, it is now widely accepted that the Antarctic, the Moon and other celestial objects, and the Area are subject to common ownership, rendering them part of the 'global commons', the 'common heritage of mankind', or common property.

[8] Surabhi Ranganathan, 'Global Commons' (2016) 27(3) European Journal of International Law 693, 693; also John G Sprankling, *The International Law of Property* (OUP 2014) 117; cf Executive Order 13914, 'Encouraging International Support for the Recovery and Use of Space Resources' (6 April 2020), where it is stated: 'Outer space is a legally and physically unique domain of human activity, and the United States does not view it as a global commons.'

[9] John Vogler, *The Global Commons—A Regime Analysis* (Wiley 1995) 64, 70, 102–03.

[10] One scholar has objected to the characterization of the Antarctic, the Moon and other celestial objects, and the Area as 'common property' because 'property' focuses on ownership, while 'common

epistemological mileage may be gained by retaining 'common heritage of mankind' as a label if the regulation of common spaces and natural resources can be achieved without it.[11] Therefore, 'common property' is the more apposite label here because it enables the discussion to focus on the regulation of new property rather than the resistance to calling common spaces and natural resources the 'common heritage of mankind'.

The remainder of this section chronicles the development of the current regulatory regimes or arrangements under international law for the Antarctic (Section 2.1), the Moon and other celestial objects (Section 2.2), and the Area (Section 2.3), and demonstrates how they are unapologetically driven by profit-maximization for some instead of benefit-sharing for all. It is remarkable how separate attempts at some form of communal regulation of different types of common property have all given way to some form of nominally supervised regulation of private property. The capitalist capture of common property regulation in international law casts serious doubt on the ability of existing regulatory instruments to promote and secure the sustainable use of common property, and, more fundamentally, on the defensibility of treaty-based regulatory regimes in time to come.

2.1 The Antarctic

Before outlining the Antarctic regulatory regime, a question that begs is whether the Antarctic, which remains subject to overlapping territorial claims asserted by more than a handful of states, is truly common property. This question can be answered in the affirmative because, notwithstanding the existence of competing territorial claims, the Antarctic bears the core attributes of new property, namely, imputable ownership, responsiveness to contextual factors, separability, and conferral of benefit.[12] First, ownership of the Antarctic is imputable to *all* states. This is because what Article IV of the 1959 Antarctic Treaty

heritage of mankind' focuses on stewardship, with stewardship better representing how common spaces and natural resources should be managed by states, see Kemal Baslar, *The Concept of the Common Heritage of Mankind in International Law* (Martinus Nijhoff 1998) 14–16, 50–52. Baslar does not explain why states as property owners are more prone to mis-regulate common spaces and natural resources to satisfy their electors, while states as stewards are not. Ownership is an attribute of new property; it is not a predictor of how new property will be regulated, see Chapter 1, Section 4.1. Therefore, what Baslar is truly concerned with is how states purport to regulate common property, and not the label of 'common property' *per se*.

[11] Bin Cheng, *Studies in International Space Law* (OUP 1997) 374.

[12] Chapter 1, Sections 4.1–4.4.

does is 'freeze' the competing territorial claims of Norway, Chile, Argentina, the UK, France, Australia, and New Zealand,[13] by specifying that there will be no 'renunciation by any Contracting Party of previously asserted rights of or claims to territorial sovereignty in Antarctica'.[14] Article IV only recognizes the *fact* of pre-existing territorial claims, and not the *validity* of such claims. The prolonged non-recognition by other states of the validity of asserted territorial claims over Antarctica, coupled with the prolonged non-pursuit of these claims by the claimant states, locks *all* states into a stalemate where *no* state can establish ownership over any part of the Antarctic. The result is sovereign Antarctic ownership by none, and common Antarctic ownership by all. Second, the Antarctic is a continent which contains a vast amount of natural resources such as icebergs, fish, seals, and other marine living resources. It is highly responsive to the demands of a consumer market for Antarctic produce as well as those of a scientific market for biodiversity and climate change research, is easily separable from its imputed state owners, and confers benefit on its imputed state owners and their nationals in the form of monetary gains from Antarctic trade or educational gains from Antarctic research. Therefore, when depicted in terms of new property, the Antarctic is common property.[15]

The Antarctic regulatory regime consists of one treaty and three protocols. Together, the 1959 Antarctic Treaty mentioned above, the 1972 Convention for the Conservation of Antarctic Seals (CCAS),[16] the 1980 Convention on the Conservation of Antarctic Marine Living Resources (CCAMLR),[17] and the 1991 Protocol on Environmental Protection to the Antarctic Treaty (Environmental Protection Protocol)[18] are known as the Antarctic Treaty System (ATS). The ATS is overseen by a Secretariat which organizes an annual meeting, the Antarctic Treaty Consultative Meeting (ATCM), attended by representatives of the original parties to the 1959 Antarctic Treaty, as well as representatives of other treaty parties who conduct substantial research activities in the Antarctic.[19] While third party states may participate in these annual

[13] Jonathan Charney, 'The Antarctic System and Customary International Law' in Francesco Francioni and Tullio Scovazzi (eds), *International Law for Antarctica* (2nd edn, Kluwer Law International 1996) 51, 91.

[14] (signed 1 December 1959, entered into force 23 June 1961) 402 UNTS 71 (1959 Antarctic Treaty) art IV(1)(a).

[15] Support for characterizing the Antarctic as common property can be found in Charney (n 13) 56 where it is posited that when the Antarctic is '*res communis* or a part of the world's commons, rules of international law normally associated with such areas would be applicable'.

[16] (signed 1 June 1972, entered into force 11 March 1978) 1080 UNTS 175.

[17] (signed 20 May 1980, entered into force 7 April 1982) 1329 UNTS 47.

[18] (signed 4 October 1991, entered into force 14 January 1998) 2941 UNTS 9.

[19] See generally Secretariat of the Antarctic Treaty, 'ATCM and Other Meetings' <www.ats.aq/e/atcm.html> accessed 30 April 2024.

meetings, only treaty parties can take part in any decision-making. On paper, the ATS comes across as a promising starter regulatory regime for common property, articulating positive obligations on states parties to use the Antarctic for peaceful and scientific purposes,[20] to submit annual reports on the environmental impact of their activities in the Antarctic,[21] and to ensure that Antarctic seals and marine living resources are not captured or harvested to the point of over-depletion.[22] In practice, the absence of any accountability mechanism in the ATS has promoted the liberal use of Antarctic resources. China conducts military activities in the Antarctic—in express violation of Article I(1) of the 1959 Antarctic Treaty[23]—without open challenge from other state parties.[24] Illegal and unreported fishing in Antarctic waters earns no sanction from the CCAMLR Commission.[25] And Japan continues hunting whales in the Antarctic in the name of scientific research,[26] even *after* the International Court of Justice ruled by a majority in 2014 that the Japanese kills were not for scientific research and had to stop.[27] To be fair to the ATS states parties (which include China and Japan) who meet annually to initiate, debate, and formulate new, albeit non-binding, resolutions, the official desire to advance Antarctic regulation has not diminished. But to be frank, more resolutions do not denote progress when the states parties display a persistently dismal track record of abiding by the treaties that they sign and the resolutions that they pass.

ATS states parties tend to adopt resolutions at the annual ATCM that purport to regulate the Antarctic as common property benefitting the common good, but end up preserving the individual preferences and practices of

[20] 1959 Antarctic Treaty art I(1); 1991 Environmental Protection Protocol art 2; also 1980 CCAMLR Preamble.

[21] 1991 Environmental Protection Protocol art 17.

[22] 1972 CCAS arts 1, 3, and Annex; 1980 CCAMLR art II.

[23] Art I(1) provides: 'Antarctica shall be used for peaceful purposes only. There shall be prohibited, *inter alia*, any measures of a military nature, such as the establishment of military bases and fortifications, the carrying out of military maneuvers, as well as the testing of any type of weapons.'

[24] Craig Hooper, 'New Polar Strategy Must Focus on China's Long March to Antarctica' *Forbes* (10 January 2021); also Ian Bremmer, 'China's Ambitious Plans in Antarctica have Raised New Suspicions' *Time* (28 April 2023).

[25] CCAMLR, 'Illegal, Unreported and Unregulated (IIU) Fishing' <www.ccamlr.org/en/compliance/illegal-unreported-and-unregulated-iuu-fishing> accessed 30 April 2024.

[26] Mostafa Rachwani, 'Japan's New Whaling "Mother Ship" Being Built to Travel as Far as Antarctica' *The Guardian* (16 February 2023); Damian Carrington, 'Japan Killed 50 Whales in Antarctic Protected Area, Data Shows' *The Guardian* (4 September 2018); Mari Yamaguchi, 'Japan Says It Has "Achieved Its Plan" by Killing 333 Antarctic Whales' *The Independent* (1 April 2017); also 'Japan to Resume Whaling in Antarctic Despite Court Ruling' *BBC News* (28 November 2015).

[27] *Whaling in the Antarctic (Australia v Japan: New Zealand intervening)* [2014] ICJ Rep 226, 299–300. Australia based its claim against Japan's whaling activities in the Antarctic on art VIII and the Schedule of the 1946 International Convention for the Regulation of Whaling (signed 2 December 1946, entered into force 10 November 1948) 161 UNTS 72. The founding treaty and protocols of the ATS contain no specific references to whales or to whaling, although art I(1) of the CCAMLR includes 'fin fish', like whales, in the definition of 'Antarctic marine living resources'.

Antarctic-faring states parties. This may be because a supermajority of ATS states parties are developed nations or nations with large economies[28] that can muster the resources to fund unilateral Antarctic expeditions and activities. A brief survey of ATCM responses and resolutions recorded in the last four decades suggests that ATS states parties favour nominal Antarctic regulation that does not interfere with activities that enable them to recover or maximize returns on their investment or involvement in Antarctic exploration. In response to a Chilean report that 'geological specimens of scientific value are increasingly being removed from Antarctica for non-scientific purposes',[29] the 1994 ATCM made no move to identify, let alone sanction, the wrongdoers, brushing off common property theft with the prosaic reminder that 'the removal of fossils, minerals, meteorites, volcanic bombs and ventifacts should be done for scientific purposes only'.[30] The 2004 ATCM adopted a resolution to 'highly support' the CCAMLR Commission for urging ATS states parties to issue licences to fishing vessels less likely to cause marine pollution.[31] However, the presence of a large number of nylon line fragments in the Antarctic waters observed in a 2019 study[32] indicated that marine pollution from fishing activities, which the CCAMLR Commission was tasked to oversee, remained rampant. It is doubtful if highly supportive words were ever converted into highly supportive action that would have greatly reduced licensing fees collected by states parties with sizeable Antarctic fishing industries. The 2014 ATCM adopted a resolution to promote a 'risk-based assessment of tourism and non-governmental activities'.[33] This resolution was passed to 'promote environmental protection', and it left the details and the implementation of the risk-based assessment to the states parties. It seems that none of the states parties, such as the UK, the Netherlands, and the US, that are home to Antarctic tour operators ever took this resolution seriously. There is currently no limit on

[28] Out of the twenty-eight ATS states parties, twenty (marked with *) possess developed or large economies: Argentina*, Australia*, Belgium*, Brazil*, Bulgaria, Chile, China*, Czechia, Ecuador, Finland*, France*, Germany*, India*, Italy*, Japan*, South Korea*, Netherlands*, New Zealand*, Norway*, Peru, Poland, the Russian Federation*, South Africa*, Spain*, UK*, US*, Ukraine, and Uruguay.

[29] Secretariat of the Antarctic Treaty, 'Final Report of the Eighteenth Antarctic Treaty Consultative Meeting' (11–22 April 1994, Kyoto, Japan) para 96 <www.ats.aq/devAS/Meetings/DocDatabase?lang=e> accessed 30 April 2024.

[30] ibid para 97.

[31] Resolution 1 (2004) in Secretariat of the Antarctic Treaty, 'Final Report of the Twenty-Seventh Antarctic Treaty Consultative Meeting' (24 May–4 June 2004, Cape Town, South Africa) 222 <www.ats.aq/devAS/Meetings/DocDatabase?lang=e> accessed 30 April 2024.

[32] Ana LDF Lacerda and others, 'Plastics in Sea Surface Waters around the Antarctic Peninsula' (2019) 9(3977) Nature 1, 5.

[33] Resolution 6 (2014) in 'Final Report of the Thirty-Seventh Antarctic Treaty Consultative Meeting' (28 April–7 May 2014, Brasília, Brazil) 285 <https://documents.ats.aq/ATCM37/fr/ATCM37_fr001_e.pdf> accessed 30 April 2024.

the number of cruise ships or tourists who can visit Antarctica, and booming numbers give short shrift to environmental protection through risk-based tourism assessments.[34] There is therefore little reason to suppose that additional tourism-related resolutions adopted at more recent ATCMs[35] will actually be implemented by the states parties.

The capitalist capture of Antarctic regulation is evident in the stark discrepancy between what ATS states parties pledge to do, and what they actually do about Antarctic regulation. When Antarctic-oriented industries such as fishing and tourism are concentrated in the hands of developed states, and when those states deviate time and again from their own recommendations for common property regulation, Antarctic regulation becomes passably communal in form, but strikingly individualistic in substance. The pursuit of self-interest in the Antarctic, be it a greater profit margin or a greater latitude in the conduct of activities, is seeded in the ATS, which lacks any accountability mechanism, and is strengthened by habitual disregard for ATCM resolutions. It is also sheltered from view and from criticism by the composition of the ATCM, which is currently dominated by states with an active interest in Antarctic exploration and who stand to gain from minimal regulatory oversight and rebuke. A probable explanation for the generous silence conferred on Japanese whaling exploits at each ATCM is the expectation held by other ATS states parties that a collective blind eye will be turned if and when they decide to pursue an uncommon course of action in the Antarctic. The ATS regime has managed to elude external challenge for so long because it 'has never been subjected to a serious test'.[36] However, the status quo can be overturned should access to the Antarctic widen, and more states develop and maintain an active interest in Antarctic activities pertaining to trade, the environment, and national and global security. It is hoped that, when the 1959 Antarctic Treaty is due for renegotiation in 2048, the prediction that '[p]ressures to undertake new activities in Antarctica and to expand participation in decision-making may produce major changes ... [and] may give rise to new law that builds on the existing law or substantially changes that law' will come to pass.[37]

[34] Paige McClanahan, 'Tourism in Antarctica: Edging Toward the (Risky) Mainstream' *The New York Times* (26 February 2020).

[35] See eg Resolution 3 (2021) 'Site Guidelines for Visitors' in Secretariat of the Antarctic Treaty, 'Final Report of the Forty-Third Antarctic Treaty Consultative Meeting' (14–24 June 2021, Paris, France) 363 <www.ats.aq/devAS/Meetings/DocDatabase?lang=e> accessed 30 April 2024.

[36] Baslar (n 10) 254.

[37] Charney (n 13) 101.

2.2 The Moon and other celestial objects

There are two regimes governing the use of the Moon and other celestial objects. The first regime comprises the 1967 Outer Space Treaty and the 1979 Moon Treaty. Article I of the 1967 Outer Space Treaty declares 'the Moon and other celestial bodies . . . the province of all mankind', while Article II provides that 'the Moon and other celestial bodies [are] not subject to national appropriation, by claim of sovereignty, by means of occupation, or by any other means'. Article 11(1) of the 1979 Moon Treaty declares that '[t]he moon and its natural resources are the common heritage of mankind', while Article 11(3) provides in part that '[n]either the surface nor the subsurface of the moon, nor any part thereof or natural resources in place, shall become the property of any State, international intergovernmental or non-governmental organization, national organization or non-governmental entity or of any natural person'. Additionally, Article 11(5) records in part that 'States Parties to this Agreement hereby undertake to establish an international regime, including appropriate procedures, to govern the exploitation of the natural resources of the moon as such exploitation is about to become feasible'. To date, the articulation of 'an international regime' as envisaged by Article 11(5) of the 1979 Moon Treaty has not materialized. The second regime comprises the Artemis Accords, which lays down 'principles for cooperation in the civil exploration and use of the Moon, Mars, comets, and asteroids for peaceful purposes'. The Artemis Accords is a thirteen-provision aspirational manual on 'best practices' in space exploration for NASA and its partner states.[38] For example, section 9(1) provides that '[t]he Signatories *intend* to preserve outer space heritage, which they consider to comprise historically significant human or robotic landing sites, artifacts, spacecraft, and other evidence of activity on celestial bodies in accordance with mutually developed standards and practices' (emphasis added). Drafted in permissive language, unlike the Outer Space and Moon treaties, the Artemis Accords cannot be violated even if Signatory action does not reflect or live up to Signatory intent.

The Outer Space and Moon treaties, on the one hand, and the Artemis Accords, on the other, represent distinct rather than complementary regimes for the following reasons. First, the US has explicitly rejected the 1979 Moon Treaty, which depicts the Moon and other celestial objects as 'the common heritage of mankind', as an 'effective or necessary instrument to guide nation states regarding the promotion of commercial participation in the long term

[38] Artemis Accords s 1.

exploration, scientific discovery, and use of the Moon, Mars, or other celestial bodies'.[39] To this end, the Artemis Accords expressly affirms the 1967 Outer Space Treaty, the 1968 Rescue Agreement, the 1972 Liability Convention, and the 1975 Registration Convention, but not the 1979 Moon Treaty.[40] Second, affirmation of the Outer Space Treaty in the Artemis Accords seems perfunctory. Section 10(2) of the Artemis Accords clarifies that 'the extraction of space resources does not inherently constitute national appropriation under Article II of the Outer Space Treaty', when Article II expressly forbids national appropriation through 'use . . . or by any other means', which surely includes the extraction of space resources. It is not possible to reconcile section 10(2), which denies that the extraction of space resources amounts to national appropriation, and Article II, which regards such activity as national appropriation, by sheer assertion of compatibility.[41] Third and finally, the Outer Space and Moon treaties advance the notion of the Moon and other celestial objects as common property to be used for the benefit of all, while the Artemis Accords paves the way for the *commercial* use of the Moon and other celestial objects for the benefit of *some*. Despite scattered references to 'humankind' in the Preamble and in the provisions, the Artemis Accords was concluded shortly after the US announced that 'commercial entities' should no longer be discouraged by uncertainties surrounding their ability to engage in 'commercial exploration' of outer space resources.[42] The Artemis Accords thus signifies approval for commercial entities like SpaceX (US), Boeing (US), Blue Origin (US), and Virgin Galactic (UK) to explore and extract outer space resources for profit,[43] something which the Outer Space and Moon treaties do not contemplate, let alone endorse.

Joining the dual-regime set-up is a private initiative by the Hague Institute for Global Justice, which presented the Building Blocks for the Development of an International Framework on Space Resource Activities (Hague Building Blocks) in 2019.[44] Advocating the 'principle of adaptive governance' for outer

[39] Executive Order 13914 (n 8).

[40] Artemis Accords Preamble.

[41] According to Michael Byers and Aaron Boley, *Who Owns Outer Space—International Law, Astrophysics, and the Sustainable Development of Space* (CUP 2023) 159, '[t]he Trump Administration clearly wanted the Artemis Accords to provide strong support for the US position that the OST does not preclude property rights over extracted resources, and that in the absence of international rules on the conduct of Space mining, these activities may be regulated solely through national laws'.

[42] Executive Order 13914 (n 8) was issued on 6 April 2020, and the Artemis Accords was signed barely six months later, on 13 October 2020.

[43] Matthew Weinzierl and Mehak Sarang, 'The Commercial Space Age is Here' *Harvard Business Review* (12 February 2021).

[44] (adopted 12 November 2019) <www.universiteitleiden.nl/en/law/institute-of-public-law/institute-of-air-space-law/the-hague-space-resources-governance-working-group> accessed 30 April 2024.

space resources like the Moon and other celestial objects, the Hague Building Blocks arguably bridge the divide between the Outer Space and Moon treaties and the Artemis Accords. Supplying a rudimentary foundation of 20 provisions for an international framework for 'space resource activities that takes into account all interests and benefits of all countries and humankind', the Hague Building Blocks reiterate the 'principle of non-appropriation under Article II [of the Outer Space Treaty]',[45] and give effect to the principle by subjecting the lawfulness of resource extraction and acquisition to future 'domestic legislation, bilateral agreements and/or multilateral agreements'.[46] In juxtaposing the non-appropriation of outer space resources such as the Moon and other celestial objects, against the growing interest among states, state agencies, and private entities in their extraction and use, the Hague Building Blocks seek to regulate 'the commercialization of space resources'.[47] Notably, an earlier version of the Hague Building Blocks envisaged the acquisition of 'internationally recognized property rights' in the Moon and other celestial objects, although the final version only contains references to 'resource rights'. The drafters were persuaded that the term 'resource rights' gave states greater flexibility in defining the 'legal content' of rights over outer space resources.[48] The preference for one label over another does not impede the viewing and regulation of the Moon and other celestial objects as common property because 'property' is not a self-evident term; it demands definition through the methodical identification of 'property' attributes. Like Antarctica, the Moon and other celestial objects are common property belonging to the genus of new property because not only is their ownership imputable to all, they are the source of raw materials that respond to the demands of a scientific market for lunar and interplanetary research and an entertainment market for television series and films on life beyond Earth.[49] Additionally, they are easily separable by great distance from their imputed state owners, and they confer benefits on their imputed state owners and their nationals in the form of security and educational gains from outer space surveillance and research.[50]

[45] Hague Building Blocks art 8.3.
[46] Hague Building Blocks art 8.1.
[47] Olavo de O Bittencourt Neto and others (eds), *Building Blocks for the Development of an International Framework for the Governance of Space Resource Activities—A Commentary* (Eleven 2020) 50.
[48] ibid 53.
[49] One memorable offering is *The Silent Sea*, a Korean series about a crew of astronauts retrieving dangerous samples from a research facility on the Moon, and which premiered on Netflix on 24 December 2021. Another is *Passengers*, a Hollywood film about people travelling on a massive spacecraft to a new planet that they will call home, and which was released in theatres on 21 December 2016.
[50] Chapter 1, Sections 4.1–4.4.

As the Hague Building Blocks, as well as the Outer Space and Moon treaties, are placeholders for a more thorough, communal international regulatory regime, and as the Artemis Accords are purely aspirational,[51] the use of the Moon and other celestial objects is, at this point in time, nominally regulated at best.[52] And the greatest beneficiaries of the status quo are the states, state agencies, and commercial entities with the technological and financial capacity for space-faring expeditions that may culminate with space resource extraction and utilization. The projected rewards that accompany this competitive advantage are staggering. NASA has set its sights on mining an asteroid—Psyche—that is believed to contain vast reserves of precious metals, worth an estimated USD 10,000 quadrillion, in 2026.[53] Other asteroids believed to contain iron, nickel, and cobalt exceeding Earth's reserves have also been discovered,[54] with the promise of trillions of dollars in profit for pioneer space miners.[55] There is no mention of NASA or the US altruistically harnessing the tiniest fraction of these anticipated rewards 'for the benefit of all humankind'.[56] The lure of great riches for first movers explains why the speculative (no asteroid has been mined to date) and very costly nature of space mining has not deterred space mining startups, which are mostly located in the US,[57] or repeated attempts to launch into space.[58] Moreover, in the ongoing race for space

[51] Byers and Boley (n 41) 157–61.

[52] ibid 171–73. It is therefore surprising that dominant literature tends to deem a clearly deficient international law on lunar and celestial object regulation adequate, see Sprankling (n 8) 177–89; also Matt Craven, '"Other Spaces": Constructing the Legal Architecture of a Cold War Commons and the Scientific-Technical Imaginary of Outer Space' (2019) 30(2) European Journal of International Law 547, 548.

[53] Jamie Carter, 'NASA Heads for "Psyche", a Mysterious Metallic Asteroid that Could be the Heart of a Dead Planet' *Forbes* (12 June 2019).

[54] Juan A Sanchez and others, 'Physical Characterization of Metal-Rich Neat-Earth Asteroids 6178 (1987 DA) and 2016 ED85' (2021) 2(5) The Planetary Science Journal 205.

[55] Andrew Wong, 'Space Mining Could Become a Real Thing—and It Could be Worth Trillions' *CNBC* (15 May 2018).

[56] Artemis Accords Preamble: 'Noting *the benefit for all humankind* to be gained from cooperating in the peaceful use of outer space' (emphasis added). Instead, NASA, a US agency, has been awarding contracts to US companies to conduct lunar activities according to its press releases, see NASA, 'NASA Awards SpaceX Second Contract Option for Artemis Moon Landing' (16 November 2022) <www.nasa.gov/humans-in-space/nasa-awards-spacex-second-contract-option-for-artemis-moon-landing> accessed 30 April 2024; NASA, 'NASA Selects Blue Origin as Second Artemis Lunar Lander Provider' (19 May 2023) <www.nasa.gov/humans-in-space/nasa-awards-spacex-second-contract-option-for-artemis-moon-landing/> accessed 28 June 2024; for contracts awarded to other US companies see NASA, 'Latest Contract Releases' <www.nasa.gov/office/procurement/latest-contract-releases> accessed 30 April 2024. The gesture is reciprocated as these US private contractors lend a financial boost to NASA activities, see Robert Hart, 'Meet the Billionaires Helping NASA Return to the Moon' *Forbes* (14 February 2024).

[57] Denise Chow, 'High Risk, High Reward: Startups Are Still Eager to Mine Space Rocks' *NBC News* (9 April 2023).

[58] Kantaro Komiya and Joey Roulette, 'Japan's ispace Says Moon Lander Unexpectedly Accelerated and Likely Crashed' *Reuters* (26 April 2023): 'Japan's top government spokesperson Hirokazu Matsuno

supremacy,[59] states jealously guard space technology from each other for real or imagined fear of espionage.[60] Immense potential profit and prestige drive the capitalist capture of outer space regulation, rendering it extremely unlikely that space-faring states and private entities will share, or commit to sharing, their technology or exploits with non-space-faring states and entities for the common good. And the absence of any technology trickle-down will only widen the gap between the haves and the have-nots in the race to space because states lacking the means to develop a space industry also lack the means to investigate and challenge the impact and equity of space resource distribution in the present age of unchecked space activities conducted by their wealthier, savvier counterparts. Therefore, the prospect of an enhanced treaty regime to regulate the Moon and other celestial objects communally as forecasted in the 1979 Moon Treaty and in the Hague Building Blocks is slim.[61] Such a regime is unlikely to appeal to space-faring states who have, by virtue of their competitive advantage and the lack of informed objectors, confidently laid claim for decades to common property as though it were private property.[62]

2.3 The Area

The Area refers to 'the seabed and ocean floor and subsoil thereof, beyond the limits of national jurisdiction'.[63] It lies beneath the High Seas, a vast expanse of ocean that is 'not included in the exclusive economic zone, in the territorial sea or in the internal waters of a State, or in the archipelagic waters of

said while it was sad that the mission did not succeed, the country wants ispace to "keep trying" as its efforts were significant to the development of a domestic space industry.'

[59] Mary W Roeloffs, 'Modern Space Race: Japan Pledges $6.6 Billion for Developing Space Sector as U.S. and China Plan Historic Missions' *Forbes* (21 November 2023).

[60] Luke Harding, 'The Space Race is Back on – but Who Will Win?' *The Guardian* (16 July 2021); also Saadia M Pekkanen, 'Governing the New Space Race' (2019) 113 American Journal of International Law Unbound 92, 95.

[61] One commentator predicts that '"Space Law 3.0" will be a private law system of contracts between operators', Brian L Israel, 'Space Resources in the Evolutionary Course of Space Lawmaking' (2019) 113 American Journal of International Law Unbound 114, 118.

[62] Countries other than the US have also been awarding contracts to nationals for lunar exploration and construction, behaving as though the Moon were their own backyard, see Jeff Foust, 'European Space Agency (ESA) Awards Contracts for Moon and Mars Exploration' *SpaceNews* (15 October 2020). Other countries, notably China, have announced their plans for lunar missions and installations, behaving, again, as though the Moon were their own backyard, see 'China Plans More Moon Missions After Finding New Lunar Mineral' *Bloomberg News* (10 September 2022). All this unchecked backyard jostling has, unsurprisingly, led to accusations and denials of lunar grab, see 'China Rejects NASA Accusation It Will Take Over the Moon' *Reuters* (4 July 2022).

[63] UNCLOS art 1(1).

an archipelagic State'.[64] The Area bears the core attributes of new property, and, by virtue of the fact that it is 'beyond the limits of national jurisdiction' like the High Seas, is already accepted as common property in the existing literature.[65] Like the Antarctic and the Moon and other celestial objects, ownership of the Area is imputable to all states. Additionally, the Area is highly responsive to a consumer market eyeing its supposed abundance of mineral deposits such as polymetallic nodules, and to a scientific market for marine biological diversity research. The Area is also separable from its imputed state owners by being located far beyond the physical borders of each state's national jurisdiction, and it confers a benefit on its imputed state owners and their nationals in the form of profit from trade in mined marine resources and in the form of knowledge advancement concerning the functioning, sustenance, and conservation of marine life and marine ecosystems.[66] Use of the Area is governed by UNCLOS Part XI containing 59 provisions, the 1994 UNCLOS Agreement containing ten provisions, and an Annex to implement UNCLOS Part XI, and, once it enters into force, the Agreement on the Conservation and Sustainable Use of Marine Biological Diversity of Areas Beyond National Jurisdiction (BBNJ Agreement) containing 60 provisions.[67] Possibly supplementing this trio of international instruments in the future is a set of regulations on the 'exploitation of mineral resources in the Area' (future Area Mining Code). The latest (2019) version of the future Area Mining Code contains 107 provisions, ten annexures, four appendices, and a Schedule on the Code's terms and scope.[68]

Compared to the slight regulation of the Antarctic and the Moon and other celestial objects, the Area appears, at first glance, to be substantially regulated. There are 169 parties to UNCLOS, 151 parties to the 1994 UNCLOS Agreement, and the conclusion of the BBNJ Agreement has been hailed as a historic feat.[69] Yet, despite the comparably strong support from states for both UNCLOS and the 1994 UNCLOS Agreement, states are *not* on the same page with regard to the regulation of the Area. In an illuminating study, Ranganathan narrates the genesis of UNCLOS and of the 1994 UNCLOS

64 UNCLOS art 86.

65 Schachter (n 1) 71; Nico Schrijver, 'Managing the Global Commons: Common Good or Common Sink?' (2016) 37(7) Third World Quarterly 1252, 1254.

66 Chapter 1, Sections 4.1–4.4.

67 The BBNJ Agreement, which was adopted on 19 June 2023, represents the culmination of discussions and negotiations that began in 2004, <https://treaties.un.org/doc/Treaties/2023/06/20230620%2004-28%20PM/Ch_XXI_10.pdf> accessed 30 April 2024.

68 ISA, 'Draft Regulations on Exploitation of Mineral Resources in the Area' <www.isa.org.jm/wp-content/uploads/2022/06/isba_25_c_wp1-e_0.pdf> accessed 30 April 2024.

69 Karen McVeigh, 'High Seas Treaty: Historic Deal to Protect International Waters Finally Reached at UN' *The Guardian* (5 March 2023).

Agreement, revealing that the proposal to label the Area as the 'common heritage of mankind', which later became Article 136 in Part XI of UNCLOS, was opportunistic and ultimately divisive.[70] Arvid Pardo, the Maltese diplomat fondly remembered as the 'father of the Law of the Sea Conference',[71] was tasked by his government to come up with a topic to table before the United Nations General Assembly. Pardo found his topic at a cocktail reception, via a member of the US delegation, who cautioned that the matter of seabed mining, of which Pardo knew little, should not be dismissed out of hand.[72] Pardo later admitted that pitching seabed riches as common property to trigger global interest had much more to do with 'putting Malta on the map',[73] and less to do with mapping the equitable distribution of the benefits of seabed mining among states.[74] The promise, though not necessarily concrete proof, of seabed riches and their distribution ended up playing on developing states' fear of resource grab by developed states, and turned UNCLOS Part XI into a metaphorical shield wielded by the developing states to block developed states' discomfort with proclaiming the Area common property.[75] Any victory scored by the presence of Part XI in UNCLOS was arguably Pyrrhic because most developed states with the capacity for seabed mining rejected Part XI and refused to accede to the entire treaty.[76] The European Union recorded major reservations to Part XI, while the US did not even sign the UNCLOS.[77] With the abandonment of Part XI as the conceptual regulatory framework for the Area by the developed states, whose financial and other resources would greatly facilitate any communal regulation of common property, an alternative arrangement had to be sought. And the alternative to UNCLOS Part XI was the 1994 UNCLOS Agreement.

Notably, the Preamble to the 1994 UNCLOS Agreement reaffirms that the Area belongs to 'the common heritage of mankind'. This, along with the first sentence of Article 2(1) which stipulates that '[t]he provisions of this Agreement and Part XI [of UNCLOS] shall be interpreted and applied together as a single instrument', suggests that the 1994 UNCLOS Agreement is a natural extension

[70] Ranganathan (n 8) 704–14.
[71] UN Press Release SEA/1619 (16 July 1999).
[72] Arvid Pardo, 'The Origins of the 1967 Malta Initiative' (1993) 9 International Insights 65, 66.
[73] ibid 65.
[74] ibid 69.
[75] Ranganathan (n 8) 711–14.
[76] Vogler (n 9) 70. This also meant that whatever Pardo's initial aspirations, UNCLOS did not 'radically . . . change the traditional law of the sea which, we believe, reflected the interests of only a few members of the international community', see 'The Origins of the 1967 Malta Initiative' (n 72) 69.
[77] United Nations Treaty Collection, 'Declarations and Reservations' <https://treaties.un.org/pages/ViewDetailsIII.aspx?src=TREATY&mtdsg_no=XXI-6&chapter=21&Temp=mtdsg3&clang=_en> accessed 30 April 2024.

of UNCLOS Part XI. However, the willingness of Part XI objectors like the EU and the US to ratify the 1994 UNCLOS Agreement more strongly suggests that the latter instrument embodies an entirely different ideology and set of provisions from the former instrument.[78] Moreover, the second sentence of Article 2(1) qualifies the first by stipulating that '[i]n the event of any inconsistency between this Agreement and Part XI, the provisions of this Agreement shall prevail'. Therefore, as far as the Area is concerned, the ruling instrument is the 1994 UNCLOS Agreement, and not UNCLOS Part XI. The chief contribution of the 1994 UNCLOS Agreement is delineating the mandate and the role of the ISA in regulating activities in the Area.[79] In particular, the 36-member ISA Council is responsible for reviewing, approving, and overseeing contract applications for seabed mining activities in the Area. Despite the 1994 UNCLOS Agreement containing an entire section on decision-making by the ISA Council,[80] there is little transparency on how and why certain contract applications are approved and whether these applications actually comply with appropriate environmental and marine safety standards. And despite the admirably diverse composition of the ISA Council,[81] it is questionable whether Nauru and the Netherlands are truly on par as fellow ISA Council members during ISA Council decision-making moments.

To date, the ISA has approved twenty-nine exploration contracts in the Area, of which only four are sponsored by developing states. And of the four sponsors, Nauru, Tonga, and Kiribati fronted contracts that will be executed by The Metals Company, a Canadian entity.[82] Separately, the contract sponsored by the Cook Islands will be executed by the Cook Islands Investment Corporation (a state-owned enterprise) in a joint venture with Global Sea Mineral Resources, a Belgian entity.[83] To the extent that the ISA Council, in practice, confers upon developed states and their entities an oligopoly over resource mining in the Area, while developing states and their entities are relegated to the sidelines as

[78] Martti Koskenniemi and Marja Lehto, 'The Privilege of Universality—International Law, Economic Ideology and Seabed Resources' (1996) 65 Nordic Journal of International Law 533, 552 where the authors observed that 'the need [of the 1994 UNCLOS Agreement] to attain universal application now required privileging the north'; see also Joanna Dingwall, *International Law and Corporate Actors in Deep Seabed Mining* (OUP 2021) 54–55.

[79] The ISA was established in UNCLOS arts 156–58. The Annex in 1994 UNCLOS Agreement articulates the workflow of the ISA.

[80] See Annex in 1994 UNCLOS Agreement, Section 3.

[81] ISA, 'Composition of the Council' <www.isa.org.jm/organs/the-council/> accessed 30 April 2024. The composition is fairly evenly split between developed and developing states, with representatives from all geographic regions.

[82] Louisa Casson and others, 'Deep Trouble—The Murky World of the Deep Sea Mining Industry' <www.greenpeace.org/static/planet4-international-stateless/c86ff110-pto-deep-trouble-report-final-1.pdf> accessed 30 April 2024, 9–13.

[83] ibid 15–17.

shell sponsors and contracting parties, the Area is currently regulated as though it were the 'common heritage of *select* mankind'.[84] And the cracks brought on by selectivism are starting to show, casting aspersions on the ISA's legitimacy as the regulatory authority for the Area. The ISA Secretary-General, British lawyer Michael Lodge, has recently come under fire for allegedly pressuring the ISA Council to let The Metals Company start its mining activities in the Area in 2024.[85] This allegation comes in the wake of revelations that The Metals Company had previously received confidential information from ISA personnel on valuable seabed tracts in the Area, giving the company a significant edge in its contract applications.[86] A number of ISA Council members, such as Germany, France, Spain, Chile, New Zealand, and several Pacific nations, are against the commencement of any mining activity in the Area in the absence of a mining code.[87] In Chile's view, it will take another fifteen years to finalize a future Area Mining Code, and there is no way for The Metals Company, or any other company, to mine in the Area in the meantime.[88] It remains unclear whether and when a fractured ISA Council can and will resolve this tug-of-war between private and communal interest in the Area as common property.

Current ISA regulation (or mis-regulation some might venture) of the Area appears beholden to the free market forces of demand and supply. The near exclusive grant of seabed mining contracts to the corporate nationals of developed states, the endorsement of some of the poorest developing states sponsoring mining applications crafted by and for the benefit of corporate nationals of developed states, and the preferential treatment accorded to a certain corporate national of a certain developed state all signal the capitalist capture of the Area. Furthermore, the ISA Council, which is the main decision-making body of the ISA,[89] is likelier to be preoccupied with the nuts and bolts of a future Area Mining Code, and its publication, so that mining activities in the Area can commence. While there are meetings on capacity building for

[84] (emphasis added).

[85] Eric Lipton, 'Leader of International Seabed Mining Agency Admonished by Diplomats' (n 6).

[86] Eric Lipton, 'Secret Data, Tiny Islands and a Quest for Treasures on the Ocean Floor' (n 6).

[87] Karen McVeigh, 'Row Erupts Over Deep-Sea Mining as World Races to Finalise Vital Regulations' *The Guardian* (21 March 2023).

[88] Maurizio Guerrero, 'Opposition Grows Among Countries as Seabed-Mining Efforts Push Ahead' *PassBlue* (1 January 2023).

[89] The ISA Assembly, comprising 167 member states plus the EU, is regarded as the 'supreme/political organ' and final approving authority of the ISA. However, s 3(4) of the 1994 UNCLOS Agreement does not allow the Assembly to overrule a decision of the Council, giving the latter de facto final decision-making power: 'Decisions of the Assembly on any matter for which the Council also has competence or on any administrative, budgetary or financial matter shall be based on the recommendations of the Council. If the Assembly does not accept the recommendation of the Council on any matter, it shall return the matter to the Council for further consideration. The Council shall reconsider the matter in the light of the views expressed by the Assembly.'

developing countries organized under the auspices of the ISA,[90] the ISA Council has never, in its twenty-nine years of existence and in fulfilment of its mandate, taken the concrete step of devising '[r]ules and regulations and procedures on the equitable sharing of financial and other economic benefits from activities in the Area'.[91] The priorities of the ISA Council are the clearest manifestation of what the supporters of UNCLOS Part XI compromised on when they signed the 1994 UNCLOS Agreement. Common management of common property for the common benefit under Part XI had given way to capitalist management of common property for the contractors' benefit under the 1994 UNCLOS Agreement.[92] In light of the above, the prediction that 'the ISA's pre-eminent role within the Convention's deep seabed regime, of which its far-reaching regulatory and supervisory powers are a prominent feature, provides the means by which the regime can secure its common heritage goals, as a matter of process',[93] seems overly optimistic. Even if we assume that the 1994 UNCLOS Agreement reflects no particular ideology,[94] the 'process' within has consistently begotten outcomes which authorize the use of common property for the benefit of a select few, leaving 'common heritage goals' by the wayside. It remains to be seen if layering the BBNJ Agreement over the 1994 UNCLOS Agreement, the former of which requires states parties to submit proposals on 'area-based management tools' in the Area to a Scientific and Technical Body for review and approval,[95] will eventually produce more equitable outcomes in state-sponsored applications for deep seabed mining. Having witnessed how the various regulatory regimes for common property have succumbed to capitalist capture, the discussion now takes a closer look at whether these regimes nonetheless sustainably regulate specific common resources found in open waters and in outer space.

3. When treaties are not enough

Common property is currently regulated by treaty-based or treaty-like regimes. The Antarctic has its ATS quartet of treaties, the High Seas and the

[90] ISA, 'ISA Secretariat Holds the First 2023 Meeting of National Focus Points for Capacity Development' (19 May 2023) <www.isa.org.jm/news/isa-secretariat-holds-the-first-2023-meeting-of-national-focal-points-for-capacity-development/> accessed 30 April 2024.
[91] 1994 UNCLOS Agreement s 9(7)(f).
[92] Koskenniemi and Lehto (n 78) 553, 549.
[93] Dingwall (n 78) 145.
[94] cf Koskenniemi and Lehto (n 78) 542–43.
[95] BBNJ Agreement arts 17, 17 bis, and 18.

Area have UNCLOS and the 1994 UNCLOS Agreement,[96] while the Moon and other outer space resources have the Outer Space and Moon treaties, as well as the 2020 Artemis Accords. With the exception of the NASA-led Artemis Accords, the other treaties impose binding obligations on ratifying states. As most, if not all, states enter into treaties with the aim of maximizing commitments from other states while limiting their own exposure to liability for non-compliance, treaties usually represent the lowest common denominator of conflicting interests, drawn up in the least provocative language. As such, treaties may supply broad regulatory strokes, but are unlikely to prescribe detailed regulatory directions. These directions, if they exist, tend to be non-binding and may be found in resolutions adopted at periodic meetings of treaty member states. I argue that the current treaty-based or treaty-like regimes for regulating resources located in or on common property fall short because the main extractors of common resources are private corporate actors, not states. Not only do they fail to urge states to effectively coordinate the use of existing and emerging common resources, or to control the activities of their corporate nationals (Section 3.1), they also fail to effectively integrate sustainability concerns, pitting resource exploitation against resource conservation in an eternal zero-sum game (Section 3.2).

3.1 Theatres of imminent resource wars

The current regulatory regimes for common resources found in the oceans and in outer space have turned common property into theatres of imminent resource wars. Relying on current harvesting and planned utilization practices of specific examples of common resources in the Antarctic, the High Seas, and in outer space, this section showcases regime failure, or at the very least regime frailty at sea (Section 3.1.1), as well as in outer space (Section 3.1.2).

3.1.1 At sea

Regime failure or frailty when it comes to the harvesting of icebergs in the Antarctic, and the depletion of stocks of krill in Antarctic waters and fish in the High Seas, can be seen in the corporate scramble to cash in on common resources.

[96] The 1994 UNCLOS Agreement is likely to be supplemented by the BBNJ Agreement once it enters into force and may be supplemented by an Area Mining Code.

Icebergs. Most of the world's freshwater supply is contained in Antarctic ice. And given how fresh water is a finite resource, it was always a matter of time before the more forward-looking and enterprising amongst us explored the feasibility of harvesting Antarctic icebergs to secure fresh water supply, be it for consumption or for other commercial uses. The states parties to the ATS appear indifferent towards the mass harvesting of Antarctic icebergs. There is no reference whatsoever to iceberg harvesting in any of the founding instruments. Article IX(1)(f) of the 1959 Antarctic Treaty, which obliges states parties to consult periodically on the 'preservation and conservation of living resources', is inapplicable because use is the opposite of 'preservation and conservation', while icebergs are not 'living resources'. Even the 1991 Environmental Protection Protocol is uninstructive because while Article 7 expressly prohibits '[a]ny activity relating to mineral resources, other than scientific research', icebergs are not minerals, which means any activity relating to them is permitted. The omission of iceberg harvesting from the 1991 Environmental Protection Protocol is puzzling because states parties recognized back in 1989 that 'uncontrolled activities relating to the exploitation of Antarctic icebergs could also have an adverse effect on the unique Antarctic environment and its dependent and associated ecosystems'. And so, they expressed 'the desirability that commercial exploitation of Antarctic ice *not occur*, in any case, prior to examination by the Contracting Parties to the Antarctic Treaty of the issues posed by such activity'.[97] Absent concrete steps to control 'activities relating to the exploitation of Antarctic icebergs', the path to regime failure is clear. With small-scale commercial harvesting of icebergs in domestic waters on the rise, large-scale commercial operations involving Antarctic icebergs are likely to follow.

Iceberg harvesting is dangerous. RMS *Titanic* sank after colliding with an iceberg in the Atlantic Ocean. Nonetheless, in the wild waters of iceberg harvesting where it is a case of 'finders keepers', the pull of profiting from a seemingly endless supply of a free resource has spawned generations of 'iceberg cowboys'.[98] Harvesting mostly off the coasts of Newfoundland in Canada, and Illulisat in Greenland, iceberg cowboys, who can sell millions of litres of iceberg water per year at a premium price, hunt and capture an iceberg as though it were a wild animal. First, they slowly approach a smaller iceberg that

[97] Secretariat of the Antarctic Treaty, 'Final Report of the Fifteenth Antarctic Treaty Consultative Meeting' (9–20 October 1989, Paris, France) Recommendation XV-21 (Use of Antarctic Ice) <https://documents.ats.aq/ATCM15/fr/ATCM15_fr001_e.pdf> accessed 30 April 2024, emphasis added.

[98] Matthew Birkhold, 'The Iceberg Cowboys Who Wrangle the Purest Water on Earth' *Geoscience* (27 January 2023).

has calved off a larger glacier in a fishing boat. Then, they use long rods with metal hooks to prod the iceberg and check that it doesn't have underwater projections before dragging it towards the boat. Once the iceberg is close enough, the cowboys fling a net over it to wrap it tight, winch it onboard the vessel by lowering a crane with a hook, and drop it onto the deck, where it is rinsed and hacked into smaller chunks. All of this takes place without any apparent regulatory oversight. While the harvesting of icebergs in Canadian and Greenlandic waters requires a licence from the provincial or the main government, there is no cap placed on the number of licences awarded or on the quantity of ice harvested. For a while, iceberg cowboys were joined by iceberg connoisseurs, who marketed iceberg water as a responsible luxury. One of these connoisseurs, former Wall Street analyst Jamal Qureshi who founded the now defunct Svalbarði, sold iceberg water from Svalbard, Norway to wealthy customers in Beijing, Dubai, and Los Angeles for a princely USD 166 a bottle. Svalbarði was in business after a simple handshake agreement in 2015 between Qureshi and the governor of Svalbard since '[t]here were no regulations before [he] showed up'.[99] Svalbarði soon became the talk of the town, and it is unclear what put Svalbarði out of business recently. It could have been the excessive price tag for its iceberg water, or its excessive (and scientifically dubious) claim that one must 'Taste the Arctic to Save the Arctic' since drinking 'ultra-premium water from Svalbard [is] helping fight climate change'.[100] The continued absence of any domestic or international regulations to prevent the over-harvesting of icebergs is concerning. Iceberg cowboys and connoisseurs and the current scale of their operations may not pose an immediate threat to the decimating of Antarctic icebergs, but a German start-up, Polewater, has announced an ambitious proposal to tow Antarctic icebergs to places like South Africa to combat water scarcity.[101] As more water supply entrepreneurs set their sights on the Antarctic and harmful activities proliferate, regime failure will become even more pronounced. And as states wait and watch the reduction of white surfaces on Antarctic icebergs that reflect the sun's rays they are complicit in the raising of global temperatures and in the fostering of climate change.

Krill and fish. Krill are shrimp-like crustaceans, about the size of a paper clip, which occupy the bottommost rung of the Antarctic food chain. It is the most abundant species on Earth, which probably explains why a CCAMLR executive said that krill is 'one of the few resources that is still underexploited in

[99] Matthew Birkold, '$166 Water Could Dictate International Iceberg Law' *The Atlantic* (31 October 2019).
[100] Svalbarði <https://svalbardi.com> accessed 30 April 2024.
[101] Polewater, 'Solution' <www.polewater.com/en/solution/> accessed 30 April 2024.

a very big way in the global oceans'.[102] Krill are a vital food source for Antarctic wildlife such as whales, penguins, and seals, play an integral part in the carbon cycle by removing up to 12 billion tonnes of carbon from the Earth's atmosphere, and are a supposedly superior source of omega-3 fatty acids to fish oil according to the billion-dollar health supplements industry. The CCAMLR estimates that the annual catch of krill in Antarctic waters is 'around 0.3% of the unexploited biomass of krill' with a total allowable catch of 'about 5.6 tonnes annually'.[103] Given that there are 400 million tonnes of krill residing in Antarctic waters, the annual harvest appears negligible. Moreover, the catch limit of 620,000 tonnes introduced by the CCAMLR Commission in 2010 to prevent the concentration of krill fishing across four areas has not yet, according to catch reports submitted by krill vessels, been breached. This may be why the CCAMLR Commission, in its latest Schedule of Conservation Measures adopted in late 2022, merely imposes a notification-of-intent-to-fish requirement on krill fisheries,[104] and not individual fishing quotas. Today, the confidence that krill is not susceptible to overfishing, that current catch limits promise sustainable use of a common resource, and that voluntary reporting of catch volumes by krill vessels is reliable is being called into question. Conservationists highlight that krill fishing tends to be concentrated in select pockets of Antarctic waters, resulting in an anomalous situation where a fraction of an area can be over-fished, without that area's prescribed catch limit being breached. Decreasing krill populations have a knock-on effect on species that feed on krill, and on other species higher up in the food chain, which can badly affect the entire Antarctic ecosystem.[105] Additionally, current catch limits which are area-based and more than a decade old do not appear to account for the fact that krill are a migratory species that do not stay within set boundaries, and whose numbers fluctuate over time. Absent any updated and dynamic assessment of krill biomass, and a more thorough examination of the impact of krill fishing on the Antarctic ecosystem, the sustainability of current krill fishing practices is not established.[106] Finally, in 2020, more than half the krill harvested from Antarctic waters were caught by Aker Biomarine, a biotech

[102] Richa Syal, 'Licence to Krill: The Destructive Demand for a "Better" Fish Oil' *The Guardian* (7 September 2021).

[103] CCAMLR, 'Krill Fisheries and Sustainability' <www.ccamlr.org/en/fisheries/krill-fisheries-and-sustainability> accessed 30 April 2024.

[104] CCAMLR, 'Schedule of Conservation Measures', Conservation Measure 21-03 (1029), Annex 21-03/A and Annex 21-03/B, 95–101 <www.ccamlr.org/en/system/files/e-schedule2022-23.pdf> accessed 30 April 2024.

[105] Syal, 'Licence to Krill: The Destructive Demand for a "Better" Fish Oil' (n 102).

[106] Richa Syal, 'Krilling for Oil' (6 September 2021) <www.oceansinc.earth/krilling-for-oil> accessed 30 April 2024.

company backed by Norwegian billionaire Kjell Inge Røkke. Røkke is known for his success in the fisheries industry, as well as his brief imprisonment for the corrupt procurement of a boat licence.[107] Aker Biomarine calls itself 'the world's leading supplier of krill, the natural powerful and health-promoting source of nutrients from the pristine waters of Antarctica'.[108] Aker Biomarine insists that its krill harvesting methods and catch volumes, neither of which are disclosed in its long and latest annual report, are sustainable.[109] What is apparent, though, is that Aker Biomarine is committed to maximizing its krill catch volumes, and in turn, its profit and status as 'the world's leading supplier of krill'. There are few other reasons why Aker Biomarine would commission the construction of a specialized krill fishing vessel whose length (130 metres) exceeds that of a soccer field (100 metres).[110]

Fish stocks in the High Seas are a common resource accessible by all.[111] Fishing in the High Seas is regulated by four pithy provisions in UNCLOS, all of which defer the direction and the details on the 'conservation and management of living resources' to inter-state cooperation.[112] Back when UNCLOS was signed in 1982, states devoted little attention to regulating fishing in the High Seas due to technological limitations on access and the belief that fish stocks there were insignificant.[113] However, the negotiation and conclusion of the BBNJ Agreement, which establishes the framework for the 'conservation and management of living resources' to preserve marine biological diversity in the Area and in the High Seas, suggests that technological capabilities and beliefs have changed. Relying on informal inter-state cooperation to regulate a burgeoning and profitable High Seas fishing industry is not optimal. And available data strongly suggests that the currently barely regulated High Seas fishing industry is fraught with opaque and unsustainable corporate practices and activities.[114] According to a 2020 study, unreported corporate fishing activities in

[107] 'Rokke to be Released from Jail' *IntraFish* (25 September 2007).

[108] Aker Biomarine <www.akerbiomarine.com> accessed 30 April 2024.

[109] Aker Biomarine, 'Annual Report 2020', <www.akerbiomarine.com/hubfs/Aker%20Biomarine%20Annual%20Report%202020.pdf> accessed 30 April 2024.

[110] 'Vard to Build New Krill Fishing Vessel for Aker Biomarine' *Ship Technology* (15 February 2017).

[111] UNCLOS art 116 provides in part that '[a]ll States have the right for their nationals to engage in fishing on the high seas . . .'.

[112] UNCLOS arts 117–20.

[113] Rashid U Sumaila and others, 'Winners and Losers in a World Where the High Seas is Closed to Fishing' (2015) 5(8481) Nature 1, 1.

[114] This data is sourced from public databases as well as satellite imaging, the latter allowing real-time tracking of vessel activity in the High Seas, see Global Fishing Watch <https://globalfishingwatch.org/map/?latitude=21.3427880283446&longitude=-21.703099042749272&zoom=0.6977892660286947&start=2023-02-25T00%3A00%3A00.000Z&end=2023-05-25T00%3A00%3A00.000Z&dvIn[0][id]=context-layer-graticules&dvIn[0][cfg][vis]=false&dvIn[1][id]=context-layer-high-seas&dvIn[1][cfg][vis]=true&sidebarOpen=false> accessed 30 April 2024.

and underreported corporate catch species and volumes from the High Seas meant that in 'an assessment of forty-eight different high seas fish stocks . . . three-quarters are considered depleted or overfished'.[115] The top 100 identified corporate fisheries are responsible for nearly 40 per cent of reported fishing activities in the High Seas,[116] while eight of the top ten corporate fisheries are non-public-listed companies headquartered in China (six), the US (one), and Taiwan (one).[117] Non-public-listed companies are under no obligation to publicize or justify their revenues, fishing methods, or catch volumes. And when the largest corporate actors are able to evade public scrutiny in their day-to-day operations, it is no wonder that the High Seas fishing industry is characterized by very low accountability.[118] This accountability deficit also accommodates unsustainable corporate practices that do not live up to corporate messaging. Parlevliet & van der Plas, a renowned Dutch company fishing in the High Seas, has pledged, in baffling language, to 'leave the capital in the sea but our customers can benefit from the interest'.[119] It then proceeded to fish for cod, haddock, saithe, and redfish by trawling in the High Seas pocket of the Norwegian Sea, contributing to a steady decline in fish stocks in that area. Of the various fishing methods in use, trawling is widely regarded as the most destructive to marine life.[120] Trawling involves dragging massive, weighted nets across the sea floor. It enables fishers to catch large quantities of fish at one go, but it is also indiscriminate in its catch, netting non-target species such as turtles and sea corals, and destroying entire marine communities along the way. Far from 'leav[ing] the capital in the sea', Parlevliet & van der Plas appears to be leaving nothing in the sea in order to maximize its profits, epitomizing the corporate scramble to cash in on fish stocks as a common resource.

3.1.2 In outer space

Just like the journey to the Antarctic and to the High Seas, which not every state and corporate actor is able and willing to undertake, physical access is a natural barrier to entry for states and corporate actors when it comes to the extraction and use of outer space resources. For those with the means to overcome that costly barrier, they are or will be rewarded with negligible constraints on

[115] Gabrielle Carmine and others, 'Who is the High Seas Fishing Industry?' (2020) 3 One Earth 730, 730.

[116] ibid 732.

[117] ibid 733. The only two public-listed corporate fisheries in the top ten are headquartered in South Korea.

[118] ibid 736.

[119] Parlevliet & van der Plas, 'Our Mission' <www.pp-group.nl/en-us/home/id/2> accessed 30 April 2024.

[120] Nina Chestney, 'Trawling Could Harm Oceans Like Ploughing Land' *Reuters* (6 September 2012).

their space-faring activities, and the promise of immense profits should their exploits bear fruit. The current nascent corporate scramble for minerals and the increasingly crowded scramble among satellite operators for orbital pathways, largely unchecked by a failed or frail regime, is a precursor to a larger-scale outer space common resource war.

Minerals. While minerals like iron, nickel, iridium, gold, and magnesium have yet to be mined in commercially viable quantities from the Moon and other celestial objects, the flurry of state-sponsored and corporate-led expeditions to space in recent years heralds the looming reality of mineral mining in outer space.[121] An extension of a space expedition is the establishment of a base on the Moon or another celestial object, which the Outer Space and Moon treaties, the Artemis Accords, and the Hague Building Blocks all envisage. The 1967 Outer Space Treaty stipulates reciprocal access to 'stations, installations, equipment and space vehicles on the Moon and other celestial bodies',[122] while the 1979 Moon Treaty permits states parties to 'establish manned and unmanned stations on the moon'.[123] The contemporary term for a base, in possible anticipation of mining or other extractive activities in outer space, is a 'safety zone'. The Artemis Accords depicts a 'safety zone' as an area where 'notification [of activities] and coordination [with any relevant actor] will be implemented to avoid harmful interference',[124] while the Hague Building Blocks defines it as an area around 'an area identified for a space resource activity, as necessary to assure safety and to avoid any harmful interference with that space resource activity'.[125] In the context of mineral mining on celestial bodies, 'safety zones' are essentially areas carved out by sovereign or corporate miners for their exclusive use for an unknown duration. Notably, the Artemis Accords caters for the expansion of 'safety zones' on the basis that '[i]f the nature of an operation changes, the operating Signatory should alter the size and scope of the corresponding safety zone as appropriate'.[126] As the space race gains momentum, one of two scenarios may come to pass. First, the lunar and celestial body surfaces are studded with 'safety zones' erected by different states and companies, each mining for minerals and minding their own business in peaceful co-existence. Second, as more companies enter the space race and room for new 'safety zones' starts to shrink, older corporate miners, who

[121] Byers and Boley (n 41) 130–37.
[122] Art XII.
[123] Art 9(1), see also arts 8(3), 10(3), 11(3), 12, 15(1).
[124] Section 11(7).
[125] Building Block 11.3.
[126] Section 11(7)(c).

are not bound by any treaty obligations, may look to expand their 'safety zones' and shut out the competition. As '[s]afety zones could amount to the *de facto* appropriation of the lunar surface, particularly if established for prolonged periods',[127] and as there are no existing lines drawn on the area limits of 'safety zones', the second scenario where miners clash over the equitable division of celestial surfaces seems more probable.[128] Some commentators prefer to wait and see how a resource war in space mining will play out,[129] while others are already urging corporate space miners to include arbitration clauses in their space mining contracts in the event of disputes over 'property rights'.[130]

Orbital pathways. An orbital pathway is the circular way in which something moves around an object in outer space.[131] Orbital pathways around Earth are a common resource, free for use by all states, but also finite because there is a limit to how far a pathway can be from Earth to remain within the Earth's orbit, and a limit to how many satellites (the main users of orbital pathways) can operate within a given orbital pathway. The use of orbital pathways by satellite operators is authorized by licences granted by the International Telecommunication Union (ITU), a United Nations agency.[132] Licences for specific orbital pathways and their accompanying radio frequencies that allow satellites to collect and transmit information to and from Earth are allocated in the first instance to the ITU's 193 member states. A corporate satellite operator in need of a licence then approaches an ITU member state for assistance, whereby that ITU member state will, if the licence acquisition price is right, notify the ITU that it wishes to assign its allocated orbital pathway and accompanying radio frequency to that corporate satellite operator.[133] Satellites can be put to many uses, including capturing images of Earth to sharpen meteorological forecasts, beaming television signals around the world, and collecting big data ranging from traffic congestion to the tracking of military targets which

[127] Jack Wright Nelson, 'Safety Zones: A Near-Term Legal Issue on the Moon' (2020) 42(2) Journal of Space Law 604, 608.

[128] The construction of a lunar base is a long-term project. China, for example, predicts that it will take close to 30 years to complete its planned lunar base, even if a basic version may be available by 2028, see Xin Ling, 'China's Moon Ambitions Take Shape with Construction Road Map for Research Station', *South China Morning Post* (25 April 2023). It is more than probable that other space-faring nations and companies will act on similar ambitions in the interim, resulting in multiple takers for one lunar surface.

[129] See for instance Sprankling (n 8) 189.

[130] Laura Y Zielinski, 'Disputes over Space Mining on the Horizon?' (18 January 2023) <www.ibanet.org/disputes-over-space-mining-on-the-horizon> accessed 30 April 2024.

[131] NASA, 'What is an Orbit?' <www.nasa.gov/audience/forstudents/k-4/stories/nasa-knows/what-is-orbit-k4.html> accessed 30 April 2024.

[132] ITU, 'About International Telecommunication Union (ITU)' <www.itu.int/en/about/Pages/default.aspx> accessed 30 April 2024.

[133] Sprankling (n 8) 191.

can then be sold to interested parties. The growing appetite for big data in an era of information obsession plus overload, and the lower cost of launching and/or operating a satellite today, have drawn many corporate actors, including those from developing countries, into an increasingly crowded satellite race.[134] Ten years ago, there were around 1,000 satellites orbiting around Earth. Today, there are more than 8,000 satellites and the numbers look set to multiply over the next ten years.[135] At present, the largest satellite constellation in the world belongs to billionaire Elon Musk's SpaceX, with more than 4,000 satellites in orbit.

The ITU does not limit the number of satellites that can orbit in a licensed pathway. But when an orbital pathway holds many satellites from a licensee, it starts to resemble 'an interstate highway in a rush hour in a snowstorm with everyone driving much too fast'.[136] To alleviate the problem of satellite congestion, each of SpaceX's 4,000 plus satellites is equipped with a collision-avoidance system, and a total of 26,037 avoidance manoeuvres were performed by these satellites from 2020 to 2022. Perhaps wishing to put the collision-avoidance system to a true test, SpaceX plans to deploy more than *40,000* satellites in the next decade.[137] Adding to SpaceX's startling numbers are mega-constellations belonging to or planned by other commercial satellite operators such as OneWeb Satellites, Telesat Lightspeed, Boeing Satellite Systems, and Project Kuiper by Amazon.[138] And given that no collision-avoidance system is foolproof, the more congested the orbital pathways, the higher the incidence of satellite collisions. The by-product of satellite collision is orbital debris.[139] Orbital debris can worsen the congestion problem in an orbital pathway by forming obstacles that create more collisions with moving satellites and more debris, or it can stray to adjacent orbital pathways and contribute to congestion and collisions there. Existing treaties do not address the removal of orbital debris, and only the Artemis Accords encourages its Signatories, but not its Signatories' corporate nationals, to 'plan for the mitigation of orbital debris'.[140]

[134] Stephanie Bailey, 'Why Africa is Sending More Satellites Into Space' *CNN* (6 October 2021).
[135] Tereza Pultarova, 'How Many Satellites Can We Safely Fit in Earth Orbit?' (27 February 2023) <www.space.com/how-many-satellites-fit-safely-earth-orbit> accessed 30 April 2024.
[136] ibid quoting Dr Jonathan McDowell, an astronomer and astrophysicist based at the Harvard-Smithsonian Center for Astrophysics, who had a main-belt asteroid—'4589 McDowell'—named after him in 1993.
[137] ibid.
[138] Tom Leins, 'Out of this World: The International Satellite Broadband Battle Intensifies' (25 October 2021) <https://blog.telegeography.com/out-of-this-world-the-international-satellite-broadband-battle-intensifies> accessed 30 April 2024.
[139] Byers and Boley (n 41) 78.
[140] Section 12(1); for a summary of other non-binding arrangements regarding space debris, see Byers and Boley (n 41) 79–83.

While the ITU's licensing practice for orbital pathways and radio frequencies thus far has been commendably even-handed,[141] it lacks the mandate to order licensees to pick up their own litter in outer space. As orbital debris accumulates and orbital pathways become too cluttered for service, the ITU will find it increasingly difficult to approve licences for later entrants to the satellite race. And when access to a common resource has to be denied on the basis of overcrowding, it is a sign of regime failure, and a sign that the true battle for orbital pathways among corporate satellite operators begins.

3.2 The worsening tension between resource exploitation and resource conservation

Treaties and instruments purporting to regulate common property in Antarctic resources, outer space resources, and resources in the Area and in the High Seas share a common trait. They all provide that common resources should be accessed and used in a way that does not harm the surrounding environment and that is sustainable. In the case of the Antarctic, the 1991 Environmental Protection Protocol permits the non-scientific use of Antarctic resources other than mineral resources,[142] so long as it is grounded in 'the protection of the Antarctic environment and dependent and associated ecosystems and the intrinsic value of Antarctica'.[143] Additionally, the 1980 CCAMLR recognizes the tension between common resource exploitation and common resource conservation by providing that '[a]ny harvesting and associated activities in the area to which this Convention applies shall be conducted in accordance with the provisions of this Convention and with the following principles of conservation', namely, the 'prevention of decrease in the size of any harvested population to levels below those which ensure its stable recruitment', the 'maintenance of the ecological relationships between harvested, dependent and related populations of Antarctic marine living resources', and the 'prevention of changes or minimization of the risk of changes in the marine ecosystem which are not potentially reversible over two or three decades'.[144] In the case of

[141] In this regard, the ITU is guided by the commitment to equitable use and distribution of common property in orbital pathways and radio frequencies, with special consideration given to the needs and capabilities of developing countries, as enshrined in its Constitution, see arts 1(1)(b), 1(2)(d), 10(4), 12(1)(1), 17(1)(1), 21(2), and 44(2).

[142] Art 7 provides: 'Any activity relating to mineral resources, other than scientific research, shall be prohibited'. In other words, the 1991 Environmental Protection Protocol does not prohibit non-scientific activities relating to non-mineral resources.

[143] Art 3(1).

[144] Arts II(3)(a)–(c).

common resources in outer space, both the Outer Space and Moon treaties oblige states to prevent the disruption and contamination of the outer space environment when pursuing outer space activities,[145] while the Artemis Accords and the Hague Building Blocks urge the sustainable use of space resources.[146] And in the case of common resources in the Area and in the High Seas, the 1994 UNCLOS Agreement authorizes the ISA to administer the resources of the Area,[147] while being '[m]indful of the importance of the [UNCLOS] for the protection and preservation of the marine environment and of the growing concern for the global environment'.[148] Going beyond 'mindfulness', UNCLOS stipulates that the right of member states and their nationals to fish in the High Seas[149] is qualified by a duty on the part of member states to cooperate with other member states to adopt and implement measures for the conservation and management of the living resources of the High Seas.[150]

Despite the presence of treaty provisions that call for a balance between resource exploitation and resource conservation, conservation goals often take a back seat. Although the 1980 CCAMLR and 1991 Environmental Protection Protocol are framed as conservation and protection treaties, they have not brought about demonstrably sustainable fishing practices in the Antarctic. The CCAMLR Commission has not been able to effectively counter whaling, unreported fishing catches, pollutive fishing activities, and the overfishing of krill in the name of conservation. Similarly, whatever the stated conservation aspirations of the Outer Space and Moon treaties, as well as the Artemis Accords and Hague Building Blocks, the current practice of states staking claims on lunar soil to build lunar bases, of state agencies openly targeting supposedly mineral-rich asteroids for exclusive gains, and of corporate nationals leaving orbital pathways littered with space debris is the antithesis of sustainable use.[151] Perhaps the largest discrepancy between the conflicting objectives of

[145] 1967 Outer Space Treaty art IX; 1979 Moon Treaty art 7(1).

[146] S 1 of the Artemis Accords provides in relevant part: 'Adherence to a practical set of principles, guidelines and best practices in carrying out activities in outer space is intended to increase the safety of operations, reduce uncertainty, and promote the sustainable and beneficial use of space for all humankind'. Block 4.2(f) of the Hague Building Blocks provides: 'The international framework should be designed to: promote the sustainable, rational, efficient and economic use of space resources'.

[147] Annex, s 1(1).

[148] Preamble.

[149] Art 116.

[150] Arts 117–19.

[151] Adding to outer space pollution in the form of space debris created by satellite collisions, a surge in black carbon particles and carbon dioxide emissions is anticipated when space tourism takes off, which could 'cause potentially significant changes in the global atmospheric circulation and distributions of ozone and temperature', see Byers and Boley (n 41) 38–41, citing Martin Ross and others, 'Potential Climate Impact of Black Carbon Emitted by Rockets' (2010) 37(24) Geophysical Research Letters L24810.

resource exploitation and resource conservation, which the 1994 UNCLOS Agreement and UNCLOS attempt to reconcile, can be observed in the ongoing tussle within the ISA over the commencement of environmentally destructive mining operations in the Area, and how a significant number of fish stocks in the High Seas are already depleted from overfishing. Whatever the contracting states' or their delegate-drafters' intentions, it is apparent that incorporating environmental protection or conservation provisions into treaties regulating the use of common property and common resources does not beget the sustainable use of that property or those resources. On the contrary, common property and common resource exploitation seem to proceed in the absence of any conservationist goals.

The tragedy of selfish practices eclipsing sustainable ones, despite treaty directives for balance, is not unique to common property. It is also observable in the field of foreign investment where newer generation investment treaties contain best-effort provisions urging contracting states to ensure that foreign investors in their territory operate investments that neither pollute the environment, nor abuse human or labour rights.[152] In practice though, pollutive and abusive practices on the part of foreign investors do not appear to be on the decline, casting serious doubt on the signalling effect of token sustainability provisions in regulatory treaties.[153] It may be tempting to posit at this juncture that sustainability provisions and goals are naturally marginalized in treaties whose object and purpose is not conservation, but the use or promotion of a resource. The Outer Space and Moon treaties on the use of space resources, the 1994 UNCLOS Agreement and UNCLOS on the use of resources in the Area and in the High Seas, and investment treaties on the reciprocal promotion and protection of foreign investment are arguably examples of treaties that cannot accommodate or advance dual objects and purposes.[154] However, the overexploitation of Antarctic resources, in the presence of the

[152] See for instance art 810 of the Free Trade Agreement between Canada and the Republic of Peru (signed 29 May 2008, entered into force 1 August 2009), which provides: 'Each Party should encourage enterprises operating within its territory or subject to its jurisdiction to voluntarily incorporate internationally recognized standards of corporate social responsibility in their internal policies, such as statements of principle that have been endorsed or are supported by the Parties. These principles address issues such as labour, the environment, human rights, community relations and anti-corruption. The Parties therefore remind those enterprises of the importance of incorporating such corporate social responsibility standards in their internal policies.'

[153] Mavluda Sattorova, 'The Foreign Investor as a Good Citizen: Investor Obligations to do Good' in Jean Ho and Mavluda Sattorova (eds), *Investors' International Law* (Hart 2021) 45, 50–64.

[154] It is therefore most peculiar when the authors of an incisive monograph enumerating the deficiencies of regulating common property in outer space via treaties maintain that '[t]he ideal outcome would be a binding treaty that is widely ratified, including by the major spacefaring states', Byers and Boley (n 41) 179–80.

1991 Environmental Protection Protocol and the 1980 CCAMLR, whose object and purpose is resource conservation, signifies that stand-alone conservation treaties may not succeed where conservation provisions in regulatory treaties have failed. Therefore, while the BBNJ Agreement was concluded after much negotiation and fanfare, it is doubtful, in light of the precedent set by the 1991 Environmental Protocol and the 1980 CCAMLR for Antarctic resources, if the BBNJ Agreement, when it enters into force, will actually advance the conservation of marine living resources in the High Seas. If neither conservationist treaty provisions nor stand-alone conservation treaties can bring about the sustainable use of common property, it is time to look beyond treaties for better ways to regulate common property.

4. Some lessons from common pool resource management for common property regulation

Common pool resources, such as fisheries and forests to name but two examples, bear two principal traits. The first is the difficulty and cost of excluding beneficiaries from accessing that common pool, and the second is the subtraction of one entity's consumption from the total quantity of resources available to others.[155] Common pool resources are closely analogous to common property as new property because it would be impractical to block any state or corporate national with the requisite means from accessing the Antarctic, outer space including the Moon and other celestial objects, as well as the High Seas and the Area. Moreover, when the Antarctic, outer space and oceanic resources such as icebergs, krill, minerals, orbital pathways, and fish are harvested or utilized, the quantity of resources available to others is correspondingly reduced by the amount that was harvested or utilized. In fact, the late Nobel laureate and economic scientist, Elinor Ostrom, whose scholarship anchors this section, observed two decades ago that '[i]n addition to the prototypic local resources, the oceans, the gene pool, and the atmosphere are all common-pool resources'.[156] When the High Seas, the Antarctic, and outer space double up

[155] Marco A Janssen and Elinor Ostrom, 'Adoption of a New Regulation for the Governance of Common-Pool Resources by a Heterogenous Population' in Jean-Marie Baland and others (eds), *Inequality, Cooperation, and Environmental Sustainability* (Russell Sage Foundation/Princeton University Press 2007) 60, 65.

[156] Nives Dolšak and Elinor Ostrom, 'The Challenge of the Commons' in Nives Dolšak and Elinor Ostrom (eds), *The Commons in the New Millennium* (The MIT Press 2003) 3, 3. According to economics literature, common property may be regarded as '[c]ommons [which] typically involves some form of communal ownership' and to the extent that common property is 'public commons', there is no restriction on who can use it. In other words, common property management upholds non-discriminatory

as repositories of common pool resources, and when common pool 'prototypic local resources' have been managed for much longer than common property as new property, precedent from common pool resource management in domestic settings may guide nascent common property regulation in international law. After all, much of international law's foundational content, such as sovereignty, state responsibility, and treaties, were adapted from domestic laws.[157]

The objective of this section is not to canvas and dissect the extensive literature on common pool resource management, or to critique the vast array of case studies on common pool resource management.[158] Rather, I rely on the distilled markers of successful common pool resource management models to assess the true extent of the deficiencies of current common property regulation regimes, and for insights to a possible workaround to those deficiencies (Section 4.1). I then consider the prospect of the main drivers of common property regulation—states—acclimatizing to such a workaround (Section 4.2).

4.1 Adapting a blueprint for common property regulation

The presence of rules is integral to any common pool resource management model, though some models succeed while others fail.[159] This indicates that rules alone, be they captured in customary practice or in a written agreement, do not secure effective and enduring common pool resource management. According to Ostrom, successful common pool resource management models possess the following seven markers:[160]

(i) *Clearly defined boundaries*
Individuals or households who have rights to withdraw resource units from the CPR must be clearly defined, as must the boundaries of the CPR itself.

use, see Brett M Frischmann, *Infrastructure—The Social Value of Shared Resources* (OUP 2012) 8, also 99–114.

[157] Hersch Lauterpacht, *Private Law Sources and Analogies of International Law* (Longmans 1927) 91–119, 134–43, 155–80.
[158] For an updated bibliography, see Ana Espinola-Arredondo and Felix Muñoz-Garcia, *Common Pool Resources—Strategic Behaviour, Inefficiencies and Incomplete Information* (CUP 2022) 199–202.
[159] Janssen and Ostrom (n 155) 66.
[160] Elinor Ostrom, *Governing the Commons—The Evolution of Institutions for Collective Action* (CUP 1990, 2020 reprint) 90.

(ii) *Congruence between appropriation and provision rules and local conditions*
Appropriation rules restricting time, place, technology, and/or quantity of resource units are related to local conditions and to provision rules requiring labour, material, and/or money.

(iii) *Collective-choice arrangements*
Most individuals affected by the operational rules can participate in modifying the operational rules.

(iv) *Monitoring*
Monitors, who actively audit CPR conditions and appropriator behaviour, are accountable to the appropriators or are the appropriators.

(v) *Graduated sanctions*
Appropriators who violate operational rules are likely to be assessed by graduated sanctions (depending on the seriousness and context of the offense) by other appropriators, by officials accountable to these appropriators, or by both.

(vi) *Conflict-resolution mechanisms*
Appropriators and their officials have rapid access to low-cost arenas to resolve conflicts among appropriators or between appropriators and officials.

(vii) *Minimal recognition of rights to organize*
The rights of appropriators to devise their own institutions are not challenged by external governmental authorities.

To date, out of the seven markers identified by Ostrom, only two are fully present in common property regulation. They are (i) the existence of clearly defined boundaries, since there is consensus over the spatial boundaries of the Antarctic, outer space, and the High Seas and since common property as defined in this monograph is owned by all states and accessible to all states and their nationals; and (vii) minimal recognition of rights to organize since states are free to regulate common property as they please. Three of the seven markers are partially present. There is some (ii) congruence between appropriation and provision rules and local conditions, because while the applicable treaties exhort the need for sustainable use of finite resources, the setting of harvesting or licensing quotas based on outdated information on prevailing conditions undercuts any warning against overuse. There is also some degree of (iii) collective-choice arrangements since common property is largely regulated by operational rules found in treaties which only state-appropriators, but not corporate-appropriators (who outnumber states), can modify. And then there is qualified (iv) monitoring because collected data such as voluntary catch reports, vessel activity, and space debris distribution appears to be used for purely informative, and not appropriator-behaviour auditing, purposes. Finally, two of the seven markers are absent from common property regulation. With the exception of the BBNJ Agreement which is not yet in force, none of the other treaties and instruments that constitute the regulatory regimes for the Antarctic, outer space, and the High Seas provide for (v) graduated sanctions or (vi) conflict-resolution mechanisms.

Common property regulation does not and most probably will not approximate the standard blueprint for a successful common pool resource management model. Common property is loosely, and arguably poorly, regulated, precisely because states have deliberately chosen not to penalize monitored deviant behaviour with graduated sanctions, and not to formalize disputes over common property usage with the establishment of conflict-resolution mechanisms. As a result, existing rules in common property regulation are followed or disregarded at will, since none of these rules can be enforced, in any tangible manner, against the rule-breakers. Calling for states to renegotiate their treaties to insert more exacting provisions on sanctions and dispute settlement is unrealistic because states have made it clear time and again that their preferred model, or the least objectionable one, for common property regulation is that of voluntary compliance. Therefore, while sanctions and conflict-resolution mechanisms are integral to a successful common pool resource management model, they are not suitable benchmarks for common property regulation which is and will continue to be centred around voluntary compliance. Conversely, the markers of (ii) congruence between operational rules and local conditions, (iii) collective-choice arrangements, and (iv) monitoring can sit well with a model of voluntary compliance. This is because the volition of states and their corporate nationals to comply or not with operational rules and recommendations on common property can be conditioned from the ground-up,[161] which may in turn bring about better congruence between operational rules and local conditions, more sustainable collective-choice arrangements, and closer and more consequential monitoring.

Ground-up volition conditioning entails educating the ultimate individual consumers of common resources on the importance of sustainable harvesting of these resources. There are already sporadic attempts to steer consumers towards sustainably caught fish and seafood, particularly in upscale restaurants,

[161] Alex Farrell and M Granger Morgan, 'Multilateral Emission Trading: Heterogeneity in Domestic and International Common-Pool Resource Management' in Nives Dolšak and Elinor Ostrom (eds), *The Commons in the New Millennium* (The MIT Press 2003) 169, 209.

and through labelling and premium pricing by upmarket vendors, but sustainability consciousness is not sufficiently widespread. When sustainability messaging, just like global warming messaging, penetrates mass consciousness, consumers of iceberg water, krill supplements, seafood, satellite-transmitted data, and other resources drawn from common property will start factoring sustainability into their purchases. And when suppliers need to adapt to a growing sustainability-conscious consumer market, changes will be triggered throughout entire supply chains so that states and corporate actors are morally and monetarily incentivized to monitor and call out unsustainable harvesting practices. A sustainability-conscious consumer market will also prompt national and transnational regulators to ensure that the overall catch or usage by appropriators complements regular, contemporaneous scientific updates on the biomass or condition of a given resource. Progress on ground-up volition conditioning, to the extent that it can positively influence voluntary collective-choice arrangements between states, regulators, corporate actors, and consumers outside of the treaty framework, is bound to be frustratingly slow and uneven. However, pitching sustainability to foster consumer correction is surely an improvement over perpetuating the currently unsustainable corporate capture of common property regulation. To this end, all that remains to be considered is the likelihood of states accepting ground-up volition conditioning as the future of common property regulation.

4.2 Potential state support for a modified approach to common property regulation

In response to the deficiencies of current common property regulation regimes, some commentators have proposed a complete halt to all harvesting and usage, and for common property to be conserved as a world park.[162] While such a proposal may excite environmentalists, it compels the abandonment, dismantling, or extreme revision of existing treaty governance frameworks and is probably far too drastic to appeal to states. In contrast, ground-up volition conditioning enables change to occur while preserving the existing treaty governance framework, regardless of how lacking or lacking in teeth such a framework may be. In the case of common property regulation, change is represented by the voluntarily sustainable harvest and use of common resources by states and corporate actors alike. The prospect of state support for change through

[162] Vogler (n 9) 84; Baslar (n 10) 258.

ground-up volition conditioning is fair to good because such an approach has taken hold on at least two earlier occasions and is now starting to bear fruit.

Ground-up volition conditioning has spurred the return of looted cultural property by museums and states, and the switch by individuals and automobile manufacturers to the purchase and production of electric vehicles which reduce climate change by lowering carbon emissions. For more than 50 years, the United Nations Educational, Scientific, and Cultural Organization (UNESCO) has been 'support[ing] the fight against the illicit trafficking of cultural property'. The fight appears to have benefitted less from the governing 1970 Convention on the Means of Prohibiting and Preventing the Illicit Import, Export and Transfer of Ownership of Cultural Property,[163] which 'offers no recourse and no remedy if promised repatriation does not materialize'.[164] And more from UNESCO's outreach efforts such as the conducting of numerous educational workshops across the globe,[165] the establishment of a fund to improve 'capacity building, the awareness and communication, the inventory work and the monitoring of auction houses' in 2015,[166] and the declaration of 14 November as the International Day Against Illicit Trafficking in Cultural Property in 2019.[167] The repatriation of looted cultural property has since become a topic of constant concern and commentary in both general and specialized media outlets, with the full weight of the media leaning in favour of repatriation. Extensive media conditioning has coincided with an uptick in voluntary repatriations of looted cultural property by museums and states in recent years,[168] achieving what the 1970 UNESCO Convention and other legal instruments, on their own, could not.

Similarly, the ongoing transition from petroleum to electric vehicles is more probably the result of ground-up volition conditioning than of top-down directives. The 1992 United Nations Framework Convention on Climate

[163] (signed 14 November 1970, entered into force 24 April 1972) 823 UNTS 231 (1970 UNESCO Convention).

[164] My phrase, Chapter 2, Section 2.2.1.

[165] UNESCO, 'Training' <www.unesco.org/en/fight-illicit-trafficking/training?hub=416> accessed 28 June 2024.

[166] UNESCO, 'Fund of the Convention' <www.unesco.org/en/fight-illicit-trafficking/support?hub=416> accessed 28 June 2024.

[167] UNESCO, 'International Day against Illicit Trafficking in Cultural Property' <www.unesco.org/en/days/against-illicit-trafficking?TSPD_101_R0=080713870fab20009695cee851ae9e0f1ed769a940a3239dd2903b816f0c8fd3ea5f0c4fc81a6fe608e90245b8143000324a17ce2e2cb6a59320a88252934f7d498e005cb54e57273b92605511dbae687b5d0935bc3103717a463d14b377efd9> accessed 30 April 2024.

[168] See for instance Sarah Cascone, 'The Met Museum Returns More Looted Art to Greece and Turkey, Including 15 Antiquities Seized From Disgraced Dealer Subhash Kapoo' *Artnet* (3 April 2023) <https://news.artnet.com/art-world/the-met-returns-more-looted-art-to-greece-and-turkey-2278882> accessed 30 April 2024; Antoinette Radford, 'Vatican Returns Parthenon Sculptures to Greece' *BBC News* (25 March 2023).

Change,[169] the accompanying 1997 Kyoto Protocol,[170] and the 2015 Paris Agreement (which supersedes the Kyoto Protocol)[171] are widely regarded as significant drivers of any reduction in global carbon emissions.[172] However, it was not until the noticeable effects of global warming, the appearance of instant media sensations and prominent environmental activists like teenager Greta Thunberg, and the release of a relatively glitch-free and affordable electric car—the 'Model S'—by US car manufacturer Tesla in 2018 that the importance of switching to sustainable, zero-carbon energy sources started to be imprinted into mass consciousness. And as consumer appetites for electric vehicles grow, other automobile manufacturers have started releasing competitors to the 'Model S'. Today, electric vehicles are available from Japanese car manufacturers like Nissan and Honda, Chinese car manufacturers like Wuling and Geely, and German car manufacturers like Mercedes-Benz and Porsche. Witnessing an increase in both demand and supply of electric vehicles, some governments have started to install more public charging stations to presumably ease and further encourage the switch from petroleum to electric vehicles. As more convert to electric vehicles, a net reduction in carbon emissions and a net gain for climate change will follow.

Apart from precedent, a ground-up volition conditioning approach also enables states to focus on the crux of common property regulation: sustainable harvest and use. Energies and attention during inter-state conferences can then be devoted to ensuring that catch and usage limits are up-to-date, and that the processes for allocating access to and extraction of common resources are sufficiently flexible so that they can adapt swiftly to changing circumstances.

5. Conclusion

There are no quick fixes to the unfinished compromise that mars the regulation of common property in international law. The geographical vastness of and accessibility challenges posed by common property, the diverse aptitudes of states and their nationals for extracting resources located in or on common property, and the resulting unwillingness of assembled states to formulate sanctionable obligations have become a recipe for treaty governance

[169] (signed 9 May 1992, entered into force 21 March 1994) 1771 UNTS 107.

[170] (signed 11 December 1997, entered into force 16 February 2005) 2303 UNTS 162.

[171] (signed 12 December 2015, entered into force 4 November 2016) 3156 UNTS 1.

[172] Philippe Sands and others, *Principles of International Environmental Law* (4th edn, CUP 2018) 317–31.

frameworks that appear rigorous on paper but are relaxed in practice. The ATS and its numerous annual supplementary resolutions may convince the casual observer that the Antarctic and its resources are comprehensively regulated, but not the careful observer who puzzles over the apparent liberty of states and corporate actors to catch and kill without consequence. The dual-track Outer Space and Moon treaties, and the Artemis Accords and Hague Building Blocks, may present a choice between traditional and contemporary regimes on the shared usage and distribution of common property, but states and corporate actors then and now continue to conduct lunar and other space-faring expeditions with individual means and for anticipated individual gains. The 1994 UNCLOS Agreement may convey the impression that divisions over UNCLOS Part XI between member states have been healed with a reasonably detailed framework for sustainable seabed mining, but mining proposals have been greenlighted in the absence of credible evidence of environmental conscionability.

These highly permissive treaty governance frameworks have induced the corporate capture of common property regulation in international law. The ability to access and commercialize free and seemingly abundant resources without being constrained by enforceable rules, and to do so with minimal to no interference from their home states, has not only fuelled but also normalized the self-serving corporate scramble for common property. And as corporate actors pull ahead in their scramble with more advanced technologies, more effective extraction techniques, more efficient processing facilities, and maximized usage of a given resource, the distance between the regulators and the regulated widens. In addition to their limited written mandates, corporate expertise or daring may explain why regulatory institutions such as the CCAMLR Commission, the ITU, and the ISA appear ill-equipped against illicit, pollutive, and destructive corporate activities on common property. Barring the exceptional resistance by some member states of the ISA Council to the proposed commencement of seabed mining activities by The Metals Company in 2024, which appears to have stalled the project for the time being, international law has been indulgent towards corporate actors with designs on common property.

That said, the greatest strength and the greatest vulnerability of corporate actors operating within a permissive treaty framework is the consumer market for the end products of commodified common property. An uninformed consumer base will be complicit in unsustainable corporate practices and the inequitable use of common property. Conversely, an environmentally conscious consumer base can, by voting with their pockets, rewrite corporate and eventually state approaches towards common property from the bottom-up. With this in mind, it is by no means necessary for states to resort to revised or brand new treaties in the search for an optimal regulatory blueprint for common property regulation in international law. It is far less onerous to decide whether to actively foster sustainability-conscious consumers by leveraging the expertise, resources, and networks of global agencies like the United Nations Environment Programme, or to passively trail a newer generation of green consumers, whose preferences and purchases are increasingly shaped by curated sustainability-oriented feeds and targeted messaging in the expansive metaverse of social media. With the future direction of common property regulation nestled in changing consumer perspectives, I now turn to the third and final category of new property whose very existence is predominantly dependent on changing contextual parameters—contingent property.

4

Contingent Property

1. Introduction

Contingent property is possibly the most provocative category of new property. Unlike cultural property or common property, which denote the various manifestations of mankind's tangible and intangible heritage and of globally shared resources respectively, contingent property lacks permanence. What was disregarded as property may subsequently be regarded as property, and what was regarded as property may subsequently be disregarded as property. The provocation lies in the transience of the property label, and in understanding why and when it attaches or detaches. Contingent property is so called because its status as property rests on the calculated assimilation of a person, a thing, or a right to property. Absent any move to assimilate, the property label does not attach. Assimilation may be undertaken for various reasons, such as the pursuit of redress for injured rights on the more familiar terms of uncompensated expropriation, or the formulation of a claim to control a limited and valuable resource from a distance.[1] It may be tempting to surmise at this early juncture that every person, every thing, and every right can be assimilated to property,

[1] Georgy Kantor and others, 'Property and Ownership: An Overview' in Georgy Kantor and others (eds), *Legalism: Property and Ownership* (OUP 2017) 18.

New Property in International Law. Jean Ho, Oxford University Press. © Jean Ho 2024.
DOI: 10.1093/9780191976117.003.0005

rendering the category of contingent property so malleable as to be meaningless. The reality is far more nuanced. Assimilation is neither attempted nor accomplished in the abstract, but in a context which fosters assimilation for the specific purpose of securing the legal protection of scarcity-driven value. Jurisdictional rights, slaves, investment contracts, and digital assets, which once embodied or currently embody scarcity-driven value, are some examples of contingent property that can be protected by the laws on property regulation. Contingent property is a chameleon, adapting its form to the applicable context, and constantly testing the observation of boundaries that separate property from non-property.

This chapter introduces contingent property as a category of new property in international law, and evaluates the extent to which assimilation to property offers a more rewarding avenue for redressing violations to a person, a thing, or a right. It further demonstrates that while international law has been applied to regulate contingent property, practice has been sporadic and uneven, resulting in an international law that is adequate as a remedial law in some contexts, and lacking in others. Section 2 takes a closer look at the motivations and conditions for assimilating a range of things and rights to property and how the assimilation breeds expectations regarding the corrective function of contingent property. Section 3 showcases the extent to which these expectations are met across different types of contingent property, namely, jurisdictional rights, humans and human rights, and economic rights. Drawing on the different types of contingent property canvassed in the preceding section, Section 4 ventures that international law's capacity for contingent property regulation and protection reflects a symbiotic relationship between the emergence of contingent property and the development of international law content, which can either sustain or suppress contingent property. Section 5 concludes.

2. The push to 'propertize' and the corrective function of contingent property

The decision to assimilate a person, a thing, or a right to property, or the push to 'propertize', is typically undertaken to declare ownership over and legitimize control and use of that person, that thing, or that right.[2] Illustrations of 'propertization' include the slave trade where a person is bought and sold and

[2] ibid 7–9.

put to work by the slave-holder,[3] the commodities trade where a commodity is harvested and sold or utilized at will by the commodities holder,[4] and the demand for monetary compensation for injury to or interference with the exercise of 'propertized' rights by the rights holder.[5] While 'propertization' offers a way to manage competition and conflict over the usage of a scarce resource by pinpointing the imputable owners and controllers of that resource,[6] it encounters varying degrees of success. Even children are schooled in this message. One memorable instance of an unsuccessful attempt to 'propertize' is found in the award-winning tale of a boy, Wilfred, who runs into a moose and decides to make the moose his.[7] Wilfred names the moose 'Marcel' in an assertion of ownership and imposes a long list of rules on Marcel in an assertion of control. To Wilfred's dismay, Marcel does not come when called and pays highly selective heed to Wilfred's rules. Worse, Wilfred chanced upon other people who believed that the moose belonged to them. Eventually, as 'Wilfred admitted, he never really owned the moose anyway'. In seeking to 'propertize' the moose, Wilfred expected to enjoy benefits conferred by the moose that he had not enjoyed before, such as 'knocking down things that are out of Wilfred's reach' (Rule 16) and 'rescuing your owner from perilous situations' (Rule 73). Similarly, the push to 'propertize' in the real world comes with the expectation that the assimilation of a person, a thing, or a right to property will boost unfettered usage, which in turn potentially enhances redress for any interference with such usage. Therefore, in remedying the purportedly inferior protection of a person, a thing, or a right with the superior protection of its 'propertized' form, contingent property exists to perform a corrective function. This section first discusses the latitude underscoring the push to 'propertize' in order to outline how the expectation of contingent property's corrective function is formed (Section 2.1). I then consider the limits that determine the success of any attempt to 'propertize' in order to ascertain whether the expectation of contingent property's corrective function can be met (Section 2.2).

[3] See below Section 3.2.1.

[4] Jatin Dua, 'A Sea of Profit—Making Property in the Western Indian Ocean' in Georgy Kantor and others (eds), *Legalism: Property and Ownership* (OUP 2017) 182–87.

[5] See below Sections 3.1, 3.2.2, and 3.3.

[6] Jedediah Purdy, 'People as Resources: Recruitment and Reciprocity in the Freedom-Promoting Approach to Property' (2007) 55(4) Duke Law Journal 1047, 1050; Tom Lambert, 'Jurisdiction as Property in England, 900-1100' in Georgy Kantor and others (eds), *Legalism: Property and Ownership* (OUP 2017) 115, 130.

[7] Oliver Jeffers, *This Moose Belongs to Me* (HarperCollins 2012).

2.1 The latitude to 'propertize'

The argument that property is a highly fluid legal construct capable of absorbing other legal constructs is not new. It has been long been advanced by some leading private law scholars studying the distinction between property and contract.[8] In his seminal article, 'Property in Thin Air', Gray posited that '[n]o quantum step differentiates contract from "property"; for "property" has no clear threshold'.[9] Nearly two decades later, Lee reiterated Gray's point with the observation that 'property does not exist as a reified "thing" with stable features and structure; it is a relative rather than an absolute concept'.[10] She added that property is essentially 'a state endorsed power relation that regulates access to valuable resources', and in order for a resource to attract such state protection, it 'must minimally be capable of being excluded from the rest of the world'.[11]

[8] One notable exception to the 'propertization' of private law contracts lies in the common law tort of conversion which, to date, can only be invoked to redress unlawful third party interference with or disposal of the *physical* assets of contracting parties: see the landmark judgment of *OBG v Allan* [2007] 2 WLR 920 paras 94–107 (*per* Lord Hoffman delivering the majority judgment for the House of Lords). When viewed against the position in civil law jurisdictions like France, where economic loss occasioned by contractual interference by third parties is recoverable under the general tort claim of *responsabilité civile delictuelle* or delictual civil responsibility, see Muriel Fabre-Magnan, *Droit des Obligations 2—Responsabilité civile et quasi-contrats* (5th edn, Presses Universitaires de France 2021) 135–36, the common law position seems unduly restrictive by leaving an injured party without a viable course of action for redress. However, historical limitation of the tort of conversion to tangible property, see Simon Douglas, 'The Nature of Conversion' (2009) 68(1) Cambridge Law Journal 198, 199–202, and various policy reasons, such as the protective priorities of tort law and problems of proof, foster ongoing support for the non-extension of the common law tort of conversion to purely economic loss, see Christian Witting, 'Distinguishing Between Property Damage and Pure Economic Loss in Negligence: A Personality Thesis' (2001) 21(3) Legal Studies 481, 493–505; Michael J R Crawford, 'Contract As Property: Triangles and Tragic Choices' (2023) 82(1) Cambridge Law Journal 83, 101–09. This position may soon change as the UK Law Commission recommended the extension of the tort of conversion to intangible digital assets in a recent report: see UK Law Commission, 'Digital Assets: Final Report' (Law Com No 412, 2023) para 9.63 <www.lawcom.gov.uk/project/digital-assets/> accessed 30 April 2024, which I discuss in Section 3.3.3 below.

[9] Kevin Gray, 'Property in Thin Air' (1991) 50(2) Cambridge Law Journal 252, 303.

[10] Pey-Woan Lee, 'Inducing Breach of Contract, Conversion and Contract as Property' (2009) 29(3) Oxford Journal of Legal Studies 511, 513; additionally Lutz-Christian Wolff, 'The Relationship Between Contract Law and Property Law' (2020) 49(1) Common Law World Review 31, 47–50; Roger Cotterrell, 'The Law of Property and Legal Theory' in William Twining (ed), *Legal Theory and Common Law* (Basil Blackwell 1986) 90, 92; even grudgingly, James E Penner, *The Idea of Property in Law* (OUP 2000) 165, 182. For US scholarship favouring the contract–property overlap under US constitutional law, see Thomas W Merrill, 'The Landscape of Constitutional Property' (2000) 86 Virginia Law Review 885, 991; Cass R Sunstein, 'On Property and Constitutionalism' (1993) 14 Cardozo Law Review 907, 908, 911–12, 933; Duncan Kennedy and Frank Michelman, 'Are Property and Contract Efficient?' (1980) 8 Hofstra Law Review 711, 714, 739; Bruce Ackerman, *Private Property and The Constitution* (Yale University Press 1977) 26–29; but cf Richard A Posner who maintains the distinction between contract and property in *Economic Analysis of Law* (9th edn, Wolters Kluwer 2014) chs 3–4.

[11] Lee, ibid 513.

When separability, which is also one of the four core attributes of new property,[12] enables an attempt to 'propertize', it follows that anything that can be 'excluded from the rest of the world' can, in principle, be 'propertized'. Wildlife is illustrative. Traditionally regarded as common property, wild animals become the exclusive property of whoever captures or reduces them to possession.[13] The capture of fish by a fisherman in the High Seas, for instance, suffices to turn the fish into his exclusive property, which he can then legally dispose of as he wishes. Capture does not, however, 'propertize' wildlife in all cases. A hunter who captures a giant panda living in the mountain ranges in central China will not be able to claim the panda as his exclusive property, as all giant pandas are already the exclusive property of the state. That said, the latitude to 'propertize' remains considerable because the list of resources that can be 'excluded from the rest of the world' and potentially converted into one's exclusive property, whereby one embodies another of the four core attributes of new property by becoming the identifiable, imputable owner of that resource,[14] is open. Apart from wildlife, non-living natural resources (such as land, water, and oil) which can be segregated with physical barriers or siphoned, as well as legal, economic, and other man-made resources which can be subjected to exclusive access and use, are all potential targets of 'propertization'.

In addition to being separable with an identifiable, imputable owner, targets of 'propertization' tend to confer a benefit, typically monetary, on their owners. This is the third of four core attributes of new property.[15] The fisherman who 'propertizes' fish from the High Seas can feed his family with part of his catch and sell the rest for profit. The iceberg connoisseurs who 'propertize' icebergs from the Antarctica can bottle and market iceberg water for a premium.[16] And the individuals who 'propertize' their exclusive access to and use of other resources can monetize their exclusive access and use if the price and the conditions are right. In other words, an object is unlikely to become a target of 'propertization' if no value whatsoever attaches upon its assimilation to property. And once 'propertization' occurs with a view to acquiring whatever value a target brings, this triggers a desire in the owner of contingent property to preserve and guard against any diminution or deprivation of this value through legal means. Absent 'propertization', the fisherman whose catch of the day could have sold for a thousand dollars at the fish market has no viable legal

[12] See Chapter 1, Section 4.3.
[13] Dua (n 4) 184–86.
[14] See Chapter 1, Section 4.1.
[15] See Chapter 1, Section 4.4.
[16] See Chapter 3, Section 3.1.1.

recourse against a rival fisherman who steals or damages his catch. In contrast, when his catch is 'propertized', the law permits recourse against the wrongdoer for property theft or property damage in order to recover the value of the catch. The pursuit of value, and the seemingly better security afforded by laws protecting property owners, nurse an expectation that contingent property corrects any imbalance in the vindication of injury to non-property and to property. The assimilation of a person, a thing, or a right to property becomes highly strategic. The stronger the expectation that a claim in property is the best or the only way to redress an injury, the stronger the push to 'propertize'. That said, the expectation regarding contingent property's corrective function is not always met. The discussion now turns to consider the constraints on the push to 'propertize' and how they may undermine the corrective role that contingent property plays.

2.2 The limits to 'propertize'

As alluded to in the preceding section, conflicting ownership claims may serve as a bar to the creation of contingent property. Ownership can be asserted over common property, but not over property with a specific, imputable owner. This is because common property belongs to all, including the person asserting ownership over a portion of it, and can, as a matter of practice, be 'excluded from the rest of the world' by capture or other means of exclusion. In contrast, other types of property already belong to a specific, imputable owner, who, by virtue of the power of ownership, has had that property 'excluded from the rest of the world'. Such property is not available for further exclusion, which means a later contender for ownership will not be able to further carve out for his exclusive use property which has already been earmarked for another's exclusive use. Asserting ownership over property already owned by another by capture, segregation, possession, or other means becomes a non-starter. Ownership, in addition to being a core attribute of contingent property as a category of new property, is thus an important limit on 'propertization'.

The second important limit on 'propertization' is the presence or absence of a context which recognizes the assimilation of a person, a thing, or a right to property, and which redresses injury to a person, a thing, or a right as injury to property. Contingent property is particularly sensitive to contextual factors, the fourth and final core attribute of new property,[17] because not only is an

[17] See Chapter 1, Section 4.2.

appreciation of property typically context-driven,[18] context can also stimulate the creation of contingent property as well as hasten its demise. A prime example of contextual factors making or breaking contingent property can be found in slavery, explored in greater detail in Section 3.2.1 below, where humans were once owned, subject to exclusive use, and traded like property, but not anymore.[19] In a context where slavery is officially outlawed and where even historical links to slave-owning are condemned,[20] no human attracts legal protection as the property of another. Another example can be found in drug applications and carbon allowances which are currently denied the status of property under some domestic laws,[21] but may, should circumstances change, acquire that status under those laws in the future. When the existence and extinction of contingent property is determined by the prevailing context, the list of contingent property remains open and dynamic. The variety of prevailing contexts also remains open and dynamic because contexts can be formed in an instant, when a novel attempt at assimilation immediately receives a warm reception from those at whom the attempt is pitched, or crystallized over an extended period of time to reflect the aggregate of a given community's political and social consciousness and values.

When one attempts to assimilate a person, a thing, or a right to property in order to benefit from the supposedly superior legal protection that the law confers on property and property holders, any expectation towards contingent property's corrective function will only be met if ownership is established and if the applicable context admits the assimilation. These limits are cumulative. If there is an effective assertion of ownership but no context in which interference with ownership privileges can be redressed, the label of contingent property

[18] Jedediah Purdy, *The Meaning of Property—Freedom, Community, and the Legal Imagination* (Yale University Press 2010) 88; Lee (n 10) 517–18, 528.

[19] There is an ongoing dialogue on how, despite formal worldwide abolition, slavery continues to thrive in the form of bonded or coerced labour, affecting millions of men, women, and children around the world. As modern slavery does not engage the push to 'propertize', it is beyond the scope of this chapter and of this monograph to weigh in on this dialogue. For a recent, book-length treatment of how modern slavery lurks beneath a raft of anti-slavery conventions and national laws, see Justine Nolan and Martijn Boersma, *Addressing Modern Slavery* (University of New South Wales Press 2019).

[20] Aamna Mohdin and Rhi Storer, 'Tributes to Slave Traders and Colonialists Removed across UK' *The Guardian* (29 January 2021); also Sally Weale, 'Cambridge College Seeks to Remove Memorial to Patron with Links to Slave Trade' *The Guardian* (15 November 2021); Jeremy Young, 'Balliol College Oxford Apologies for 300 Years of Taking Slavery Cash' *The Times* (21 March 2021); Sean Coughlan, 'Harvard Abolishes "Master" in Titles in Slavery Row' *BBC News* (25 February 2016).

[21] See *Apotex Holdings Inc. & Anor v United States of America*, ICSID Case No ARB(AF)/12/1), Award (Veeder, Rowley, Crook) (25 August 2014) (*Apotex v US*) para 7.55 where the tribunal agreed with the US that drug applications are not recognized as property under US laws, and *Koch Industries, Inc. & Anor v Canada*, ICSID Case No ARB/20/52 (award pending) (*Koch Industries v Canada*), Counter-Memorial on Jurisdiction and the Merits (17 February 2022) paras 137–51 where Canada submitted that carbon allowances are not recognized as property under Ontario laws.

does not attach and the corrective function of contingent property does not materialize. Similarly, if the applicable context accommodates the assimilation, but the claimant is unable to prove ownership over contingent property, there is no basis for expecting redress for any injury to or interference with someone else's property. It follows that a failure to abide by either or both limits of 'propertization' corresponds to a failure in the push to 'propertize'. Returning to the story of Wilfred and the moose, we see that there was neither an effective assertion of ownership over the moose by Alfred, nor a context which acknowledged Wilfred's attempt to treat the moose as his property. Wilfred was unable to defeat prior claims of ownership asserted by other villagers over the moose so that his use and enjoyment of Marcel could be 'excluded from the rest of the world'. Wilfred also had nowhere to go to confirm and consolidate his authority over Marcel, resigning himself instead to a fate whereby '[t]he moose would agree to all of Wilfred's rules whenever it suited him'.[22] Therefore, any expectations Wilfred entertained from the outset for assimilating the moose to his property were largely wishful thinking and largely unmet. *This Moose Belongs To Me* may be a children's tale, but it manages to convey expectations regarding contingent property's corrective function in pithy terms.[23] The discussion will now showcase the extent to which these expectations are met across different types of contingent property where the push to 'propertize' has followed different trajectories.

3. The types of contingent property

One of the hazards of identifying different types of contingent property in a monograph on new property is the expectation from readers that the list ought to include whatever they may consider contingent property, or is otherwise exhaustive. So it is imperative for me to clarify that this section, this chapter, and this monograph makes no claim to being all-encompassing, or exhaustive. Rather, my objective is to offer a modest range of illustrations of contingent property—past, present, and prospective—so that others can extrapolate additional or new types of contingent property from this selection. The curation is not due to constraints of time or space, but a way to reinforce the highly context-driven nature of contingent property, which results in a highly dynamic list of contingent property that can shorten or lengthen depending on

[22] Jeffers (n 7).
[23] Kantor and others, 'Property and Ownership: An Overview' (n 1) 2–6.

the point in time that the list is consulted. The list of contingent property will always remain open because present contexts accommodating certain types of contingent property may disappear, while future contexts accommodating as yet unknown types of contingent property have yet to appear.

Striking illustrations of contingent property include, but are not limited to, jurisdictional rights which confer the power on rights holders to perform legal functions, such as apprehending and punishing wrongdoers (Section 3.1), humans and human rights where persons and rights attached to personhood are conferred a monetary value for the purposes of trade or vindication for violation (Section 3.2), and economic rights which entitle rights holders to seek monetary compensation for injury to or interference with those rights (Section 3.3). Jurisdictional rights, humans and human rights, and economic rights are assimilated to property in contexts which recognize these rights as scarce resources of considerable monetary value. However, these contexts do not necessarily facilitate the legal protection of these rights as jurisdictional, human, or economic rights, thereby nudging their assimilation to contingent property in order to leverage on the existing legal protection accorded to property rights. In some cases, expectations regarding contingent property's corrective function are clearly met; in other cases, the outcome is or may be equivocal.

3.1 Jurisdictional rights

Jurisdictional rights first emerged as property in eleventh-century England. Prior to this, virtually anyone had the right to apprehend wrongdoers. Wrongdoers 'needed to be confronted in force, and either killed on the spot or made to find sureties to guarantee their compliance' by 'communal expeditions'.[24] These 'communal expeditions' had to be led by senior local men, with any breaking of ranks by lone rangers punishable with disobedience to the king, and stood a high chance of incurring the vengeance of escaped wrongdoers. The promise of violence, the risk of displeasing the king, and the open invitation for revenge turned the exercise of jurisdictional rights via 'communal expeditions' into a burden, not a privilege. As a result, little value attached to jurisdictional rights and the paucity of takers ensured the absence of competition over the ownership of these rights.

Two key events altered a landscape of abundance in the tenth century, where the availability of jurisdictional rights outstripped willing rights holders, into a

[24] Lambert (n 6) 122.

landscape of scarcity in the eleventh and twelfth centuries, where rights supply could not meet rights demand. The first was the onset of a military crisis brought about by intensified Scandinavian raiding activities on the English coast, leading to an urgent need for revenue to repel the Scandinavian threat.[25] The second was the creation of a new class of royal officials known as sheriffs who were individuals with the right to collect revenues flowing from the performance of legal functions, such as extracting fines from thieves or hunting down fugitives.[26] In the race to collect as much revenue as possible for the king and be rewarded for it, the sheriffs clashed with the feudal lords who were keen to perform legal functions on their own lands and be rewarded accordingly. After all, prevailing laws sketched 'a broad principle that those who invest effort in the performance of legal functions ought to share in any profits that arise from those functions'.[27] There were now far more takers of jurisdictional rights than there were jurisdictional rights to go around. Competition between sheriffs and lords, and ensuing disputes, over scarce and valuable rights to perform legal functions prompted the assimilation of jurisdictional rights to property, and the establishment of property regimes to govern access to these rights.[28]

This abbreviated account of how jurisdictional rights came to be regarded and regulated as property in eleventh- and twelfth-century England[29] nonetheless suffices to present a stark contrast to how jurisdictional rights are regarded and regulated today. In most modern societies, the right to perform legal functions such as the arrest and imprisonment of criminals and the imposition and collection of fines is largely vested in national state organs and agencies. Instances of wholly private or vigilante dispensation of justice are extremely rare.[30] Even judges and arbitrators hearing disputes submitted to international courts and tribunals are acting on authority delegated by states through treaties and instruments pursuant to which these courts and tribunals

[25] ibid 136, 138.
[26] ibid 136.
[27] ibid 137.
[28] ibid 143.
[29] For a fuller picture, see ibid 121–42.
[30] Even in Brazil, where indigenous communities can administer their own civil and criminal justice systems, the right to do so can be traced back to the Brazilian Constitution, which deems any judicial authority exercised by indigenous communities to be authority that stems from and is delegated by the state, see Constitution of the Federative Republic of Brazil, art 231 (in part) and 232 (in full) respectively: 'Indians shall have their social organization, customs, languages, creeds and traditions recognized, as well as their original rights to the lands they traditionally occupy, it being incumbent upon the union to demarcate them, protect and ensure respect for all of their property.'; 'The Indians, their communities and organizations have standing under the law to sue to defend their rights and interests, the public prosecution intervening in all the procedural acts.'

are constituted, and must stay within the mandate which they have been conferred. Jurisdictional disputes between different adjudicatory bodies arise from time to time, but these can be resolved by the application of rules designed to settle disputes over jurisdictional rights as jurisdictional rights,[31] and not as property. Therefore, although jurisdictional rights have an imputable owner (be it the state or a delegated rights holder), are separable (such being the exclusive performance of legal functions by the rights holder), and confer a benefit (on the rights holder in the form of revenue collection or remuneration), they are no longer regarded and regulated as property. This is because the modern day legal context has evolved so much from that of the middle ages that past disputes over who bore greater entitlement to exercise jurisdictional rights have been replaced by present default state exercise and control of jurisdictional rights. Contingent property, which is exceptionally responsive to contextual factors, ceases to exist when the prevailing context offers no cause for its continued existence.

The assimilation of jurisdictional rights to property in medieval England clearly met the corrective function of contingent property at a time when the perception and protection of jurisdictional rights as a scarce and valuable resource was not reflected in existing laws. According to Lambert, the medieval mind viewed entitlement to collect revenue upon the performance of legal functions as one stick in 'the standard bundle of rights' that a lord had over his land.[32] The supposed viewing of property as a bundle of rights during the medieval period,[33] made property the nearest equivalent to jurisdictional rights, whereby the rules regulating access to and allocation of property were equally applicable to jurisdictional rights. Without the assimilation of jurisdictional rights to property, there would have been no regime to regulate or

[31] *Forum non conveniens*, or the invitation to a court to decline to exercise jurisdiction on the ground that there is a more appropriate forum in which the dispute should be heard, may be invoked by a dispute where there is jurisdictional conflict between national courts in different countries, see generally Ronald A Brand and Scott R Jablonski, *Forum Non Conveniens: History, Global Practice, and Future Under the Hague Convention on Choice of Court Agreements* (OUP 2007) chs 1, 7. In international arbitration, where disputes are submitted to a tribunal of party-appointed arbitrators for final settlement, jurisdictional conflicts and challenges are normally resolved by the arbitrators who are empowered by applicable arbitral institutional rules to decide on their own jurisdiction, see for instance the 2021 Arbitration Rules of the International Chamber of Commerce, art 6(5): 'In all matters decided by the Court under Article 6(4), any decision as to the jurisdiction of the arbitral tribunal, except as to parties or claims with respect to which the Court decides that the arbitration cannot proceed, shall then be taken by the arbitral tribunal itself.'

[32] Lambert (n 6) 131.

[33] It has been suggested that the leasehold, where the discrete rights of the owner and the rights of the lessor are bundled up in the same piece of property, was, for reasons that are beyond the scope of this monograph, unique to England in all of medieval Europe, see Alexandar Volokh, 'Property Rights and Contract Form in Medieval Europe' (2009) 11(2) American Law and Economics Review 399, 404–09.

protect jurisdictional rights. Up until a fundamental change in contexts, contingent property corrected a situation of insoluble conflicts over the exercise of jurisdictional rights into one of principled and peaceful resolution of conflicts over the exercise of jurisdictional rights in accordance with property laws.

3.2 Humans and human rights

The equation of slaves to human property was assumed without much ado during periods and in places when slavery flourished, until it became obsolete with the gradual abolition of slavery over the course of nearly two centuries.[34] The initial, seemingly effortless, push to 'propertize' humans was only reversed by a long and drawn-out journey to de-'propertize' humans the world over. In sharp contrast, the 'propertization' of human rights, especially economic, social, and cultural rights which still lack established avenues for redress and compensation for violation, remains a work-in-progress. The following discussion juxtaposes an account of slaves as contingent property (Section 3.2.1) with an account of soft law human rights as contingent property (Section 3.2.2) to elicit the considerations and challenges involved in treating humans and human rights as property from past to present. The comparison will also shed light on the strength, real or projected, of contingent property's corrective function in either context.

3.2.1 Slaves

The most remarkable aspect of how slaves came to be regarded and treated as property is probably the near absence of any scholarly or judicial attempts to justify the assimilation. Modern day scholars define slavery by simply reporting on a widely held assumption that slaves are the property of slave owners,[35] while contemporary umpires of slave owners saw fit to simply accept and apply, without question, laws that deemed slaves the property of slave

[34] For a chronology of measures taken at both the national and international level from 1772 to 1962 outlawing slavery, see Paul E Lovejoy, *Transformations in Slavery—A History of Slavery in Africa* (3rd edn, CUP 2011) 285–92.

[35] See generally, Stephanie E Jones-Rogers, *They Were Her Property—White Women as Slave Owners in the American South* (Yale University Press 2019) chs 1, 4; specifically Hannah Skoda, 'People as Property in Medieval Dubrovnik' in Georgy Kantor and others (eds), *Legalism: Property and Ownership* (OUP 2017) 235, 236; Kevin Bales, 'Contemporary Coercive Labour Practices—Slavery Today' in David Eltis and others (eds), *The Cambridge World History of Slavery vol. 4 AD 1804- AD 2016* (CUP 2017) 655, 655; Paul Finkleman, 'Slavery in the United States - Persons or Property?' in Jean Allain (ed), *The Legal Understanding of Slavery: From the Historical to the Contemporary* (OUP 2012) 106, 112.

owners.[36] Slavery was not universally accepted.[37] Even within the US, slavery was mostly practised in the southern states like Louisiana, but outlawed in other states like Pennsylvania. Moreover, if one considers that 'property involves relationships between people with respect to things',[38] the stripping of a slave's personhood for its demotion to a thing, and its interaction with the slave owners as the latter's property, were hardly self-evident or self-explanatory phenomena. Amid assumptions, one extended defence of the institution of slavery was published in 1857 by US writer George Fitzhugh. Fitzhugh justified the assimilation of slaves to property in moral and in economic terms, asserting that 'property in man' not only liberates slaves from the predicament of '[t]he free labourer [who] must work or starve', it also imparts value to other forms of property since it '[g]ive[s] you... ten thousand acres of land ... ; and with your artificial wants you are poorer than Robinson Crusoe, or the lowest working man, if you have no slaves to capital, or domestic slaves'.[39] Fitzhugh's dismissal of free labour in favour of slavery was welcomed by American slave owners, but pilloried by anti-slavery campaigners.[40] It suffices to note for present purposes, without taking a stance on Fitzhugh's apologia, that the assimilation of slaves to property, however presumptuous and controversially defended, once represented the divisive status quo.

One plausible explanation for the scantily reasoned, yet well-entrenched assimilation is the presence of laws enforcing the notion that slaves are property. These laws were underscored by the existence of a thriving slave trade where there was consistent demand for and supply of slaves. While many slaves were tricked into slavery and subjected to abominable treatment, the prevailing

[36] *Prigg v Pennsylvania* (1842) 41 US 539, 540 where Story J, delivering the majority opinion of the US Supreme Court, held that a federal statute, the Fugitive Slave Act of 1793, trumped a Pennsylvanian state law that prohibited negros from being transported out of Pennsylvania (which did not uphold slavery) into slavery in other states: 'It is historically well known that the object of the clause in the Constitution of the United States relating to persons owing service and labour in one state escaping into other states was to *secure to the citizens of the slaveholding States the complete right and title of ownership in their slaves as property* in every State in the Union into which they might escape from the State where they were held in servitude. The full recognition of this right and title was *indispensable to the security of this species of property* in all the slaveholding States, and indeed was so vital to the preservation of their domestic interests and institutions that it cannot be doubted that it constituted a fundamental article without the adoption of which the Union could not have been formed' (emphasis added). According to acclaimed political historian, Sean Wilentz, the 'propertizing' of humans as slaves in the US stemmed from a compromise by the Constitution's framers to tolerate slavery without officially endorsing it. The resulting ambiguity locked slavers and anti-slavers into an endless struggle over slavery, see *No Property In Man—Slavery and Antislavery at the Nation's Founding* (Harvard University Press 2019) ch 3.

[37] Pamela Crossley, 'Dependency and Coercion in East Asian Labor, 1800-1949' in David Eltis and others (eds), *The Cambridge World History of Slavery vol. 4 AD 1804- AD 2016* (CUP 2017) 540, 546.

[38] Skoda (n 35) 237.

[39] George Fitzhugh, *Cannibals All! Slaves Without* Masters (Harvard University Press 1966) 18–20.

[40] Comer Vann Woodward, 'George Fitzhugh, *Sui Generis*' in Fitzhugh, *Cannibals All! Slaves Without Masters* ibid vii, xxviii–xxxi.

legal and social contexts in slave-owning regions protected slave owners and their human property, offering meagre means of escape for disgruntled slaves,[41] and enabling the slave trade to prosper. As depicted by Jones-Rogers in her critically acclaimed exposé on American female slave owners entitled *They Were Her Property*, the slave trade economy was so resilient because it was so pervasive:[42]

> Not only did slave-owning women participate in the public haggling over black bodies in the slave pen, the slave yard, and the auction block, they frequently subjected enslaved people to the terror of the slave market in the privacy of their homes. While slave traders, auctioneers, and brokers prepared enslaved people for sale by the sides of country roads, in southern auction houses, and in slave-trading establishments, white women talked with friends and family members about their labor needs and their desire to buy or sell enslaved men, women, and children. They were often able to fulfil that desire without visiting a brick-and-mortar marketplace because this process took place—or at least began—in their homes.

Yet, the once pervasive slave trade economy was headed for extinction when the numbers and voices of anti-slavers started to eclipse the persistence of stakeholders in the slave trade. This occurred in the US in the nineteenth century when the slave trade was abolished, and in the rest of the world in the twentieth century when Saudi Arabia became the last country to outlaw slavery.[43] The attachment of the property label to humans when the prevailing legal and social contexts accommodated a slave trade economy, and the subsequent detachment of this label when the prevailing contexts no longer tolerated slavery, makes slaves the archetype contingent property that is highly responsive to contextual factors. Contingent property's profound dependence on its context for substance and sustenance may trigger interest in pinpointing when exactly contexts change so that it can be said with certainty whether contingent property has commenced or ceased existence. In the case of slavery, this is not a straightforward exercise. When slaves are property in the eyes of the law because enough segments of a population do not find the notion of one person possessing and controlling another in order to put the latter to work or up for sale objectionable, slaves can only stop being

[41] One way of escaping slavery is manumission, where the slave pays his or her owner the price he or she is apparently worth, thereby purchasing his or her freedom, see Skoda (n 35) 252.
[42] (n 35) 82.
[43] Lovejoy (n 34) 286, 291.

property in the eyes of the law when enough segments of the population feel otherwise.[44] There is no single turning point or catalyst for change, only a protracted series of turning points as anti-slavery sentiments gain adherents over time and assume mainstream, dominant status in the slavery dialogue. Context, while indispensable to the identification of contingent property, can also impede the identification of contingent property at a given point in time. Slaves were property before the anti-slavery movement took root, arguably property as the anti-slavery movement gained momentum, and no longer property once the anti-slavery movement achieved its ultimate goal of worldwide abolition. As the anti-slavery movement lasted around two centuries, slaves were both property and not property during this entire period, depending on who you asked.

Leaving aside the propriety of owning slaves, the push to 'propertize' slaves enabled slave owners to sidestep any moral conundrum associated with putting a trading price on another human being, and with demands to the authorities for the capture and return of runaway slaves. The former conundrum arises from the fact that slave owners will not dream of putting a price on their family members and selling them to willing buyers on the auction block or in their own backyards, prompting questions over the basis for the discriminatory treatment of human beings. 'Propertizing' slaves offers a fix that is simple, though by no means satisfactory from the perspective of anti-slavers, since slaves as contingent property are no different from livestock or other forms of property to which monetary value can be attached. The latter conundrum arises from the state enacting laws on the one hand to deter the holding of human beings in captivity against their will, while enacting laws on the other to forcibly return runaway slaves to captivity.[45] 'Propertizing' slaves dehumanizes them to the extent that the law recognizes the right of free men, but not slaves, to resist and to be freed from captivity. Had slave owners expected valuable assets in the form of complete dominium over their slaves, these expectations were fully met by the assimilation of slaves to property. The demise of the institution of slavery removed the dubious rationales for assimilating slaves to property. Eventual rejection of the 'propertization' of certain human beings

[44] Jean Allain and Robin Hickey, 'Property and the Definition of Slavery' (2012) 61(4) International and Comparative Law Quarterly 915, 932.

[45] In the US, the contrast in treatment of free men and slaves was evident in the 1791 Fifth Amendment to the Bill of Rights, which provides in part that '[n]o person shall ... be deprived of life, liberty, or property, without due process of law', and in the Fugitive Slave Act of 1850 s 6, which provides that 'when a person held to service or labor in any State or Territory of the United States, has heretofore or shall heretofore escape into another State or Territory of the United States, the person or person to whom such service or labor may be due ... may pursue and reclaim such fugitive person'.

was followed by reticence in the 'propertization' of certain human rights, to which the discussion now turns.

3.2.2 Soft law human rights

Human rights conform to a hierarchy.[46] Topping the hierarchy are human rights such as the right to life, to liberty, to freedom of expression, and to freedom of religion, collectively known as civil and political rights, that are enshrined in national constitutions and in international conventions and enforceable by affected individuals through settled avenues for redress.[47] Elsewhere in the hierarchy are human rights such as the right to education, to social security, to sanitation, and to water, collectively known as economic, social, and cultural rights, which are articulated in various international conventions but which lack effective mechanisms for enforcement.[48] The relative ease of redressing violated civil and political rights as human rights and the relative difficulty of doing the same for economic, social, and cultural rights renders aspirational this latter grouping of human rights. Their appearance in international conventions that confirm their importance without providing any means of safeguard, other than voluntary reporting by signatory states, deems them soft law human rights which are not legally binding. When soft law human rights holders are unable to attract concrete legal protection under international law for violation, it nudges them to reframe these rights in order to strengthen and succeed on any claim for legal protection. Notably, economists have long advocated the assimilation of human rights to property rights, since human rights, like property rights, represent 'tools or parameters of social interaction'.[49] Soft law human rights are therefore potential targets for 'propertization', and one example of this is the soft law human right to water.

In *Urbaser S.A. & Anor v Argentina*, the right to water was raised in Argentina's counterclaim, where it sought a ruling from an arbitral tribunal

[46] Theodore Meron, 'On A Hierarchy Of International Human Rights' (1986) 80 American Journal of International Law 1, 2; also Fernando Suárez Müller, 'The Hierarchy of Human Rights and the Transcendental System of Right' (2019) 20(1) Human Rights Review 47, 56–57; Tom Farer, 'The Hierarchy of Human Rights' (1992) 8(1) American University International Law Review 115, 115; cf UNICEF, 'What are Human Rights?' <www.unicef.org/child-rights-convention/what-are-human-rights#:~:text=Whether%20civil%2C%20political%2C%20economic%2C,no%20hierarchy%20of%20human%20rights> accessed 30 April 2024.

[47] Farer, 'The Hierarchy of Human Rights' ibid 118.

[48] ibid.

[49] Michael Veseth, 'The Economics of Property Rights and Human Rights' (1982) 41(2) American Journal of Economics and Sociology 169, 174, 170. For an extreme libertarian justification for the assimilation of human rights to property, see Murray N Rothbard, *Man, Economy, and State with Power and Market* (2nd edn, Ludwig von Mises Institute 2009) 1337–40.

constituted under the Argentina–Spain investment treaty[50] that the claimants' failure to comply with the terms of a water concession covering the Province of Buenos Aires deprived the Buenos Aires population of clean water and simultaneously 'violated human rights obligations clearly applicable to companies'.[51] Argentina stopped short of arguing that the right to water created a binding legal obligation under international law and conceded that 'international law does not provide a cause of action for the Counterclaim'.[52] The vagueness of Argentina's counterclaim became its undoing as the tribunal, after referencing multiple international human rights conventions, pointed to 'the lack of any legal ground based on international law that would entitle a group of individuals to raise a claim for performance for delivery of water and sewage services directed against a company or any other private party'.[53] The upshot of this failed counterclaim is a soft law right to water, inherent in every human being, that becomes impossible or unrealistic to redress even when violated. Individuals have no claim in international law against private companies that violate this right,[54] nor can they pursue direct recourse under international law against their home states for allowing their right to water to be violated.[55] They may seek redress from the home state of the transgressing company if they can attribute the company's actions or omissions to its home state under the Articles on State Responsibility.[56]

[50] Agreement Between the Argentine Republic and the Kingdom of Spain on the Reciprocal Promotion and Protection of Investments (signed 3 October 1991, entered into force 28 September 1992).

[51] ICSID Case No ARB/07/26, Award (Bucher, Martínez-Fraga, McLachlan) (8 December 2016) (*Urbaser v Argentina*) para 1206.

[52] ibid.

[53] ibid paras 1220, 1196–98.

[54] The proposed use of arbitral tribunals to hear claims involving human rights violations brought by individuals against private companies in the 2019 Hague Rules on Business and Human Rights Arbitration offers a redress mechanism where none previously existed. However, the Hague Rules deliberately do not clarify whether soft law human rights violations can form the object of a claim, see Centre for International Legal Cooperation, 'The Hague Rules on Business and Human Rights Arbitration' 3 <www.cilc.nl/cms/wp-content/uploads/2019/12/The-Hague-Rules-on-Business-and-Human-Rights-Arbitration_CILC-digital-version.pdf> accessed 30 April 2024.

[55] The United Nations Guiding Principles on Business and Human Rights articulate an obligation on states to 'take appropriate steps to ensure, through judicial, administrative, legislative or other appropriate means, that when such [human rights] abuses occur within their territory and/or jurisdiction those affected have access to effective remedy', Foundational Principle 25 <www.ohchr.org/sites/default/files/documents/publications/guidingprinciplesbusinesshr_en.pdf.> accessed 30 April 2024. Access to remedy does not appear to extend to the affected vis-à-vis the home state in situations where the home state falls short on this aspirational obligation.

[56] 2001 Articles on Responsibility of States for Internationally Wrongful Acts, UN Doc A/RES/56/83 (2001) arts 5, 8. The possibility of foreign victims invoking international law against companies' home states for attributable human rights violations has been canvassed by eminent scholars, see Robert McCorquodale and Penelope Simons, 'Responsibility Beyond Borders: State Responsibility for Extraterritorial Violations by Corporations of International Human Rights Law' (2007) 70(4) Modern Law Review 598, 606–15; Muthucumaraswamy Sornarajah, 'Linking State Responsibility for Certain Harms Caused by Corporate Nationals Abroad to Civil Recourse in the Legal Systems of Home States'

The 'propertization' of soft law human rights, such as the right to water, can only proceed if these rights embody the core attributes of new property, namely, imputable ownership, conferral of a benefit, responsiveness to contextual factors, and separability.[57] Three of the four attributes are easily discerned, as soft law human rights are intrinsic to every human being as owners of those rights, confer a benefit in the form of the particular right that is claimed as its owner's entitlement, and are susceptible to a push to 'propertize' in contexts where these rights are recognized but cannot be effectively enforced as human rights. This leaves the final attribute of separability, which does not require a transfer of ownership in new property as defined in this monograph.[58] Contrary to conservative views, human rights are separable from their owners.[59] Even if a person cannot transfer their right to water, to sanitation, to education, or to adequate housing to another person, they can, in disregard of personal dignity, relinquish them temporarily or permanently. While few may choose to abandon or waive their soft law human rights, the fact that such a choice can be made is what matters when determining whether soft law human rights can be assimilated to property. When soft law human rights are contingent property, they benefit from the same legal protection available to property. In concrete terms, the avenue for redress for unlawful property interference becomes the avenue for redress for soft law human rights violations. Where individuals are empowered to bring claims for hard law human rights violations against states, such as before the European Court of Human Rights, soft law human rights violations may be reframed as unlawful interference with property rights, or unlawful expropriation, under Article 1 of Protocol 1 to the European Convention of Human Rights (ECHR).[60] To reimagine *Urbaser v Argentina* where Urbaser's actions are attributable to Spain,[61] the flimsy counterclaim brought by Argentina against Urbaser for soft law human rights violations

in Craig Scott (ed), *Torture As Tort—Comparative Perspectives on the Development of Transnational Human Rights Litigation* (Hart Publishing 2001) 491, 497–505.

[57] See Chapter 1, Section 4.

[58] See Chapter 1, Section 4.3.

[59] Donald van de Veer, 'Are Human Rights Alienable?' (1980) 37(2) Philosophical Studies: An International Journal for Philosophy in the Analytic Tradition 165, 165–69; cf the Preamble to the 1948 Universal Declaration of Human Rights, which recognizes 'the equal and inalienable rights of all members of the human family'.

[60] Protocol to the Convention for the Protection of Human Rights and Fundamental Freedoms (signed 20 March 1952, entered into force 18 May 1954) art 1, entitled 'Protection of Property', provides in part: 'Every natural or legal person is entitled to the peaceful enjoyment of his possessions. No one shall be deprived of his possessions except in the public interest and subject to the conditions provided for by law and by the general principles of international law'.

[61] The challenge of attributing corporate conduct to the corporation's home state is discussed in greater detail in Chapter 5, Section 3.1.1.

that gave rise to no cause of action in international law may be replaced by a firmer claim brought by Argentina against Spain for the unlawful expropriation of the former's population's right to water under general international law in an appropriate forum.[62] Prevailing in this alternative scenario would entitle Argentina, on behalf of the population of Buenos Aires, to monetary compensation from Spain for unlawful expropriation, valued at whatever amount the chosen forum determines the right to water as contingent property to be worth.

Given the absence of claims to date framing soft law human rights as new property in international law, the corrective function of contingent property remains prospective. However, the conditions for assimilating soft law human rights to property, and the realization of expectations towards contingent property's corrective function, are arguably promising. First, exercising the freedom to bring an expropriation claim for unlawful interference with contingent property and potentially obtain monetary redress accomplishes more for victims than failing to state a cognizable cause of action in international law, or waiting indefinitely for soft law human rights to crystallize into hard law.[63] The corrective function is met when legal protection for soft law human rights increases from negligible to some. Second, there is no difficulty with putting a price on soft law human rights violations as even hard law human rights violations are redressed with monetary compensation.[64] Further, there is no risk of conflation within the human rights hierarchy when relying on an expropriation claim to seek redress since soft law human rights can be pegged at a lower monetary value than rights which are supposedly higher up in the hierarchy. The corrective function is met when soft law human rights which previously could not attract any monetary compensation for violation can now do so. Third and finally, the assimilation of certain rights to property, for the purpose of seeking enhanced protection under the laws on property regulation, is not new. The assimilation has already gained considerable traction in the field of economic rights, the focus of the next section, under international law as well as under national law. Extending the assimilation to soft law human rights

[62] One possible forum for such a claim is the International Court of Justice.

[63] Gunther F Handl and others, 'A Hard Look At Soft Law' (1988) 82 Proceedings of the American Society of International Law 371. Remarks made specifically by Pierre Marie Dupuy, 387.

[64] The Practice Directions of the European Court of Human Rights <www.echr.coe.int/documents/d/echr/pd_satisfaction_claims_eng> accessed 30 April 2024: paras 1 and 5 clarify that the Court's power to award 'just satisfaction' to the injured party pursuant to art 41 of the European Court of Human Rights includes '[a]warding sums of money'. While the ability of damages awards to promote state compliance with rulings has been questioned, the propriety of the Court awarding monetary damages for proven human rights violations has not, see Veronika Fikfak, 'Changing State Behaviour: Damages Before The European Court of Human Rights' (2018) 29(4) European Journal of International Law 1091, 1092–93, 1102–07.

merely builds on existing practice. And as with economic rights, the greater the uptake on the assimilation of soft law human rights to property, the more opportunities there are to verify contingent property's projected corrective function.

3.3 Economic rights

The push to 'propertize' economic rights was borne from necessity. Economic rights satisfy the definition of new property as they are held by imputable owners, and they are transferable and assignable and thus separable from their imputable owners. Moreover, they typically confer an economic benefit on their imputable owners, and reside in contexts that place a premium on their preservation and protection,[65] even if it means assimilating them to contingent property for enhanced legal protection. Using investment contracts (Section 3.3.1), judgments on legal claims (Section 3.3.2), and digital assets (Section 3.3.3) as case studies, I explain why existing means of legal protection for each sub-genre of economic rights, prior to their assimilation to property, were inadequate. This inadequacy, coupled with the strong desire of the affected parties to seek and obtain effective redress for injured economic rights, prompted serious and enduring attempts to employ alternative means of legal protection. That the push to 'propertize' is more evident and entrenched for economic rights strongly suggests that the contexts in which claimants seek redress for injured economic rights are more conducive to the assimilation of economic

[65] See Chapter 1, Section 4. The interests involved in *Apotex v US* (n 21) test the limits of assimilating economic rights to new property. The claimants argued that their new drug applications which were submitted to the US government were intangible property and protected investments under art 1139(g) of the now defunct North American Free Trade Agreement (signed 17 December 1992, entered into force 1 January 1994, terminated 1 July 2020) (NAFTA). The tribunal found at para 7.55 that the applications were 'quasi-import licenses' and 'not commodities in the territory of the USA' but did not elaborate on why this particular manifestation of economic rights does not qualify as new property. As the claimant's applications had to be approved by the US government in order for its products to be sold by US distributors, the relevant context for any assimilation to new property was the US generic drugs market governed by US domestic laws. Applying the four-prong definition for new property set out in Chapter 1, Section 4, new drug applications are arguably not new property because while they satisfy the criteria of imputable ownership (by claimants), separability (from claimants), and conferral of benefit (in the form of monetary profit for claimants from the authorization of cross-border sales), the applications are not recognized as property in the US context within which they operate. The critical importance of context in the form of domestic laws in the recognition of new property is a double-edged sword. While domestic laws can draw a clear dividing line between property and non-property, they can also, as noted in Chapter 1, Section 2.1.3, disable any protective shield that international law can potentially cast over new property by sheer whim of legislative will. And when national security interests are starting to shape US property law, then the creation or disavowal of new property becomes purely a matter of policy, not of principle, see Matthew S Erie, 'Property As National Security' (2024) 1 Wisconsin Law Review 255, 268–94.

rights to property. And while these favourable contexts for the framing of economic rights as property augur the meeting of contingent property's corrective function, the remainder of this section will address any discrepancy between anticipation and reality.

3.3.1 Investment contracts

The push to 'propertize' investment contracts under international law stemmed from the inability of foreign investors to present a contract claim directly against host states in investment treaty arbitration.[66] Foreign investment usually enters a host state via a contract or a series of contracts concluded between host state or local entities and the foreign investor, and is often protected by an investment treaty concluded between the host state and the investor's home state. Investment treaties set out obligations owed by the states parties to qualifying investments and investors, such as the obligation not to expropriate without compensation, the obligation to provide fair and equitable treatment (FET clause), and the obligation to observe all commitments made to investors (umbrella clause), amongst others. Investment treaties also provide for the arbitration of investor–state disputes, although these disputes must concern the alleged violation of a stipulated treaty obligation by host states parties, and not a contractual obligation.

As a considerable number of investor–state disputes submitted to investment treaty arbitration are contractual in origin, claimant investors hoping to avail themselves of treaty protection for contractual breaches or interference by respondent states have to frame a contractual breach or termination as a treaty breach. And of the various treaty claims that investors can bring, publicly available arbitral awards indicate an affinity for expropriation claims.[67]

[66] Foreign investors can present a contract claim directly against host states in international arbitration provided the following conditions are met: (i) that the investor and state are parties to the underlying contract and (ii) that the underlying contract contains an arbitration clause. As states often enter into investment contracts via state or state-linked entities each bearing separate legal personalities from the state, investors may struggle to show that the state should nonetheless be bound by the arbitration clause contained in a contract which it did not sign, see Philippe Leboulanger, 'Some Issues in ICC Awards Relating to State Contracts' (2004) 15(2) ICC International Court of Arbitration Bulletin 93, 95–96. Therefore, investors may, where applicable, prefer to invoke investment treaty protection when host state measures have adversely affected their contracts as this allows them to overcome the absence of contractual privity between themselves and the host state.

[67] The treaty claim of choice for redressing payment default in government- or bank-issued bonds, which is analogous to payment default under an investment contract, also appears to be an expropriation claim. Although the mass treaty claims against Argentina for defaulting on its sovereign bond repayments were never decided on the merits because *Abaclat & Ors v Argentine Republic*, ICSID Case No ARB/07/5, Consent Award (Tercier, van den Berg, Bernárdez) (29 December 2016) settled, while proceedings in *Ambiente Ufficio S.p.A. & Ors v Argentine Republic*, ICSID Case No ARB/08/9, Order of Discontinuance of the Proceeding (Simma, Böckstiegel, Bernárdez) (28 May 2015) and *Giovanni Alemanni & Ors v The Argentine Republic*, ICSID Case No ARB/07/8, Order of the Tribunal Discontinuing the Proceeding

Expropriation in international law is traditionally defined as the substantial deprivation of benefit or enjoyment derived from physical property by the state, though modern forms of takings spotlight 'the manner of governmental interference with the contracts on the basis of which the original investment was made'.[68] So when investors bring expropriation claims that are grounded in a breach or termination of contract, the assimilation of contractual rights to property is implied.[69] The recurrence of contract-based expropriation claims is bolstered by two additional factors. One, some investment treaties limit arbitrable disputes to expropriation claims, cutting off other treaty avenues of redress for contractual breaches and terminations.[70] Two, a growing number of investment treaties explicitly require the claimant investor to demonstrate that its injured contractual rights bear property traits, before these rights can form the object of an expropriation claim.[71] Investment treaty arbitration is

(Berman, Böckstiegel, Thomas) (14 December 2015) were discontinued, sovereign bonds can be readily assimilated to contingent property and become an object of expropriation. The same goes for bank bonds as these financial instruments have imputable owners in the form of bondholders, can be separated from their owners and transferred from one bondholder to another, confer an economic benefit on their owners in the form of periodic interest payments on the principal sum invested by the bond issuer, and circulate in contexts where bond repayment is assured by the law applicable to that bond. Bond-based expropriation claims may soon play out on a large scale as disgruntled Credit Suisse bondholders threaten to sue Switzerland for writing off USD 17 billion worth of AT1 bonds after Credit Suisse's state-sponsored takeover by the Union Bank of Switzerland, see Mercedes Reuhl, 'Singapore Bondholders Prepare to Sue Switzerland over Credit Suisse' *Financial Times* (20 April 2023).

[68] Muthucumaraswamy Sornarajah, *The International Law on Foreign Investment* (5th edn, CUP 2021) 463, 465–88.

[69] *Accession Mezzanine Capital L.P. & Anor v Republic of Hungary*, ICSID Case No ARB/12/3, Award (Rovine, Lalonde, Douglas) (17 April 2015) paras 153–57; *Emmis International Holding B.V. & Ors v Republic of* Hungary, ICSID Case No ARB/12/2, Award (McLachlan, Lalonde, Thomas) (16 April 2014) para 164; *Occidental Petroleum Corporation & Anor v Republic of Ecuador*, ICSID Case No ARB/06/11, Award (Fortier, Williams, Stern (dissenting)) (5 October 2012) para 455; *Compañía de Aguas del Aconquija S.A. & Anor v Argentine Republic*, ICSID Case No ARB/97/3, Award (Rowley, Kaufmann-Kohler, Bernal Verea) (20 August 2007) para 7.5.18; *Bayindir Insaat Turzim Ticaret Ve Sanayi AS v Pakistan*, ICSID Case No ARB/03/29, Award (Kaufmann-Kohler, Berman, Böckstiegel) (27 August 2009) para 444; also *Crystallex International Corporation v Bolivarian Republic of Venezuela*, ICSID Case No ARB(AF)/11/2, Award (Lévy, Gotanda, Boisson de Chazournes) (4 April 2016) para 663.

[70] Agreement between the Swiss Confederation and the Hungarian People's Republic on the Reciprocal Promotion and Protection of Investments (signed 5 October 1988, entered into force 16 May 1989) art 10(2)(a). For an example of an even narrower scope of submission to arbitration where only disputes over the amount of compensation granted for expropriation are arbitrable, see Agreement on the Promotion and Protection of Investments (with exchanges of letters) Between China and Singapore (signed 21 November 1985, terminated 16 October 2019) art 13(3) and the first award to interpret art 13(3)—*AsiaPhos Limited & Anor v People's Republic of China*, ICSID Case No ADM/21/1, Award (Sachs, van den Berg, Alexandrov (dissenting)) (16 February 2023) paras 56–89.

[71] Comprehensive and Progressive Agreement for Trans-Pacific Partnership (signed 8 March 2018, entered into force 30 December 2018) (CPTPP) Annex 9-B art 1, which provides: 'An action or a series of actions by a Party cannot constitute an expropriation unless it interferes with a tangible or an intangible property right or property interest in an investment'; Association of Southeast Asian Nations (ASEAN) Comprehensive Investment Agreement (signed 26 February 2009, entered into force 24 February 2012) Annex 2 s 1, which is identical in substance to CPTPP Annex 9-B art 1.

thus highly conducive to the assimilation of contractual rights to property because it represents the only forum to date where individual and corporate investors can bring a treaty claim directly against a host state for expropriating its contractual rights, lending unusual gravitas and publicity to otherwise ordinary contract claims.[72]

To the extent that the assimilation of contractual rights to property secures an avenue for effective redress to injured contractual rights where none previously existed, the corrective function of contingent property is undoubtedly met. However, when 'propertizing' contractual rights is one of several options for redressing contractual breaches, terminations, or interference, then contingent property's corrective function can only be determined in light of the efficaciousness of the other options. This can be seen in the presentation of contract-based expropriation claims in investment treaty arbitration, which tend to take place alongside the presentation of contract-based FET claims and contract-based umbrella clause claims, and their relative rates of success. In an earlier study based on more than two dozen arbitral awards where investors presented both contract-based expropriation and FET claims, I found that claimants were no more likely to prevail on a contract-based FET claim than they were on a contract-based expropriation claim. The data suggests that investors tend to prevail on both claims or fail on both claims.[73] Investors bringing contract-based umbrella clause claims fare no better as most tribunals are reluctant to construe umbrella clauses in a way that elevates every contractual obligation to a treaty commitment, thereby transforming every contractual breach into a treaty breach.[74] Moreover, to eliminate the risk of over-expansive interpretation, states have been phasing out umbrella clauses from newer generation investment treaties,[75] signalling the eventual extinction of contract-based umbrella clause claims. If the prospects of contract-based expropriation claims in investment treaty arbitration are comparable to those of contract-based FET claims, and superior to those of soon-to-be-obsolete contract-based umbrella clause claims, it may be surmised, with cautious

[72] For a more detailed discussion on the distinction between treaty claims and contract claims, see James Crawford, 'Treaty and Contract in Investment Arbitration' (2008) 24(3) Arbitration International 351, 360–70.

[73] Jean Ho, *State Responsibility for Breaches of Investment Contracts* (CUP 2018) 264–68.

[74] ibid 205–14, 270.

[75] A survey of post-2000 model bilateral investment treaties reveals the absence of an umbrella clause, see the 2009 Turkish Model Bilateral Investment Treaty (BIT), the 2014 Serbia Model BIT, the 2016 Indian Model BIT, the 2019 Dutch Model BIT, the 2021 Canadian Model BIT, and the 2022 Italian Model BIT, United Nations Conference on Trade and Development, 'Model Agreements' <https://investmentpolicy.unctad.org/international-investment-agreements/model-agreements> accessed 30 April 2024.

optimism, that contingent property's corrective function is also met for investment contracts.

3.3.2 Judgments on legal claims

Judgments on legal claims record the decision of an authorized adjudicatory body on a submitted dispute, where the respective liabilities of each disputing party, if any, and the amount of monetary compensation or performance of specific acts, if any, payable or owed by one disputing party to another are set out. Judgments on legal claims can take the form of judicial decisions which are subject to appeal unless they emanate from the apex court in a given jurisdiction, or arbitral awards rendered by an arbitral tribunal which are usually final and binding on the parties to the arbitration.[76] Judicial decisions are normally enforced in accordance with the laws of the country where the decision was issued, and exceptionally in accordance with the laws of a foreign country where enforcement is sought. In the latter scenario and in the interest of preserving international comity, most countries enact legislation recognizing and enforcing foreign judicial judgments on legal claims as though these judgments were issued by local courts.[77] Arbitral awards are also enforceable in accordance with the laws of the country where enforcement is sought, but unlike the routine enforcement of judicial decisions, arbitral awards can be set aside or annulled by local courts.[78] An arbitral award requiring the payment of monetary compensation by the losing party holds significant economic value for the winning party. Therefore, when an arbitral award is vacated, especially by the courts of the country where the award was made, the inability of the winning party to monetize the arbitral award is akin to the erasure of an economic right. The winning party is effectively barred from pursuing a right that no longer exists in the eyes of local courts, necessitating a workaround to restore the economic value of the arbitral award. 'Propertizing' arbitral awards represents such a workaround, and the following two illustrations show how arbitral judgments on legal claims can be protected as contingent property.

[76] Finality is a prized feature of arbitral awards, and an important reason for the popularity of arbitration as a mode of dispute settlement. Finality, though, is not absolute, and may be overridden in limited and specified situations, see the Convention on the Recognition and Enforcement of Foreign Arbitral Awards (signed 10 June 1958, entered into force 7 June 1969) (New York Convention) art V and the Convention on the Settlement of Investment Disputes Between States and Nationals of Other States (signed 18 March 1965, entered into force 14 October 1966) art 52.

[77] See for instance the UK Foreign Judgments (Reciprocal Enforcement) Act 1933, ss 1(1), (2), (3); see also Hague Convention on the Recognition and Enforcement of Foreign Judgments in Civil or Commercial Matters (signed 2 July 2019, entered into force 1 September 2023).

[78] New York Convention (n 76), art V.

The first illustration is found in the *Case of Stran Greek Refineries & Anor v Greece*, which was decided by the European Court of Human Rights.[79] An oil concession dispute between Stran Greek and Greece was submitted to arbitration in Greece, where the arbitration court found Greece liable for 70% of the losses suffered by Stran. While an appeal by Greece to vacate the arbitral award was pending before Greece's apex court, the Court of Cassation, the Greek Parliament passed a law terminating all oil concessions previously concluded with the Greek military junta, including Stran Greek's contract, and invalidating all arbitral awards issued pursuant to these terminated concessions.[80] In the aftermath, the Court of Cassation declared the arbitral award void, and the applicants commenced proceedings before the European Commission, alleging, among other things, that their right to property, which is guaranteed under Article 1 of Protocol 1 to the ECHR, was violated.[81] The Commission agreed with the applicants that their right to property had been infringed, and subsequently referred the case to the Court in Strasbourg for a final ruling on whether Greece's setting aside of the arbitral award contravened Article 1 of Protocol 1.[82] Article 1 of Protocol 1 is entitled 'Protection of Property' and provides in part that '[e]very natural or legal person is entitled to the peaceful enjoyment of his possessions'. Before the Court in Strasbourg, the applicants advocated the assimilation of an arbitral judgment on its legal claim to property, arguing that Greece's legislative and judicial acts amounted to a 'de facto deprivation of their possessions because the result was literally to cancel the debt arising out of a final and binding arbitration award'.[83] The Court in Strasbourg agreed, finding the existence of interference with the applicants' property right and a violation of Article 1 of Protocol 1 because Greece made it 'impossible for the applicants to secure enforcement of an arbitration award having final effect and under which the State was required to pay them specified sums'.[84] The Court in Strasbourg proceeded to award the applicants in excess of USD 16 million—the amount which they were owed under the voided arbitral award—plus interest.[85]

[79] Application No 13427/87 (9 December 1994) (*Stran Greek v Greece*). See also *Case of Regent Company v Ukraine*, Application No 773/03 (3 April 2008); *Case of Kin-Stib & Majkić v Serbia*, Application No 12312/05 (20 April 2010).
[80] *Stran Greek v Greece* ibid paras 7–23.
[81] ibid para 27.
[82] ibid paras 1–2.
[83] ibid para 63.
[84] ibid paras 67, 75.
[85] ibid paras 81–83.

The second illustration is found in *Saipem S.p.A. v The People's Republic of Bangladesh*, which was decided by an investment treaty arbitral tribunal.[86] The claimant Saipem submitted a contractual dispute with a state-owned entity, Petrobangla, to an International Chamber of Commerce (ICC) arbitration seated in Dhaka, Bangladesh. Petrobangla objected to the jurisdiction of the arbitral tribunal and successfully applied to the Dhaka courts to revoke the authority of the ICC tribunal to hear the dispute. However, the arbitration went on and the ICC tribunal ruled in favour of Saipem. Petrobangla then successfully applied to the Supreme Court of Bangladesh to set aside the ICC arbitral award, with the apex court holding that the ICC arbitral award was a 'nullity in the eye of the law . . . [and] can neither be set aside nor can it be enforced'.[87] Having exhausted its options before the Bangladeshi courts, Saipem brought an expropriation claim against Bangladesh pursuant to Article 5(1)(2) of the Italy–Bangladesh investment treaty,[88] submitting that the various orders issued by the Bangladeshi judiciary were attributable to Bangladesh and amounted to an unlawful expropriation of Saipem's 'rights to arbitration and under the [ICC] Award'.[89] Notably, Article 5(1)(2) of the Italy–Bangladesh investment treaty protects any 'investment' against unlawful expropriation, while Article 1 of the same treaty defines 'investment' as 'any kind of *property* invested before or after the entry into force of this Agreement . . .' (emphasis added). Saipem was explicit in assimilating its right to payment under the ICC award to property, relying on 'the presently prevailing view pursuant to which any interference with the exercise of property (or "expropriable" rights), however defined, can amount to an expropriation'.[90] The investment treaty tribunal was explicit in its endorsement of the assimilation, and 'considers that the allegedly expropriated property is Saipem's residual contractual rights under the investment

[86] ICSID Case No ARB/05/07, Award (Kaufmann-Kohler, Schreuer, Otton) (30 June 2009) (*Saipem v Bangladesh*). See also *White Industries Australia Limited v The Republic of India*, UNCITRAL, Final Award (Rowley, Brower, Lau) (30 November 2011) para 12.3.6. Although the tribunal here did not find an expropriation of White Industries' ICC award under Article 7(1) of the now defunct Australia–India investment treaty because a decision on award enforcement was still pending before the Indian courts, the tribunal tracked the wording used in the *Saipem v Bangladesh* Award to describe the expropriation of an arbitral award, implying its acceptance that arbitral judgments on legal claims are akin to property.

[87] *Saipem v Bangladesh* ibid para 50.

[88] Agreement Between the Government of the Republic of Italy and the Government of the People's Republic of Bangladesh on the Promotion and Protection of Investments (signed 20 March 1990, entered into force 20 September 1994).

[89] *Saipem v Bangladesh* (n 86) para 84(vi). When the conduct challenged in an investment treaty claim for unlawful expropriation was carried out by a host state's judicial organ, such conduct is also known as judicial expropriation, see generally Chin Leng Lim and others, *International Investment Law and Arbitration—Commentary, Awards and other Materials* (2nd edn, CUP 2021) 423–29.

[90] ibid para 127.

as crystallized in the ICC Award'.[91] The outcome of 'propertizing' the ICC arbitral award to found an expropriation claim under the Italy–Bangladesh investment treaty was the reinstatement of the damages award made by the ICC tribunal in favour of Saipem. The investment treaty tribunal ruled that 'the amount awarded by the ICC award constitutes the best evaluation of the compensation due under the *Chorzów Factory* principle',[92] and ordered Bangladesh to pay Saipem in excess of USD 6 million plus interest.[93]

The strategic decision of the applicants in *Stran Greek v Greece* and of the claimant in *Saipem v Bangladesh* (or their counsel) to assimilate an arbitral award to property, in order to invoke Article 1 of Protocol 1 to the ECHR and Article 5(1)(2) of the Italy–Bangladesh investment treaty respectively, enabled them to revive arbitral awards voided by national courts and to effectively reclaim monetary debts which they were owed. These are instances where the corrective function of contingent property is clearly met. The exclusion of local means of redress pushed these economic rights holders to explore regional or international means of redress, and prompted them to rethink the characterization of their injured rights in order for those rights to fall within the purview of the instrument from which legal protection is sought. In the absence of explicit and unqualified protection for economic rights in general, it is unsurprising that beneficiaries of judgments on legal claims will gravitate towards property as the nearest equivalent and present their claims for payment as property claims. This is because money is one of the most widely accepted vessels of property rights,[94] so much so that a right to money may be readily understood as a right to property. This, along with a possible miscarriage of justice should a prevailing party in a legal claim be manoeuvred out of receiving its just dues, may also explain the apparent lack of resistance on the part of regional courts and international tribunals when presented with contingent property claims. These circumstances establish a reliable avenue for the fruitful redress of judgments on legal claims reframed as contingent property claims.

3.3.3 Digital assets

Digital assets is an extremely broad term that encompasses a wide variety of things such as digital files and records, domain names, email accounts,

[91] ibid para 128.
[92] ibid para 202.
[93] ibid para 216(1).
[94] David Fox, *Property Rights in Money* (OUP 2008) paras 1.73–1.86.

non-fungible tokens (NFTs), in-game digital assets, digital carbon credits, and cryptocurrencies.[95] Certain types of digital assets, like digital files and records of trademarks, copyright, patents, and trade secrets, as well as domain names, email accounts, and NFTs which usually take the form of digital art, are already recognized and regulated as intellectual property. And as there is abundant literature on the advances made in intellectual property protection,[96] there is no need to further 'propertize' intellectual property into contingent property in order to remedy the absence or the inadequacy of legal protection.[97] The focus of this section, therefore, will be on digital assets that are not simultaneously intellectual property. Cryptocurrencies in particular, given their growing popularity as a medium of exchange for goods and services, merit closer scrutiny, since it remains unclear what avenues of legal redress are available to injured cryptocurrency holders, and since largely self-regulating cryptocurrency systems which are 'designed to obscure the claims of strangers to payment transactions, to eliminate the need for adjudication in payment transactions, and to hide the real-world identity of the people behind them are not an easy object for traditional rules of property'.[98]

In a nutshell, cryptocurrencies function as 'electronic cash'.[99] However, unlike fiat currency, payment transactions involving cryptocurrencies are validated by group consensus via a self-contained cryptographic ecosystem, and not financial institutions acting as trusted third parties. Once validated, cryptocurrency transactions are irreversible. Cryptocurrencies are figuratively stored in a software hosted on the user's computer device or that of a third party internet service provider (a so-called wallet), which can only be accessed by a password known to the user (a so-called key).[100] Cryptocurrencies can also

[95] UK Law Commission (n 8) para 1.3.

[96] This is evident in book series and journal titles established by major publishers which are dedicated to issues and laws on intellectual property. See for instance Cambridge University Press' Intellectual Property and Information Law series, Routledge's Research in Intellectual Property series, and Edward Elgar's Intellectual Property Law and Practice series, as well as Oxford University Press' Journal of Intellectual Property Law & Practice, and Sweet & Maxwell's Intellectual Property Quarterly.

[97] Moreover, unlike cultural, common, and contingent property, whose recognition and regulation as new property in international law has been highly uncertain or unsatisfactory, intellectual property is readily recognized and regulated as an established property form in international law. It is therefore beyond the scope of this chapter, and of this monograph which is dedicated to the exploration of three specific categories of new property in international law, to dwell on intellectual property and its various manifestations.

[98] David Fox, 'Cryptocurrencies in the Common Law of Property' in David Fox and Sarah Green (eds), *Cryptocurrencies in Public and Private Law* (OUP 2019) 139, para 6.04.

[99] Satoshi Nakamoto, 'Bitcoin: A Peer-to-Peer Electronic Cash System' <bitcoin.org/bitcoin.pdf> accessed 30 April 2024.

[100] For a more detailed primer, see Kelvin FK Low and Ernie GS Teo, 'Bitcoins and other Cryptocurrencies as Property?' (2017) 9(2) Law, Innovation and Technology 235, 236–42.

be traded on various platforms for monetary value,[101] and this can range from around USD 0.06 for 1 Dogecoin to around USD 28,000 for 1 Bitcoin.[102] The scarcity of cryptocurrencies, some of which are offered in limited quantities in a particular cryptographic ecosystem while others are 'mined' by specially designed computers, their considerable real-world value, and the irreversibility of payment transactions soon made them an attractive target for hackers and embezzlers. Similarly, in-game digital assets and digital carbon credits which can bear immense real-world value,[103] and which are stored and traded electronically, are also susceptible to electronic theft and unauthorized electronic transfer. Existing cryptographic ecosystems and trading platforms neither enable nor enforce the recovery of stolen or wrongfully transferred digital assets, compelling injured digital asset holders to look elsewhere for compensation or satisfaction. The push to 'propertize' digital assets stemmed from the growing need for legal protection for injured asset holders and the relative ease of assimilating digital assets to property. After all, digital assets embody core attributes of contingent property as new property. Digital assets have an imputable owner traceable through transactions made on the host wallet using the host key and respond to factors from their respective ecosystems as proprietary objects of trade, exchange, and fluctuating values. They are separable from their imputable owners by virtue of their ability to be traded away or stolen, and confer a benefit on their imputable owners chiefly in the form of monetary and other gains through trade.[104] It follows that legal protection afforded to traditional property can also be afforded to digital assets as contingent property.[105]

[101] Farran Powell, '10 Best Crypto Apps & Exchanges of 2023' <web.archive.org/web/20231029201503/https://www.forbes.com/advisor/investing/cryptocurrency/best-crypto-exchanges/> accessed 30 April 2024.

[102] Coinranking, 'Cryptocurrencies Prices and Signals' <https://coinranking.com> accessed 30 April 2024.

[103] Elizabeth Howcroft, 'Insight: Crypto and Gaming Collide in High-Risk "Play-to-Earn" Economies' *Reuters* (9 April 2022); Duncan Miriri, 'Hundreds of Millions of Dollars Pledged for African Carbon Credits at Climate Summit' *Reuters* (6 September 2023). In *Koch Industries v Canada* (n 21), the claimants argued that Ontario's abrupt withdrawal from a carbon trading programme amounted to an expropriation of their Ontario-held carbon allowances pursuant to NAFTA art 1110 and valued their loss at over USD 30 million, see Memorial on Jurisdiction and the Merits (6 October 2021) paras 403–45, 489–512.

[104] See Chapter 1, Section 4.

[105] cf Robert Stevens, 'Crypto is Not Property' (2023) 139(Oct) Law Quarterly Review 615 where the author argues vigorously against 'propertizing' cryptocurrency. However, as digital assets, which include cryptocurrency, have imputable owners who possess the right to transfer these digital assets to another, they are clearly more than 'a form of information, admittedly with special factual features given to it by virtue of the system within which it makes sense' (621). Stevens' major concern with 'propertizing' cryptocurrency appears to lie in his conviction that cryptocurrency is not a 'useful' means of exchange (621, 627) and in his disdain for the commercial value attached to cryptocurrency by people partaking in 'the largest pyramid scheme ever yet dreamed up' (618, 621, 627). Personal disinclinations notwithstanding, the fact remains that cryptocurrency is now a medium of exchange, useful or otherwise, and one that possesses considerable commercial value, inflated or otherwise. Lawmakers can certainly

Despite the concern that digital assets, and especially cryptocurrencies, 'are not an easy object for traditional rules of property', current discourse backs the push to 'propertize' digital assets. A number of national courts have simply deemed cryptocurrencies property on which an actionable claim can be brought,[106] while others have found that cryptocurrencies satisfy the prevailing definition of property.[107] Commentators have been likewise encouraging, with one declaring categorically that '[c]ryptocurrencies constitute a form of intangible property',[108] and another opining confidently that 'the conclusion that bitcoins would be recognised as property in the common law was never much in doubt'.[109] In June 2023, the UK Law Commission published a report containing suggestions for legal reform to alleviate the 'legal uncertainty and complexity' brought about by the constantly evolving digital asset market. After considering the approaches taken in multiple jurisdictions towards digital asset regulation,[110] as well as the existing inclination of English courts to regard and regulate digital assets as property,[111] the Law Commission proposed the formal assimilation of digital assets to property if (i) 'it is composed of data represented in an electronic medium, including in the form of computer code, electronic, digital or analogue signals; (ii) it exists independently of persons and exists independently of the legal system; and (iii) it is rivalrous [whereby] the use or consumption of the thing by one person, or a specific group of persons, necessarily prejudices the use or consumption of that thing by one or more other persons'.[112] To ensure that the assimilation is accompanied by an effective proprietary remedy, the Law Commission also recommended the formal extension of the English tort of conversion, historically reserved for tangible property, to 'propertized' digital assets.[113]

choose to discredit 'innovative ways of holding wealth' (615) by excluding them from any form of legal recognition or regulation, but I believe the more evolutionary and progressive approach is to confront and thereby control the uses and abuses of digital assets as new property.

[106] *ByBit Fintech Ltd v Ho Kai Xin & Ors* [2023] SGHC 199 paras 31–36 (*per* Philip Jeyaretnam J).

[107] See for instance *AA v Persons Unknown* [2019] EWHC 3556 (Comm) para 59 (*per* Bryan J).

[108] Andrew Dickinson, 'Cryptocurrencies and the Conflict of Laws' in David Fox and Sarah Green (eds), *Cryptocurrencies in Public and Private Law* (OUP 2019) 93, para 5.97.

[109] Kelvin FK Low, 'Bitcoins as Property: Welcome Clarity?' (2020) 136(Jul) Law Quarterly Review 345, 349.

[110] UK Law Commission (n 8) paras 2.37–2.40 and accompanying footnotes.

[111] ibid paras 2.47–2.54.

[112] ibid para 4.5.

[113] ibid para 9.63. Should this recommendation become reality for the English courts and beyond, it would mean that the common law tort of conversion accommodates the assimilation of digital assets (a sub-genre of economic rights), but not contracts (another sub-genre of economic rights), to property, see *supra* note 8.

Absent the establishment of a legal regime or legal regulations specific to the protection of digital assets, the next best alternative is to leverage on an existing body of law and suite of remedies and adapt them to redress injury to or wrongful interference with digital assets. The assimilation of digital assets to contingent property so that the theft, destruction, or unlawful conversion of digital assets by a wrongdoer can be routinely redressed as the theft, destruction, or unlawful conversion of property belonging to the victim clearly serves a corrective function when the status quo of uncertainty in the viability of a given mode of legal redress can be replaced by certitude in the form and substance of legal redress. Corrective function notwithstanding, the reframing of digital assets as contingent property may also entail, as in the case of the UK, updates to the existing property regulation regime to better accommodate the emergence of contingent property, suggesting a symbiotic relationship between contingent property and any pre-existing property regulation regime. Drawing on select illustrations of contingent property canvassed thus far, the discussion will now briefly consider the adaptive capacity of international law when invoked to govern contingent property.[114]

4. A symbiotic relationship between international law and contingent property?

Contingent property's extreme dependence on the applicable legal context for survival is a hallmark of the relationship between international law as the regulator and contingent property as the regulated. This is evident in how international law can develop to either reinforce contingent property's emerging status as property or renounce contingent property's existing status as property. In other words, while present attempts to assimilate non-property to property can incite changes to existing international law to validate the assimilation, existing international law can also undergo changes that undermine past attempts to assimilate non-property to property, arguably giving rise to a symbiotic relationship between international law and contingent property. Contingent property can make international law, and international law can break contingent property.

One example of contingent property triggering change in international law that consolidates its status as property in the eyes of international law is the

[114] International law's overall adaptive capacity in other specialist fields and towards other categories of new property will be considered in greater detail in Chapter 5, Section 4.

prevalence of expropriation claims which are grounded in injured economic rights and submitted to investment treaty arbitration. Although the assimilation of investment contracts or judgments on legal claims to property has not led to any textual alterations in the applicable governing investment treaties which are a source of international law,[115] the assimilation is repeatedly recognized and upheld in awards rendered by investment treaty arbitral tribunals which are also a source of international law.[116] Over time, despite the absence of a system of binding precedent in investment treaty arbitration, the accretion of arbitral awards endorsing economic rights as contingent property serves as an authoritative point of reference for future claimants seeking to vindicate and future tribunals tasked to adjudicate injured economic rights under investment treaties.[117] Even if the applicable governing investment treaty does not expressly provide that contracts and judgments on legal claims can be defended as property via an expropriation claim, the weight of arbitral authority supports a permissive interpretation of the relevant treaty provisions that imparts legitimacy and normality to contingent property.

One example of international law changing to undermine and eventually eradicate the assimilation of non-property to property is the gradual outlawing of slavery where humans were deemed property. If slavery has been the rule for much of human history,[118] then international law has at the very least, and over an extended period of time, acquiesced in the characterization of slaves as contingent property. Hardening attitudes towards the morality of slavery and an uptick in anti-slavery sentiments in the nineteenth century disturbed that acquiescence. The UK has been credited with spearheading the international abolition of slavery, by concluding a series of bilateral maritime treaties granting states parties the right to search each other's vessels with a view to collectively suppressing trade in enslaved Africans.[119] The extinction of the African slave trade towards the end of the nineteenth century then paved

[115] Statute of the International Court of Justice art 38(1)(a).

[116] Ho (n 73) 63–72.

[117] ibid 79–88.

[118] *The Cambridge World History of Slavery* spans four volumes and covers the entire period from the Ancient Mediterranean World (vol 1) to AD 2016 (vol 4) (CUP, 2011, 2021, 2011, 2017). The publisher's introduction of the compendium describes slavery as 'among the most ubiquitous of all human institutions, across time and place, from earliest history until, some would argue, the present day'.

[119] Jean Allain, 'The Nineteenth Century Law of the Sea and the British Abolition of the Slave Trade' (2007) 78(1) British Yearbook of International Law 342, 357–76. For critical reflections on triumphant narratives that honour Euro-centric visions of international law in ending slavery, see Christopher Gevers, 'Refiguring Slavery Through International Law: The 1926 Slavery Convention, the "Native Labor Code" and Racial Capitalism' (2022) 25(2) Journal of International Economic Law 312, 316–24; and Christopher Gevers, 'Slavery and International Law' (2023) 117 American Journal of International Law Unbound 71, 71–76.

the way for multilateral efforts to abolish slavery and the slave trade worldwide, the most well-known being the historic Slavery Convention of 1926.[120] The widely ratified Slavery Convention defines slavery as 'the status or condition of a person over whom any or all of the powers attaching to the right of ownership are exercised',[121] and obliges states parties to 'bring about, progressively and as soon as possible, the complete abolition of slavery in all its forms'.[122] The Slavery Convention's depiction of a slave through the lens of ownership, which is paradigmatic for property, and its call for the abolition of slavery undermines the assimilation of human slaves to property, signalling the eventual eradication of the continued existence of slaves as contingent property.

The different ways in which the observably symbiotic relationship between international law and contingent property has unfolded permits tentative forecasts on the relative strength and weakness of international law's adaptive capacity vis-à-vis emerging contingent property that has not been subject to serious international dispute and adjudication. Claimants seeking redress for 'propertized' digital assets are likelier to encounter an international law with stronger adaptive capacity for contingent property because digital contingent property has already gained legal traction nationally,[123] and because international law is already accustomed to awarding redress to other forms of injured 'propertized' economic rights such as terminated contracts and voided judgments on legal claims. Conferring greater international legal protection on digital assets as contingent property becomes a swift and natural extension of a familiar practice, rather than a novel and radical endeavour. In contrast, claimants seeking redress for 'propertized' soft law human rights are likelier to encounter an international law with weaker adaptive capacity for contingent property because the hard-won battle to outlaw human property may breed suspicion towards seemingly regressive attempts to 'propertize' manifestations of human dignity such as the right to water. Moreover, the formal recognition of 'propertized' soft law human rights may present the risk of

[120] Convention to Suppress the Slave Trade and Slavery (signed 25 September 1926, entered into force 9 March 1927) 60 LNTS 254 (Slavery Convention); Protocol amending the Slavery Convention (signed 7 December 1953, entered into force 7 December 1953) 182 UNTS 51; see also Supplementary Convention on the Abolition of Slavery, the Slave Trade, and Institutions and Practices Similar to Slavery (signed 7 September 1956, entered into force 30 April 1957). The impact of the Slavery Convention continued to be felt decades later. For example, art 7(2)(c) of the Rome Statute of the International Criminal Court (signed 17 July 1998, entered into force 1 July 2002) 2187 UNTS 3 draws on the Slavery Convention to define 'enslavement' as 'the exercise of any or all of the powers attaching to the right of ownership over a person'.

[121] Slavery Convention art 1(1).

[122] ibid art 2(b).

[123] cf *Apotex v US* Award (n 21) para 7.55; *Koch Industries v Canada* Counter-Memorial on Jurisdiction and the Merits (n 21) paras 137–51.

commodification, where human rights can be voluntarily relinquished or traded for a price, begetting a commercial market for the sale and purchase of human dignity. Conferring greater international legal protection on soft law human rights as contingent property invites greater circumspection because it risks reviving the ghosts of slavery past by reducing human rights to their current market value.

5. Conclusion

Contingent property captivates because it embodies unpredictability. Whether attempts to assimilate non-property to property will encounter lasting, temporary, or doubtful success depends almost entirely on the relevant context, which is always susceptible to change. This context-driven unpredictability has important implications for the development of regulatory content in international law, as can be seen from past, present, and prospective examples of contingent property.

Past examples of contingent property include jurisdictional rights and slaves, and international law's regulatory content has developed to reflect the demise of jurisdictional rights and of slaves as contingent property. In the case of jurisdictional rights, the current default position in international law is the exclusive empowerment of adjudicatory bodies with state-delegated authority to rule on the scope of the exercise of their jurisdictional rights as jurisdictional rights. Any revenue arising from the exercise of jurisdictional rights accrues to the state or the authorized adjudicatory body and cannot be subjected to competing claims by unauthorized entities. Absent any contemporary rationale or room for 'propertizing' jurisdictional rights, international law's regulatory content focuses on jurisdictional rights as a dimension of adjudicatory power, and has nothing to say on jurisdictional rights as contingent property. In the case of the institution of slavery, which was progressively abolished in the wake of the Slavery Convention, international law's content pertaining to slaves and slavery is better described as prohibitive and eradicative, rather than regulatory. Similarly to jurisdictional rights, international law did not develop any regulatory content for slaves as contingent property because the worldwide abolition of slavery meant that it was no longer permissible under international law to be a slave or a slave-holder, let alone 'propertize' slaves.

Present examples of contingent property include investment contracts and judgments on legal claims, which have triggered the development of international law's regulatory content pertaining to these sub-genres of economic rights as contingent property. The regulation of 'propertized' investment contracts via unlawful expropriation claims submitted to investment treaty arbitration, and of 'propertized' arbitral awards via unlawful expropriation claims submitted to both the European Court of Human Rights and to investment treaty arbitration, has generated a substantial body of arbitral and judicial case-law analysing the propriety of the assimilation to property, as well as providing points of references for successful or unsuccessful contract-based or judgment-based unlawful expropriation claims. The durability of contracts and judgments on legal claims as contingent property in international law may be foreseen in the ongoing development of regulatory content on these forms of contingent property that, at least in the case of investment treaty arbitration, occur even outside the bounds of a strict, textual treaty mandate. Even in a world without investment treaties, which surely constitutes a fundamentally changed context, the presence of past arbitral *jurisprudence* endorsing investment contracts and arbitral awards as property which forms part of the corpus of international law arguably ensures that contract-based and judgment-based unlawful expropriation claims remain valid causes of action.

Prospective examples of contingent property include soft law human rights and digital assets. Protection of the former will severely test international law's adaptive capacity to develop regulatory content to provide effective redress for injured rights, while protection of the latter is more likely to tap into international law's existing regulatory content on investment contracts and arbitral awards as contingent property. While compelling justifications for the 'propertization' of soft law human rights, such as offering victims actual redress over aspirational rhetoric, exist, genuine reservations towards the commodification and monetization of human dignity obstruct the push to 'propertize' and breed inertia when it comes to invoking international law to redress 'propertized' human rights. The hanging of the status of soft law human rights as contingent property in a state of limbo should not discourage the believers in contingent property. Rather, it serves as a testament to the diverse ways in which contingent property comes to be, ceases to be, and is ultimately a creature of context. Having zeroed in on the respective regulatory regimes of contingent property, common property, and cultural property in this and the preceding two chapters, I now zoom out to consider, in the fifth and final substantive chapter of this monograph, international law's broader response to new property interference.

5

The Regulation of Actors and Actions Affecting New Property

1. Introduction

New property introduces a new cast of actors engaging in new forms of property interference. Newness, as the preceding three chapters depicting cultural, common, and contingent property have shown, does not only signify never-before-seen phenomena. Rather, newness can also signify novel perspectives on an existing state of affairs. In the same way that traditional cultural expressions, orbital pathways, and investment contracts existed prior to their

New Property in International Law. Jean Ho, Oxford University Press. © Jean Ho 2024.
DOI: 10.1093/9780191976117.003.0006

respective assimilation to cultural property,[1] common property,[2] and contingent property in this monograph,[3] the various actors and actions affecting new property are known and documented. However, the presence of actors and actions which interfere with new property without incurring consequences prompt reflection on international law's regulatory ambit, auguring its possible expansion to accommodate new subjects of regulation. International law at present only sanctions two configurations of property interference. The first is the uncompensated taking of a foreigner's property by a host state which founds a claim before an international arbitral tribunal for unlawful expropriation. The second is the destruction of property during armed conflict by an individual which founds a prosecution before the International Criminal Court for the commission of a war crime. The adequacy of this limited regulatory ambit is by no means self-evident because property interference is neither the sole province of states or individuals engaged in armed conflict, nor is it confined to takings and the destruction of property. The illicit acquisition of cultural property by individuals during peacetime, the unsustainable exploitation of common property by state-backed commercial entities, and the monopolization of contingent property in arms-for-concessions deals negotiated by private military and security companies (PMSCs) in resource-rich strife-riven zones announce a neglected cast of property-interfering actors undertaking an overlooked range of property-interfering actions. With new property here to stay, accounting for its actors and redressing their actions become indispensable to the relevance of international law to new property.

This chapter investigates the adequacy of existing procedural and substantive redress in international law with respect to actors and actions affecting new property. It also posits that the outlook for new property regulation can only be assessed in light of any articulated shortcomings besetting the status quo. To this end, Section 2 identifies six configurations of sanctionable new property interference, featuring new property-interfering actors undertaking new property-interfering actions. Building on these configurations, Section 3 demonstrates how international law lags behind the rise of new property and its personalities by failing to provide satisfactory procedural and substantive redress for interference. Procedural redress is hampered by stringent conditions attached to the jurisdictional authority of international courts and tribunals, as well as overlapping jurisdictions across different dispute settlement

[1] See Chapter 2, Section 4.1.
[2] See Chapter 3, Section 3.1.2.
[3] See Chapter 4, Section 3.3.1.

bodies. Substantive redress is hampered by the availability of only state-centric or individual-centric remedies for property interference in narrowly defined settings. Drawing together the dawn of new problems presented in Section 2, and the current obstacles to redress reviewed in Section 3, Section 4 considers the propriety of viewing international law as a complex adaptive system capable of self-correction, and the factors that inform the promise of self-correction. Section 5 concludes.

2. Six configurations of new property interference

Apart from a claim for the unlawful taking of property against a host state by a foreign investor under general international law,[4] or pursuant to an applicable investment treaty,[5] and a prosecution for the war crime of property destruction against an individual pursuant to the Rome Statute of the International Criminal Court,[6] there are at least *six* other sanctionable configurations arising from new property interference. These additional configurations, all of which involve violations of international obligations, are not currently sanctioned by international law. This section outlines the six configurations of new property interference that appear to fall outside the regulatory ambit of international law. The first and second configurations reflect stealth dealings in cultural property (Section 2.1), where individual traders and art collectors sustain demand for smuggled art and antiquities (Configuration 1), and where states are occasionally complicit in the cultural heist (Configuration 2). The third and fourth configurations capture the unsustainable use of common property (Section 2.2), namely, the depletion of fish stocks in the High Seas by corporate fishers (Configuration 3), and the endangering of whale stocks by corporate whalers in the Antarctic (Configuration 4). The fifth and sixth configurations involve the use of force to edge out competition for contingent property (Section 2.3), in the way that trading companies once secured exclusive trade routes with gunboats (Configuration 5), and in the way that PMSCs today offer military expertise in exchange for exclusive mining contracts (Configuration 6).

[4] *SPP (Middle East) Limited & Anor v Arab Republic of Egypt & Anor*, ICC Arbitration No YD/AS/3493, Award (Bernini, Elghatit (dissenting), Littman) (11 March 1983) para 49.

[5] Jean Ho, *State Responsibility for Breaches of Investment Contracts* (CUP 2018) 157–68.

[6] (signed 17 July 1998, entered into force 1 July 2002) (Rome Statute) arts 8(2)(a)(iv), 8(2)(b)(xiii), 8(2)(e)(iv), 8(2)(e)(xii); see *The Prosecutor v Ahmad Al Faqi Al Mahdi*, ICC-01/12-01/15-171, Trial Chamber VIII, Judgment and Sentence (27 September 2016) paras 14–16, 42–48, 72, 77, where the court read cultural property destruction into art 8(2)(e)(iv) which does not specifically mention cultural property.

2.1 Illicit transactions in cultural property

Trafficking in cultural property occurs during periods of armed conflict and during peacetime. The 1970 Convention on the Means of Prohibiting and Preventing the Illicit Import, Export and Transfer of Ownership of Cultural Property[7] expressly forbids trafficking in cultural property. Article 3 provides:

> The import, export or transfer of ownership of cultural property effected contrary to the provisions adopted under this Convention by the States Parties thereto, shall be illicit.

The 1970 UNESCO Convention then proceeds to articulate a host of undertakings for states parties such as the obligation to 'prohibit the exportation of cultural property from their territory unless accompanied by [an] export certificate' (Article 6(b)), and the obligations to 'prohibit the import of cultural property stolen from a museum or religious or secular public monument or similar institution in another state party' (Article 7(b)(i)) and to 'recover and return any such cultural property imported' (Article 7(b)(ii)). Notably, the 1970 UNESCO Convention recognizes that the international obligations set out in Articles 6 and 7 may also be violated by individuals and non-state party entities. Article 8 empowers states parties to 'impose penalties or administrative sanctions on *any person responsible for infringing the prohibitions referred to under Articles 6(b) and 7(b)* above'.[8]

The fact that persons, not just states, are capable of violating obligations set out in the 1970 UNESCO Convention, and the fact that states parties are tasked with sanctioning these violations, have produced two anomalies. The first is the ability of private entities to violate international law without being sanctioned by international law. The turn to domestic law to indict the private trafficking of art and antiquities, as the following discussion will reveal, yields sub-optimal outcomes for the regulation of new property (Section 2.1.1). The second is a focus on individual indictments when illicit transactions involving art and antiquities are more often than not the result of collective effort involving reckless individuals and complicit exporting and importing states or state authorities. In a classic case of missing the wood for the trees, collective responsibility for trafficking art and antiquities lurks

[7] (signed 14 November 1970, entered into force 24 April 1972) 823 UNTS 231 (1970 UNESCO Convention).

[8] ibid art 8 (emphasis added).

behind individual defendants, lying just beyond international law's reach (Section 2.1.2).

2.1.1 Configuration 1 (private trafficking of art and antiquities)

The ability of individuals to falsify the provenance of cultural property, and the oversight of auction houses when verifying the declared provenance of cultural property consigned for resale, renders the legitimacy of every transaction involving the sale and purchase of cultural property uncertain. As the Kingsbury Case demonstrates, trafficked cultural property typically comes to light at the initiative of eagle-eyed whistle-blowing art and antiquities experts, suggesting rampancy in the unnoticed and unpunished trafficking of cultural property, their subsequent disappearance into private collections, and their provenance further obscured by anonymized transfers of private ownership. Despite the stern prohibition against the unlicensed 'import, export or transfer of ownership of cultural property' in the 1970 UNESCO Convention, the result of relying on domestic laws to sanction and deter individuals from trafficking art and antiquities has not been encouraging.

Neil Kingsbury was an English purveyor of ancient Egyptian artefacts, having successfully auctioned five pieces at Bonham's and another eight pieces at Christie's in the United Kingdom.[9] On his third outing, he consigned six pieces to Christie's, which were then scheduled for Christie's London antiquities sale on 2 May 2013. One of the six pieces featured in the Christie's catalogue was a red granite relief fragment depicting a Nubian captive that was discovered in the Mortuary Temple of Amenhotep III during excavation expeditions conducted by the Egyptian government in the early 2000s. A curator at the British Museum spotted the Nubian fragment in the catalogue and checked with a colleague in Egypt, who confirmed that the fragment had been stolen from a storage depot. When notified, Christie's withdrew all six items consigned by Kingsbury from its antiquities sale and called the police, who arrested Kingsbury on charges of fraudulent misrepresentation and possession of stolen property. The charges of fraudulent misrepresentation covered items previously auctioned off at Bonham's and at Christie's. Kingsbury previously told Christie's that he'd inherited the items from his uncle who lived in Egypt in the 1940s. The auction house accepted his account unequivocally as it marked the provenance of the six consigned artefacts in the catalogue as 'Private collection, UK, acquired Egypt 1940s; thence by descent'.[10] When pleading

[9] Martin Bailey and Melanie Gerlis, 'Guilty Plea over Antiquities' *The Art Newspaper* (5 September 2013).
[10] ibid.

guilty to most of the charges levelled against him at Uxbridge magistrate's court, Kingsbury claimed that he'd bought the consigned items from a souvenir shop in Egypt. Museum specialists believed that the other items consigned by Kingsbury could have been pilfered, like the Nubian fragment, from the storage depot in Egypt. For his part in trafficking cultural property, the court ordered Kingsbury to pay a nominal GBP 500 fine, and GBP 50 in court costs.[11] And for their part in selling trafficked cultural property, neither auction house was required to trace and recover the allegedly stolen cultural property. Ironically, the spokespersons for both auction houses, in the aftermath of the Kingsbury Case, took the opportunity to reiterate their commitment to verifying the provenance of every item they sell, as well as their intolerance for illicit trade in trafficked art and antiquities.[12]

Although Kingsbury was charged, convicted, and fined for his misdeeds, the Kingsbury Case is representative of how private trafficking in art and antiquities, despite being a clear violation of international law,[13] owes its survival to a severe regulatory deficit. The deficit manifests in three ways. First, a charge and subsequent conviction for fraudulent misrepresentation or possession of stolen property under domestic law downgrades the severity of private trafficking in cultural property. The former do not amount to violations of international law, while the latter does, and the reframing of cultural property trafficking as an ordinary domestic white-collar crime of dishonesty strips cultural property of any special status conferred by international conventions and undermines international calls for better cultural property protection and regulation. Second, the distorting effect of watered down charges and consequences neutralizes any anticipated deterrence in the private trafficking of cultural property. From the theft, to the unlicensed exportation and importation, and to the eventual receipt by a dealer in antiquities such as Kingsbury, trafficked cultural property crosses national borders and passes through the hands of a myriad of individuals before making its way to its final destination. And yet, when only one individual in a cast of many is identified, charged, and given a slap on the wrist for his role in trafficking cultural property, other traffickers in the supply chain are unlikely to be deterred from their illicit activities, and art and antiquities collectors are unlikely to be deterred in their demand for

[11] Neil Brodie, 'Egyptian Objects sold at Bonhams and Christie's London in 2013' (6 November 2015) <https://traffickingculture.org/encyclopedia/case-studies/Egyptian-objects-sold-at-bonhams-and-christies-london-in-2013/> accessed 30 April 2024. The United Kingdom is not a party to the 1970 UNESCO Convention.

[12] Bailey and Gerlis (n 9).

[13] 1970 UNESCO Convention (n 7) arts 3, 6–8.

cultural property, trafficked or otherwise. Third, domestic regulation, however unsatisfactory, is only activated when there is a whistle-blower report of suspected trafficked cultural property. With auction houses being less than meticulous in their provenance checks, counting on art and antiquities specialists to raise timely alerts turns already deficient cultural property regulation into a lottery. The situation is exacerbated by the inability of source countries of much trafficked cultural property, like Egypt, to photograph and document every artefact that is excavated and kept in storage, due to the prohibitive cost of doing so.[14] Absent images and descriptions of art and antiquities earmarked for conservation and circulated worldwide, even the most astute antiquities specialist will struggle to spot trafficked cultural property listed for sale in an auction catalogue. This severe regulatory deficit persists even when states, as traditional subjects of international law, enter the picture, as the next configuration of new property interference shows.

2.1.2 Configuration 2 (public-private trafficking of art and antiquities)

Politically unstable source states are often the weak link in the supply chain of cultural property, enabling looters to export cultural property to dealers abroad who then broker illicit transactions with 'extraordinarily wealthy individuals willing to take advantage of the chaos and desperation created by war to acquire great art and antiquities'.[15] These source states may facilitate the unlicensed export of cultural property by inadvertence, such as when it lacks the resources to track every item of cultural property in its possession, or by design. The latter scenario, where source states appear cavalier about cultural property, may seem improbable, but the Kanakaria Case demonstrates how even source states can be complicit in the trafficking of cultural property.

The Kanakaria Church is located in Northern Cyprus and housed a quartet of mosaics created in 530 AD. These mosaics depict a young Jesus sitting with his mother Mary on a throne, flanked by two archangels and framed by the busts of the twelve apostles. They are one of a handful of Byzantine mosaics to survive today. When Turkey invaded Cyprus in 1974 on the heels of a conflict between Greek and Turkish Cypriots, the Turkish occupying forces took control of Northern Cyprus including the Greek Orthodox Kanakaria Church, and established the Turkish Republic of Northern Cyprus (TRNC).

[14] United Nations Office on Drugs and Crime, 'Case Kingsbury' <https://sherloc.unodc.org/cld/case-law-doc/traffickingculturalpropertycrimetype/gbr/2013/case_kingsbury.html> accessed 30 April 2024.

[15] Mary Ellen O'Connell, 'Beyond Wealth: Stories of Art, War and Greed' (2008) 59(4) Alabama Law Review 1075, 1103.

Over the next decade, Turkey deliberately turned a blind eye to the large-scale looting of Greek Orthodox churches in Northern Cyprus,[16] condoning the public-private trafficking of cultural property. It was during this time that the Kanakaria Church's ancient mosaics were forcibly removed from the apse of the church, its specific whereabouts unknown. The mosaics resurfaced in Geneva in 1988 where they were shown by a Munich-based Turkish antiquities dealer (and a known art thief) to Peg Goldberg, an Indiana-based art gallery owner. Goldberg purchased the mosaics for USD 1.08 million, shipped them back to Indiana, and attempted to sell them to the Getty Museum in Los Angeles for a large profit. However, the museum's curator informed the Republic of Cyprus of Goldberg's offer and Cyprus asked Goldberg to return the mosaics. Goldberg refused. Cyprus then brought an action for wrongful possession against Goldberg in the United States District Court of the Southern District of Indiana, claiming the return of the mosaics to its rightful owner—the Kanakaria Church.[17] Surprisingly, given its indifference to the fate of the mosaics in the first place, the TRNC filed a motion to intervene as Plaintiff in the Kanakaria Case.[18] The motion was denied mainly on the basis that only Turkey recognized the TRNC as the legitimate government of Northern Cyprus.[19] The court applied Indiana law to the dispute and found that the Kanakaria Church had good title to the mosaics, that the mosaics were unlawfully removed from the Kanakaria Church, and that Goldberg was in wrongful possession of stolen cultural property.[20] The court ordered Goldberg to return the mosaics to Cyprus and this decision was affirmed on appeal.[21]

With the spotlight on Goldberg since she was in physical possession of the mosaics and therefore the only person who could return them to Cyprus, Turkey's role in the Kanakaria Case and its likely violation of the 1970 UNESCO Convention has escaped scrutiny. At first glance, the refusal of other states to recognize the TRNC as the legitimate governing authority of Northern Cyprus appears to exempt Turkey from any international obligation pertaining to cultural property located in Northern Cyprus. After all, the Republic of Cyprus is, in the eyes of other states, the legitimate governing authority of the whole of Cyprus. However, Northern Cyprus remains under

[16] Judith Miller and Stephen Kinzer, 'Greek Orthodox Church Icons Ravaged in the Turkish Part of Cyprus' *The New York Times* (1 April 1998).

[17] *The Republic of Cyprus & Anor v Peg Goldberg & Anor*, 717 F.Supp 1374 (1989) (*Cyprus v Goldberg 1989*).

[18] ibid 1377.

[19] William G Pearlstein, 'Claims for the Repatriation of Cultural Property: Prospects for a Managed Antiquities Market' (1996) 28(1) Law and Policy in International Business 123, 138.

[20] *Cyprus v Goldberg 1989* (n 17) 1397–1400.

[21] *The Republic of Cyprus & Anor v Peg Goldberg & Anor*, 917 F.2d 278 (7th Cir. 1990).

Turkish control. Moreover, having ratified the 1970 UNESCO Convention in 1981, well before the mosaics were shown to Goldberg in 1988, and since it clearly regards Northern Cyprus as its *territory*, it is at least arguable that Turkey has failed to 'prohibit the exportation of cultural property from [its] *territory* unless accompanied by the above-mentioned export certificate'.[22] If Goldberg and her shady associates can violate international law without being sanctioned,[23] if the Republic of Cyprus is undeserving of sanction by international law because it alerted UNESCO to the theft of the mosaics at first opportunity,[24] and if Turkey avoids sanction by international law because Northern Cyprus cannot be considered its territory, then contemporary manifestations of public-private trafficking of cultural property clearly fall outside the regulatory ambit of international law.

2.2 Unsustainable harvesting of common property

As observed in Chapter 3, existing treaties and instruments purporting to regulate common property oblige states parties, and, by extension, their nationals, to harvest common property in a sustainable manner.[25] When it comes to fishing in the High Seas, Article 117 of the United Nations Convention on the Law of the Sea provides:[26]

> All States have the duty to take, or to cooperate with other States in taking, such measures for their respective nationals as may be necessary for the conservation of the living resources of the high seas.

When it comes to catches of marine living resources in Antarctica, Article II(3)(a) of the Convention on the Conservation of Antarctic Marine Living Resources provides:[27]

> Any harvesting and associated activities in the area to which this Convention applies shall be conducted in accordance with the provisions of this Convention and with the following principles of conservation:

[22] 1970 UNESCO Convention (n 7) art 6(b) (emphasis added).
[23] cf O'Connell (n 15) 1081–88.
[24] *Cyprus v Goldberg 1989* (n 17) 1380.
[25] See Chapter 3, Sections 3.1.1 and 3.2.
[26] (signed 10 December 1982, entered into force 16 November 1994) 1833 UNTS 397 (UNCLOS).
[27] (signed 1 August 1980, entered into force 7 April 1982) 1329 UNTS 47 (CCAMLR).

(a) prevention of decrease in the size of any harvested population to levels below those which ensure its stable recruitment. For this purpose its size should not be allowed to fall below a level close to that which ensures the greatest net annual increment[.]

And when it comes to the overall conservation of the common marine environment, the recently concluded Agreement under the United Nations Convention on the Law of the Sea on the Conservation and Sustainable Use of Marine Biological Diversity of Areas Beyond National Jurisdiction[28] introduced mandatory environmental impact assessments. Article 28(1) provides:

> Parties shall ensure that the potential impacts on the marine environment of planned activities under their jurisdiction or control that take place in areas beyond national jurisdiction are assessed as set out in this Part before they are authorized.

While sustainable harvesting obligations are primarily directed at states, the duty of states to implement conservation measures 'for their respective nationals' (UNCLOS Article 117) and to scrutinize 'planned activities under their jurisdiction or control' (BBNJ Agreement Article 28(1)) serves as a constant reminder that the entities engaging in unsustainable harvesting of common property are rarely states, but their nationals. It follows that non-state entities are more than capable of violating international sustainability obligations and have in fact been doing so for years when harvesting common property. Overfishing in the High Seas (Section 2.2.1) and over-whaling in Antarctica (Section 2.2.2), to which the discussion now turns, demonstrate the unsettling trend of corporate fisheries violating international law without being sanctioned by their home states, let alone international law.

2.2.1 Configuration 3 (overt corporate overfishing in the High Seas)

Fish in the High Seas are harvested by hundreds of corporate fisheries, with the leading corporate fisheries bearing Chinese, Spanish, Japanese, and South Korean nationalities.[29] Despite all of these countries being parties to UNCLOS,[30] and three out of four being parties to the BBNJ Agreement,[31] the

[28] (signed 19 June 2023, not yet in force) (BBNJ Agreement).
[29] Sarah Gibbens, 'Can the Ocean Feed a Growing World?' *National Geographic* (15 August 2018).
[30] UNCLOS signatories <https://treaties.un.org/pages/ViewDetailsIII.aspx?src=TREATY&mtdsg_no=XXI-6&chapter=21&Temp=mtdsg3&clang=_en> accessed 30 April 2024.
[31] Japan is not a signatory to the BBNJ Agreement, see United Nations Treaty Collection, '10. Agreement Under the United Nations Convention on the Law of the Sea on the Conservation and

High Seas suffer from overfishing. This is attributable to a number of reasons. First, states parties to UNCLOS do not appear to have implemented conservationist measures, whether unilaterally, or in cooperation with other states, which are binding on their corporate nationals who fish in the High Seas. Second, the practice of states paying lip service to the sustainable harvesting of common property appears to have rubbed off onto their corporate nationals, who see fit to adopt sustainability-oriented corporate slogans while simultaneously failing to report or under-reporting their catch volumes and species to the relevant authorities.[32] Third, the absence of any best fishing practices guidelines and accountability mechanism, domestically or internationally, to reinforce such guidelines enables errant corporate fisheries to persist with destructive fishing methods, such as trawling, with impunity.[33] Of course, there are environmentally conscious corporations which voluntarily strive for sustainable fishing in accordance with standards established by international non-governmental organizations like the World Sustainability Organization,[34] but there are many more that prioritize immediate gains over conservation. Fourth, consumer awareness and preference for sustainably harvested fish may steer corporate fisheries to practise sustainable fishing, but consumer demand may just as likely be influenced by corporate premium pricing of fish caught in open waters, sustainably or otherwise.[35] Fifth, far from being chastised for overfishing in the High Seas, corporate fisheries are receiving state subsidies to carry on, all in the name of food security for national populations.[36] Overt corporate domination of industrial fishing in the High Seas, emboldened by state support or at the very least state acquiescence, has resulted in the overfishing or depletion of more than three-quarters of forty-eight different fish stocks.[37]

Sustainable Use of Marine Biological Diversity of Areas beyond National Jurisdiction, New York, 19 June 2023' <https://treaties.un.org/Pages/ViewDetails.aspx?src=TREATY&mtdsg_no=XXI-10&chapter=21&clang=_en> accessed 30 April 2024.

[32] See Chapter 3, Section 3.2.

[33] See Chapter 3, Section 3.2.

[34] One such non-profit standard-setter is Friend of the Sea, which represents 'the leading certification standard for products and services which respect and protect the marine environment', and operates as a 'project of the World Sustainability Organization', see World Sustainability Organization, 'Friend of the Sea—Certification for Sustainable Seafood, Fisheries and Aquaculture Products' <https://friendofthesea.org/friend-of-the-sea/> accessed 30 April 2024.

[35] Jocelyn Tan, 'Chefs Explain: Why the Elusive Turbot Fish is Worth Its Hefty Price Tag' *Lifestyle Asia* (10 November 2021).

[36] Sarah Gibbens, 'High Seas Fishing Isn't Just Destructive—It's Unprofitable' *National Geographic* (7 June 2018).

[37] Gabrielle Carmine and others, 'Who is the High Seas Fishing Industry?' (2020) 3 One Earth 730, 730.

The sustainable use of common natural resources, such as fish stocks in the High Seas, is arguably more critical than the sustainable use of natural resources subject to the sovereignty of one state, because common natural resources are supposed to be shared among and for the mutual benefit of all states and their peoples for generations to come. However, rampant and ongoing corporate overfishing of the High Seas shows disregard by corporations, and even states, for the common good. I argued in Chapter 3 that states have exhibited a tendency to treat common property as their own property, leveraging on any competitive edge to exploit the former as and how they see fit.[38] For Schrijver, this approach towards common property begs the question 'if the national and international resource regimes are therefore in competition: [does] the common heritage of mankind regime . . . only start where the permanent sovereignty over natural resources regimes ends'?[39] When states are minded, consciously or subconsciously, to let a sense of sovereign entitlement over common property eclipse an open commitment to share, the sustainable harvesting of common property commands limited attention because so little property is actually treated by states as common. States are unlikely to reign in their corporate nationals from overfishing in the High Seas, or establish accountability regimes that penalize states for failure to supervise and corporations for failure to act sustainably, when the High Seas is common property in word but not in deed. Corporate fisheries, which are profit- rather than policy-driven, are even less likely to desist from overfishing in the High Seas. Not only can they flout international conservation obligations without consequence under international law or domestic law, but they are also being incentivized via subsidies by their home states to continue overfishing.

2.2.2 Configuration 4 (covert corporate over-whaling in Antarctica)

Commercial whaling has been banned since 1986 by the International Convention for the Regulation of Whaling,[40] subject to one exception where states parties 'grant to any of its nationals a special permit authorizing that national to kill, take and treat whales for purposes of scientific research'.[41] The qualified ban, along with a large number of states parties supporting the ban, appears to park the matter of commercial whaling squarely within the regulatory ambit of international law. First impressions can be falsely assuring.

[38] See Chapter 3, Section 2.
[39] Nico Schrijver, *Sovereignty Over Natural Resources—Balancing Rights and Duties* (CUP 1997) 229.
[40] (signed 3 December 1946, entered into force 10 November 1948) 161 UNTS 72 (Whaling Convention) Schedule paras 6, 7, 10(e).
[41] ibid art VIII(1).

As treaty provisions are only binding on states parties who consent to be so bound,[42] it is possible for a state party to formulate a reservation to the treaty, which may modify the reserving state's obligations under that treaty.[43] That said, reservations which are 'incompatible with the object and purpose of the treaty' are invalid.[44] A number of states parties with whaling industries, like Japan, lodged objections to the ban in the Whaling Convention, even though such an objection is potentially 'incompatible with the object and purpose of the treaty', which recalls 'the history of whaling [having] seen over-fishing of . . . one species of whale after another to such a degree that it is essential to protect all species of whales from further over-fishing'.[45] Be that as it may, Japan's objection, which pertains specifically to minke whale stocks in Antarctica and which has never been withdrawn, appears to exempt Japan and its nationals from the ban.[46] And even if the validity of outright exemption is doubtful, there remains the possibility of capturing whales 'for purposes of scientific research'. Whether Japanese corporate whalers operating in the Antarctic were capturing minke whales 'for purposes of scientific research' was put to the test when Japan was sued by Australia before the International Court of Justice (ICJ) for allegedly violating the Whaling Convention.

In *Whaling in the Antarctic*,[47] Australia contended that Japan's issuance of special permits to its corporate nationals to hunt minke whales in the Antarctic pursuant to the Japanese Whale Research Program under Special Permit in the Antarctic Phase II (JARPA II) was a violation of international law because the JARPA II was not a programme 'for purposes of scientific research' within the meaning of the Whaling Convention.[48] Japan initially submitted that it enjoyed discretion in ascertaining whether or not the JARPA II pursued 'purposes of scientific research',[49] but adjusted its stance at the close of oral proceedings before the ICJ to agree with Australia (and New Zealand intervening) that the classification of the JARPA II as a programme of scientific research has to be 'objectively justifiable'.[50] In finding that there is no objective justification for the 'granting of a special permit for a programme that uses lethal sampling on a larger scale than is reasonable in relation to achieving the programme's

[42] Vienna Convention on the Law of Treaties (signed 23 May 1969, entered into force 27 January 1980) 1155 UNTS 331, arts 11–15, 18.
[43] ibid arts 19, 20.
[44] ibid art 19(c).
[45] ibid Preamble.
[46] Whaling Convention (n 40) Schedule para 3.
[47] *Australia v Japan: New Zealand intervening* [2014] ICJ Rep 226.
[48] ibid 239.
[49] ibid 252.
[50] ibid 254.

stated research objectives',[51] the ICJ ruled by a majority that the disproportionately large sample sizes of minke whales captured from the Antarctic '[do] not establish that the programme's design and implementation are reasonable in relation to achieving its stated objectives . . . [and] the special permits granted by Japan . . . in connection with JARPA II are not "for purposes of scientific research"'.[52] Japan was ordered to 'revoke any extant authorization, permit or license to kill, take or treat whales in relation to JARPA II, and refrain from granting any further permits under Article VIII, paragraph 1, of the [Whaling] Convention'.[53] The ICJ ruling in 2014 'sent shock waves in Japan' and set off a chain reaction.[54] In October 2015, Japan modified its Optional Declaration to the ICJ Statute to exclude 'any dispute arising out of, concerning, or relating to research on, or conservation, management or exploitation of, living resources of the sea' from the world court's jurisdiction;[55] in November 2015, Japan announced its decision to capture 333 minke whales from the Antarctic, in flagrant disregard of the earlier ICJ ruling;[56] in January 2019, Japan withdrew from the International Whaling Commission,[57] and even to this day, Japan strenuously (and successfully) opposes any anti-whaling language in multilateral trade agreements that it is negotiating.[58] The sum effect of Japanese resistance is the unilateral removal of corporate over-whaling in Antarctica from the purview of international law.

Unlike overfishing in the High Seas, which is openly done by corporate fisheries, over-whaling in Antarctica is covertly done by corporate whalers who are, first, cloaked with the authority of state-issued permits and, second, concealed from sanctions by their home state defending their activities against the rest of the world as scientific research. In the aftermath of *Whaling in the Antarctic*, it is convenient to regard Japan, and other states with whaling industries such as Norway, Iceland, and the Russian Federation, as the protagonists in unsustainable commercial whaling. Yet, the main driving force behind

[51] ibid 260.
[52] ibid 293.
[53] ibid 298.
[54] Malgosia Fitzmaurice, 'Whales' in Jessie Hohmann and Daniel Joyce (eds), *International Law's Objects* (OUP 2018) 547.
[55] Motohide Yoshikawa, 'Declarations Recognizing the Jurisdiction of the Court as Compulsory' (6 October 2015) <www.icj-cij.org/declarations/jp> accessed 30 April 2024.
[56] Rachel Feltman, 'A Japanese Vessel is Set to Kill 333 Whales for "Research"—but is Science Really Behind the Hunt?' *The Washington Post* (30 November 2015).
[57] International Whaling Commission, 'Statement on Government of Japan Withdrawal from IWC' (14 January 2019) <https://iwc.int/resources/media-resources/news/statement-on-government-of-japan-withdrawal> accessed 30 April 2024.
[58] Julian Ryall, 'How a Dispute Over Whaling Could Spur Japan's Exit from US Indo-Pacific Trade Pact: "Kishida has Zero Leeway"' *South China Morning Post* (15 August 2023).

Japan's pro-whaling policy is a handful of corporate whalers who employ a grand estimated total of 300 people. While whale meat was once popular in Japan due to food shortages after the Second World War (WWII), consumer demand has dropped drastically over the years and whale meat now accounts for less than 0.1 per cent of total meat consumption in Japan.[59] Despite the lacklustre figures and the absence of economic sense to prop up a whaling industry in steep decline, Japan's miniscule corporate whaling lobby has managed to persuade its home state to approve its unsustainable whaling practices, even if it means getting Japan to turn its back on international law. This is not only a testament to the ability of corporate entities to evade sanction under domestic law for the unsustainable harvesting of common property, but, more importantly, poses a serious challenge to the regulation of corporate interference with new property using international law.

2.3 Extortionate acquisition of contingent property

Contingent property, which encompasses jurisdictional, human, and economic rights, can be acquired in any number of ways.[60] Two of the more unsettling, yet understudied, methods of acquisition concern economic rights, namely, the outright use of force by corporate actors in the past to secure trading rights (Section 2.3.1), and the offer to use force by corporate actors in the present in exchange for mining rights (Section 2.3.2). These two configurations of new property interference are unsettling because they dispel the myth that states have a monopoly on the use of force. Article 2(4) of the Charter of the United Nations provides:[61]

> All Members shall refrain in their international relations from the threat or use of force against the territorial integrity or political independence of any state or in any other manner inconsistent with the Purposes of the United Nations.

While the prohibition on the use of force is directed at member states, the principle of *effet utile* in treaty interpretation, which seeks to uphold rather than destroy the object and purpose of the treaty,[62] demands the application

[59] Elaine Lies, 'Outlook Uncertain for Japan's Whaling Industry Despite Commercial Restart' *Reuters* (24 June 2019).
[60] See Chapter 4, Section 3.
[61] (signed 26 June 1945, entered into force 24 October 1945) 1 UNTS XVI (UN Charter).
[62] Richard Gardiner, *Treaty Interpretation* (1st edn, OUP 2015) 179–81.

of the prohibition to the nationals of member states. Nonetheless, a serious accountability gap remains. The steady track record of certain corporate actors using force to acquire contingent property, thereby violating international law without being sanctioned by international law, is a long-standing problem that has led to a proliferation of such activities.[63] In addition to contravening the international obligation against the use of force, corporate actors who threaten or promise force in a *quid pro quo* with their contracting partners, who are usually natural resource-rich developing states, are arguably abusing their right to enter into contracts,[64] as well as engaging in anti-competitive behaviour which is unlawful in accordance with the domestic law of most countries.[65] Although neither abusive nor anti-competitive conduct necessarily amounts to a violation of an identifiable and established international obligation,[66] their adoption by corporate actors reveals the deliberate violation of international law for self-serving ends, and underscores extortionate corporate acquisitions of new property.

2.3.1 Configuration 5 (the historical use of force by trading companies to seize trading concessions)

The Dutch Verenigde Oostindische Compagnie (VOC) and the British East India Company (EIC) epitomized the use of force by powerful trading companies from the seventeenth to eighteenth centuries to monopolize trading routes and concessions in Asia. The VOC's target was the East Indies for abundant spices, while the EIC's principal target was India for abundant cotton, tea, and spices. The VOC and the EIC represent the world's earliest incarnations of

[63] Enrique Bernales Ballesteros (Special Rapporteur), 'Final Report on the Use of Mercenaries as a Means of Violating Human Rights and Impeding the Exercise of the Right of Peoples to Self-Determination' United Nations Economic and Social Council (24 December 2003) E/CN.4/2004/15, 13.

[64] The right to enter into contracts inheres in every entity in possession of legal personality and legal standing to do so. However, when such a right is exercised in pursuit of an illegal outcome (eg contract killing), or in a manner that bends the other contracting party's will through a resort to arms, be it to coerce or to entice, there is likely an abuse of rights.

[65] Anu Bradford, 'Antitrust Law in Global Markets' in Einer R Elhauge (ed), *Research Handbook on the Economics of Antitrust Law* (Edward Elgar 2013) 284–95.

[66] The proposition that an abuse of rights constitutes a general principle of international law is a contested one (see Jan Paulsson, *The Unruly Notion of Abuse of Rights* (CUP 2020) 61–67; cf Michael Byers, 'Abuse of Rights: An Old Principle, A New Age' (2002) 47(2) McGill Law Journal 384, 397–410), while the global directive for corporate actors to refrain from 'an abuse or acquisition and abuse of a dominant position of market power, limit access to markets or otherwise unduly restrain competition, having or being likely to have adverse effects on international trade, particularly that of developing countries, and on the economic development of these countries' is currently found in sections B(i)(1) and D(1) of the non-binding United Nations Set of Principles and Rules on Competition published by the United Nations Conference on Trade and Development (2000, TD/RBP/CONF/10/Rev.2), making it an aspirational rather than a mandatory directive.

an 'aggressive multinational corporation',[67] possessing its own private army, as well as a relentless desire to sideline all its trading competitors by acquiring and maintaining its exclusive trading rights through force. For the VOC and the EIC, the best way to ensure stability and continuity in their respective trading interests was to invade the targeted territory and install a military presence there, effectively bringing that territory under corporate control. It is extremely ironic that the colonization of Asia was largely accomplished not by states, but by these powerful trading companies which conquered *states* in order to turn the latter into trading outposts. Remarkably, the use of force by the VOC and the EIC to seize trade routes and concessions for their own profit appears to have been condoned by their home states. The Dutch government entertained a request from the VOC for tax exemption so that it could maintain a 'special fund for warfare in the East Indies',[68] while the British government approved a massive bailout of the EIC when it suffered a severe cash flow crisis during its 'fifty-year-long assault on India and its rise from a humble trading company to a fully-fledged imperial power'.[69]

In stark contrast to modern attitudes against the use of force, there was a point in time when the use of force to acquire economic rights was acceptable. The legitimization of the use of force, which was 'not just coterminous with the rise of global trading empires in the seventeenth and eighteenth centuries but made them possible in the first place', was the handiwork of Hugo Grotius, a shrewd jurist employed by the VOC to justify its expansionist policy in the East Indies on moral and legal grounds.[70] Grotius deftly couched his defence of the VOC's military activities in terms of the freedom of trade and navigation. He attacked Iberian ambitions to dominate the spice trade on the basis that they compromised the VOC's freedom of trade and navigation, while simultaneously asserting that the VOC could, in the name of protecting its freedom of trade and navigation, 'crush all forms of native opposition' to its 'attempts to monopolize the trade in nutmeg, mace and cloves'.[71] Conveniently for Grotius and the VOC, '[t]hese spices were grown on small islands in Southeast Asia that easily succumbed to the [VOC's] military and naval forces'.[72] Often

[67] William Dalrymple, *The Anarchy—The Relentless Rise of the East India Company* (Bloomsbury 2019) xxxi.
[68] Martine Julia van Ittersum, *Profit and Principle—Hugo Grotius, Natural Rights Theories and the Rise of Dutch Power in the East Indies (1596–1615)* (Brill 2006) 182.
[69] Dalrymple (n 67) xxx–xxxi.
[70] van Ittersum, *Profit and Principle* (n 68) lxi.
[71] ibid.
[72] ibid.

called a 'founding father of international law',[73] Grotius's sophisticated *De Jure Pradae*, which was written to advance the VOC's commercial interests,[74] encouraged the VOC to carry on with its 'just war' in the East Indies,[75] and eventually emboldened the EIC to 'declare[] war' against an Indian prince, setting in motion the EIC's closing grip on India.[76] Grotius's endearing, if clearly partisan, treatise conferred an exalted status on corporate actors wielding military force for economic ends. The sanitizing of the use of force by the VOC and the EIC appeared to place these corporations above the reproach of international law. The corporate form and the manner in which force is used to acquire economic rights have since evolved, and attitudes towards the use of force have since hardened. Yet, corporate actors continue to evade sanction by international law when relying on force to acquire economic rights. The discussion now turns to PMSCs as the modern iteration of mighty trading companies of the past, to articulate the sixth and final configuration of new property interference.

2.3.2 Configuration 6 (the modern engagement of force by PMSCs to extract mining concessions)

Unlike trading companies, such as the VOC and the EIC, which openly used force on resource-rich nations to cower their monarchs into awarding exclusive economic rights, PMSCs acquire new property in a subtler way. PMSCs are in the business of selling military and security services to paying clients, be they private entities or states. Typically founded and led by ex-military chiefs, PMSCs maintain a security force ranging from hundreds to thousands of people, usually recruited from the military, who stand by to offer intelligence, training, protection, peacekeeping, and even armed combat services. PMSCs also possess military equipment such as weapons, aircraft, and armoured vehicles. PMSCs are, essentially, a private army for hire. They do not invade nations by using force to acquire economic rights; instead, they offer to use force to assist the client state to manage a situation that is beyond the client state's ability to handle, and which calls for external armed response. Hiring PMSCs to troubleshoot is extremely costly, and when the client is a resource-rich but financially strapped state, it is common for PMSCs to be partly remunerated

[73] For a critical take on this accolade, see Martine Julia van Ittersum, 'Hugo Grotius: The Making of a Founding Father of International Law' in Anne Orford and Florian Hoffmann (eds), *The Oxford Handbook of the Theory of International Law* (OUP 2016) 94–100.
[74] van Ittersum, *Profit and Principle* (n 68) liv.
[75] ibid 169.
[76] ibid liv; Dalrymple (n 67) 111.

in mining concessions. A concessions-for-security exchange may seem fair in principle since PMSCs should be paid for their services, but it is highly extortionate and exploitative in practice. As the Sandline Affair and its moving pieces illustrate, PMSCs are merely the vanguard of a vast corporate empire comprising a maze of numerous holding companies and subsidiaries. By leveraging on force as their currency of exchange, PMSCs wedge an opening in the client state's economy through which its corporate affiliates can steadily enter and remain. In the worst case scenario, a PMSC's corporate family establishes a controlling stake in the key sectors of a client state's economy, driving out competitors in order to monopolize entire industries.[77]

The Sandline Affair lasted from 1996 to 1997 on the island-state of Papua New Guinea (PNG),[78] and involved two PMSCs and two closely linked corporate empires. Unable to contain a local separatist movement known as the Bougainville Revolutionary Army (BRA), the then Prime Minister of PNG, Sir Julius Chan, contracted with British PMSC Sandline International in January 1997 to quash the separatist movement and recapture a huge copper mine (the Paguna mine) which had fallen into BRA hands. Sandline then subcontracted the provision of military equipment and mercenaries to South African PMSC Executive Outcomes. The contract cost the PNG USD 36 million, an amount which the country could barely afford. During negotiations over possible modes of payment, a Sandline representative reportedly proposed that Sandline and PNG 'could come to some arrangements regarding part repayment with mineral concessions', which revealed Sandline's keen interest to acquire control of the Paguna mine that it was tasked to recapture.[79] Concessions-for-security transactions were the hallmark of Sandline's subcontractor—Executive Outcomes—when it operated in sub-Saharan Africa.[80] Sandline and Executive Outcomes belong to the Branch and the Strategic Resource Corporation (SRC) groups of companies respectively.[81] The Branch group was founded by British businessman, Tony Buckingham,

[77] United Nations Security Council (UNSC), 'Final Report of the Panel of Experts on the Illegal Exploitation of Natural Resources and Other Forms of Wealth of the Democratic Republic of the Congo' (S/2002/1146) 20–21.

[78] Anthony J Regan and Sinclair Dinnen, 'The Sandline Affair: A Chronology of Significant Events' in Sinclair Dinnen and others (eds), *Challenging the State: The Sandline Affair in Papua New Guinea* (Australian National University 1997) 9–48.

[79] Sinclair Dinnen, 'Trading in Security: Private Military Contractors in Papua New Guinea' in Sinclair Dinnen and others (eds), *Challenging the State: The Sandline Affair in Papua New Guinea* (The Australian National University 1997) 124.

[80] ibid 123.

[81] Khareen Pech, 'Executive Outcomes—A Corporate Conquest' in Jakkie Cilliers and Peggy Mason (eds), *Peace, Profit or Plunder? The Privatisation of Security in War-torn African Societies* (Institute for Security Studies 1999) 87–88.

while the SRC group was founded by a former lieutenant-colonel of the South African armed forces, Eeben Barlow. The two founders first collaborated in 1993 when Buckingham hired Executive Outcomes to liberate the city of Soyo in Northern Angola, where one of Branch group's oil companies was located, from rebel occupation.[82] Success in Soyo led to other mutually beneficial collaborations, most notably in Sierre Leone in 1995 where the impoverished government hired Executive Outcomes in a desperate attempt to end a bloody civil war started by local insurgents known as the Revolutionary United Front (RUF). In exchange for repelling the RUF, Executive Outcomes extracted USD 15 million and a number of diamond mining concessions, the latter being awarded to a company in the Branch group.[83] Buckingham and Barlow pursued a similar strategy in PNG, with Executive Outcomes pocketing cash for providing military capabilities, and Sandline securing copper mining concessions on behalf of the Branch group for brokering the deal. Local opposition to the use of PMSCs to restore peace to PNG grew and, shortly after part payment had already been made, Sir Julius Chan caved into public calls to suspend the Sandline contract.[84] The contract was eventually cancelled in June 1997 by a newly elected government in PNG.[85]

The way PMSCs like Sandline and Executive Outcomes engaged force to extract mining concessions from client states is extortionate because it is no coincidence that PMSC activities are concentrated in conflict-ridden, cash-poor states that happen to possess an abundance of natural resources, such as Angola (petroleum, diamonds, minerals) and Sierra Leone (mainly diamonds, minerals).[86] By deliberately pricing the provision of military and security services beyond the reach of the state's national defence budget, while softening the blow with the option of part payment with mining concessions, states in urgent need of PMSC assistance have little choice but to accede to PMSC demands. The concessions-for-security arrangement is also exploitative in the long-run because PMSCs will strive to keep the host state or region in a state of precarious, rather than lasting, peace so as to justify their continued presence in guarding the operation of lucrative mining concessions.[87] And having enjoyed

[82] Scott Fitzsimmons, *Mercenaries in Asymmetric Conflicts* (CUP 2012) 168–69.

[83] Elizabeth Rubin, 'Saving Sierra Leone, At A Price' *The New York Times* (4 February 1999).

[84] Regan and Dinnen (n 78) 20.

[85] The cancellation precipitated a claim in arbitration by Sandline against the PNG for payment of the full contractual sum, see *Sandline International Inc v The Independent State of Papua New Guinea*, UNCITRAL, Interim Award (Somers, Kerr, Dawson) (9 October 1998) 117 International Law Reports 552, 553, 556.

[86] Alice E Fuchs, 'Searching for Resources, Offering Security . . . Private Military Companies in Sierra Leone' in Thomas Jäger and Gerhard Kümmel (eds), *Private Military and Security Companies—Chances, Problems, Pitfalls and Prospects* (VS Verlag 2007) 105.

[87] ibid 119.

the economic fruits of their military labour, profit-oriented PMSCs and their corporate affiliates have no incentive to accommodate competitors. The corporate desire to monopolize is so strong that even if the PMSC is forced to step back from a lucrative concession, which was what happened to Executive Outcomes in Angola in 1996 after pushback from the US and the UN, its corporate affiliates will step up to take its place. Executive Outcomes' diverse commercial opportunities in Angola were eventually absorbed by six affiliates from the SRC group of companies, which included another PMSC, Saracen International.[88]

There is repeated acknowledgement of the ability of PMSCs to violate international law by engaging force in potential or actual contravention of Article 2(4) of the UN Charter, while simultaneously avoiding sanction by international law.[89] However, existing instruments purporting to regulate PMSCs are either poorly subscribed,[90] consist of non-binding recommendations that only cater to armed conflict scenarios,[91] or remain in draft form with states as the primary bearers of international obligations concerning PMSC activity.[92] There are two possible reasons why international law tolerates PMSCs engaging force to acquire economic rights. The first reason is that PMSCs serve as a tool for certain states to act in a manner that is not in accordance with international law. To get around the principle of non-intervention among states in international law,[93] the US Department of Defense contracted Military Professional Resources Inc (MPRI) to train the Croatian army during the Bosnian War, and Dyncorp International (Dyncorp) to supress the narcotics trade in Columbia. For the US, MPRI and Dyncorp 'serve in an overall strategy to pursue foreign policy goals and to establish certain political regimes in certain parts of the world'.[94] States like the US with foreign policy interests which are maintained

[88] Pech (n 81) 91.

[89] Ballesteros (n 63) 13, 23; also UNSC (n 77) 20–21.

[90] International Convention Against the Recruitment, Use, Financing and Training of Mercenaries (adopted 4 December 1989, entered into force 20 October 2001) 2163 UNTS 75. To date, this instrument has only attracted seventeen signatories.

[91] International Committee of the Red Cross, 'The Montreaux Document on Pertinent International Legal Obligations and Good Practices for States related to Operations of Private Military and Securities Companies during Armed Conflict' (17 September 2008) <www.icrc.org/en/doc/assets/files/other/icrc_002_0996.pdf> accessed 30 April 2024.

[92] United Nations Human Rights Council, 'Draft of a possible Convention on Private Military and Security Companies (PMSCs) for consideration and action by the Human Rights Council' (13 May 2011) A/HRC/WG.10/1/2 <https://digitallibrary.un.org/record/707162?v=pdf> accessed 30 April 2024.

[93] Maziar Jamnejad and Michael Wood, 'The Principle of Non-Intervention' (2009) 22(2) Leiden Journal of International Law 345, 346–49.

[94] Daniel Kramer, 'Does History Repeat Itself? A Comparative Analysis of Private Military Entities' in Thomas Jäger and Gerhard Kümmel (eds), *Private Military and Security Companies—Chances, Problems, Pitfalls and Prospects* (VS Verlag 2007) 35.

by PMSCs are unlikely to support multilateral initiatives to ban, contain, or closely regulate PMSC activity. The second reason is that PMSCs have come to be regarded as a necessary evil. In a report on PMSCs published by the UK Select Committee on Foreign Affairs, the Select Committee called for 'regulation [that] takes into account PMC's capabilities and does not only concentrate on potential human rights abuses by these companies but also on their ability to prevent abuses occurring by rebels, insurgents and military forces'.[95] Without proposing any specific regulations, the report concludes on an ambiguous note, urging 'Britain to take the lead in appropriate legislation that does not drive PMCs into the wilderness but regulates those who wish to be accountable and transparent'.[96] It is debatable if excluding errant PMSCs from regulatory oversight represents a sensible step forward for either domestic or international law. In the aftermath of the Sandline Affair, which made international headlines, the South African government implemented a licensing scheme to constrain PMSC activity. Although Executive Outcomes received a licence to continue operating, Barlow proceeded to dissolve the company because the conditions attached to the licence rendered operations unprofitable.[97] In October 2020, after a twenty-year hiatus, Barlow announced the revival of Executive Outcomes on social media.[98] Unlike Executive Outcomes, its successor has no known name and no known coordinates. If PMSCs that openly leveraged on force to acquire economic rights as new property could routinely escape sanction by international law, the regulatory challenge will surely intensify with the emergence of a new breed of untraceable PMSCs that operates in the shadows.

3. Current systemic shortcomings when redressing new property interference

From the foregoing six configurations of new property interference that elude penalty, it is evident that international law has considerable regulatory catching-up to do. And part of effective regulation lies in the availability

[95] House of Commons, 'Chapter 2—The Private Military Companies Perspective' (1 August 2002) para 2.2.5 <https://publications.parliament.uk/pa/cm200102/cmselect/cmfaff/922/2061322.htm> accessed 30 April 2024.
[96] ibid para 2.5.
[97] Pech (n 81) 94–97.
[98] Iain Esau, 'Africa Awaits: Mercenary Outfit Executive Outcomes is Reborn' *Upstream* (8 December 2020) <www.upstreamonline.com/people/africa-awaits-mercenary-outfit-executive-outcomes-is-reborn/2-1-921836> accessed 30 April 2024.

of avenues and remedies to redress sanctionable new property interference. As noted in the opening paragraph of this chapter, international law at present only provides explicit avenues for redress for foreign individual claimants against host states taking property, and in the form of international criminal prosecution for individual destruction of property during armed conflict. None of the potential claimants and respondents in the six configurations of new property interference can be neatly accommodated by the two established avenues for redress. The claimants in Configuration 1 (private trafficking of art and antiquities) are the source states of cultural property and their entities, while the respondents are individual smugglers and art dealers plying their trade in peacetime. The claimants in Configuration 2 (public-private trafficking of art and antiquities) are source states and their entities, while the respondents can be individuals as well as occupying states complicit in the illicit removal and export of cultural property. The claimants and respondents in Configuration 3 (overt corporate overfishing in the High Seas) are corporate fishers who are either angling for or abusing their equitable share in common property. The claimants in Configuration 4 (covert corporate over-whaling in Antarctica) are conservationists, while the respondents are corporate whalers. The claimants in Configurations 5 (the historical use of force by trading companies to seize trading concessions) and 6 (the modern engagement of force by PMSCs to extract mining concessions) are impoverished, resource-rich states and their local communities, while the respondents are multinational corporate behemoths that employ force to monopolize contingent property to the detriment of the host state's overall economic development and the well-being of their populations. The remainder of this section explains why existing dispute settlement options fall short when redressing new property interference, by examining the procedural hurdles that potential claimants encounter (Section 3.1), as well as deficiency in the content of international law when it comes to substantive redress (Section 3.2).

3.1 Procedural hurdles

Claimants seeking redress under international law for new property interference will face two main procedural hurdles. The first is the presence of strict conditions to meet before the matter can be heard by international courts or tribunals (Section 3.1.1). The second is the burden of navigating the overlapping jurisdictions borne from multiple dispute settlement bodies possessing the mandate to regulate new property interference in international law (Section 3.1.2).

3.1.1 Conditional dispute settlement before international courts and tribunals

Presenting a claim before an international court or tribunal requires the satisfaction of cumulative procedural conditions. The claim must be brought by an eligible claimant against an eligible respondent, and normally concern the violation of an international obligation over which the given international court or tribunal is empowered by its constituting treaty to adjudicate. While standing to sue and be sued over a justiciable obligation before international courts and tribunals ought to be clearly delineated in the interests of transparency and institutional workload, existing procedural conditions appear to hinder rather than help attempts to redress new property interference. The ICJ possesses a vast jurisdictional mandate to determine, among other things, 'the existence of any fact which, if established, would constitute a breach of an international obligation',[99] such as new property interference, but limits disputing claimants and respondents to states.[100] Narrower jurisdictional mandates can be seen in specialized international dispute settlement bodies such as the International Criminal Court (ICC), the International Tribunal for the Law of the Sea (ITLOS), the Dispute Settlement Body (DSB) of the World Trade Organization (WTO), and investor–state arbitral tribunals constituted under investment treaties, each with its own distinct set of procedural conditions. The ICC only prosecutes individual defendants for the commission of international crimes,[101] such as cultural property destruction, and such destruction must have occurred during armed conflict.[102] The ITLOS' jurisdictional mandate extends to 'all disputes and all applications' arising from UNCLOS,[103] which may include common property interference, but can only be invoked by claimant states parties against respondent states parties.[104] The DSB hears disputes arising from alleged violations of the General Agreement on Tariffs and Trade,[105] the Agreement on Trade-Related Aspects of Intellectual Property

[99] Statute of the International Court of Justice (26 June 1945, entered into force 18 April 1946) 33 UNTS 993 (ICJ Statute) arts 36(2)(c), 36(1), 36(2)(a)–(b), 36(2)(d).

[100] ibid art 35(1).

[101] Rome Statute (n 6) art 25(1).

[102] ibid arts 8(2)(a)(iv), 8(2)(b)(xiii), 8(2)(e)(iv), 8(2)(e)(xii).

[103] UNCLOS (n 26) Annex VI, art 21.

[104] UNCLOS (n 26) Annex VI, art 20(1).

[105] General Agreement on Tariffs and Trade (signed 30 October 1947, provisionally applied 1 January 1948 to 1995) 55 UNTS 194, subsequently incorporated into the Marrakesh Agreement Establishing the World Trade Organization (signed 15 April 1994, entered into force 1 January 1995) (WTO Agreement) Annex 1A.

Rights,[106] and the Agreement on Trade-Related Investment Measures,[107] none of which contemplate new property interference by non-state actors, and only if these disputes are submitted by claimant WTO member states against respondent WTO member states.[108] Finally, investor–state arbitral tribunals are expressly empowered to hear claims concerning alleged violations of investment treaty obligations, which can include interference with economic rights as contingent property,[109] provided these claims are initiated by qualified investors against host states parties to the underlying investment treaty.[110]

These diverse procedural conditions severely limit claimants' access to justice for new property interference. Source states of cultural property stolen and traded abroad in peacetime, in direct contravention of the 1970 UNESCO Convention, cannot refer individuals to the prosecutorial arm of the ICC since no international crime as defined in the Rome Statute has been committed.[111] Corporate fishers and conservationists disadvantaged by the unsustainable harvesting of common property, which violate several treaties including UNCLOS, cannot bring claims directly against offending corporate actors before ITLOS, which only hears disputes brought by states against states.[112] Under-developed states and their local communities have no direct recourse against PMSCs before the DSB and investor–state arbitral tribunals because the use of force to extort economic rights, which violates the UN Charter, does not violate the various trade and investment protection obligations set out in the WTO Agreements and investment treaties. This leaves the ICJ as the most promising international dispute settlement body for new property interference claims. The test case was *Whaling in the Antarctic*, where Australia prevailed

[106] Agreement on Trade-Related Aspects of Intellectual Property Rights (signed 15 April 1994, entered into force 1 January 1995) 1869 UNTS 299 (TRIPs Agreement); WTO Agreement (n 105) Annex 1C.

[107] Agreement on Trade-Related Investment Measures (signed 15 April 1994, entered into force 1 January 1995) 1868 UNTS 186 (TRIMs Agreement); WTO Agreement (n 105) Annex 1A.

[108] WTO Agreement (n 105) Annex 2, art 1(1), also arts 2(1), 3(2), 3(3), 3(7).

[109] One example is the imposition of measures that adversely impact the profitability of an investment contract, a species of contingent property (Chapter 4, Section 3.3.1), that amount to a denial of fair and equitable treatment under the applicable investment treaty, see Ho, *State Responsibility for Breaches of Investment Contracts* (n 5) 119–37.

[110] Article 19(1) of the 2019 Dutch Model Bilateral Investment Treaty (2019 Dutch Model BIT) is fairly typical of dispute settlement clauses in investment treaties which empower qualified investors to initiate claims against a host state, but not *vice versa*: 'If a request for consultations has been submitted according to the procedures laid down in Article 18 and where such consultations do not result in a resolution of the claim within six months from the date of the written request for consultations, *the investor may submit a claim* under one of the following sets of rules on dispute settlement . . .' (emphasis added). Apart from investor–state dispute settlement, the 2019 Dutch Model BIT also provides for state–state dispute settlement, discussed above at Section 3.1.2.

[111] Rome Statute (n 6) art 14.

[112] UNCLOS (n 26) arts 287(1)(a), 291(1).

by a majority in showing that Japan's authorization of corporate whaling amounted to a violation of the Whaling Convention.[113] Leaving aside Japan's deliberate snubbing of the ICJ ban by allowing its corporate nationals to continue whaling in Antarctica, there are two considerations which temper optimism in the ICJ's role in settling disputes over new property interference.

The first is the discretionary nature of claims submitted to the ICJ. As comity is prized in international relations, the decision of one state to resort to high-profile international legal proceedings against another state is rarely straightforward and its push factors are rarely public knowledge. Although Australia has long positioned itself as an anti-whaling advocate, there were probably additional grounds which convinced Australia to differentiate itself from other anti-whaling countries, and take on Japan at the ICJ. To the extent that states are infrequent claimants in new property interference disputes and have infrequent recourse to the ICJ, most new property interferences will not be redressed by the ICJ. The second is the attributability of individual or corporate conduct to the respondent state in ICJ proceedings when the latter has not acted in violation of an international obligation. In *Whaling in the Antarctic*, Japan's JARPA II programme, which issued licences to Japanese corporate whalers, was adjudged a violation of Japan's obligations under the Whaling Convention. In an alternative reality where corporate whalers overharvest common property without licences from their home states, it is possible for home states to disavow knowledge and approval of their nationals' activities. The inability to prove that 'the person or group of persons is in fact acting on the instructions of, or under the direction or control of, [the respondent] State in carrying out the conduct'[114] entails the non-attribution of individual or corporate conduct to the respondent state under international law, and the exoneration of the respondent state from the claims brought against it in ICJ proceedings. The world of new property interference is one where individuals illegally transact cultural property, where corporate fishers overharvest common property, and where PMSCs monopolize contingent property through force, all for personal gain. Requiring claims to be brought against these actors' home states on the basis of attributed conduct, when their links to their home states may be non-existent, tenuous, or highly classified, may turn out to be the procedural condition to the ICJ's exercise of jurisdiction over new property interference disputes that proves impossible to satisfy.

[113] *Australia v Japan* (n 47) 293.

[114] 2001 Articles on Responsibility of States for Internationally Wrongful Acts (12 December 2001) UN Doc A/RES/56/83 (2001) (ASR) art 8.

3.1.2 Overlapping jurisdictions across dispute settlement bodies

The procedural challenge presented by conditional dispute settlement for sanctionable new property in international law is compounded by the prospect of overlapping jurisdictions across discrete dispute settlement bodies. Potential claimants in Configuration 6 (the modern engagement of force by PMSCs to extract mining concessions), namely host states of PMSCs and their local communities, may approach up to three dispute settlement bodies in pursuit of redress. They are the ICJ, treaty-based investment arbitration tribunals, and, when the PMSC is a US national, the US courts.

The ICJ. As the ICJ's jurisdiction can be invoked by states parties to the ICJ Statute 'in all legal disputes concerning the existence of any fact which, if established, would constitute a breach of an international obligation',[115] as well as in 'all legal disputes concerning the nature or extent of the reparation to be made for the breach of an international obligation',[116] the scope of the ICJ's mandate is broad enough to encompass claims seeking redress for new property interference that can be construed as a violation of international law. The likeliest international obligation at stake is the obligation not to use force as set out in Article 2(4) of the UN Charter. But invoking the ICJ's jurisdiction raises three complications. The first is the uncertainty of diplomatic espousal of an international claim by the PMSC's host state if the original claimants are injured local communities who have no standing as litigants before the ICJ. Requests for diplomatic espousal are not granted as of right and states have unfettered discretion whether or not to espouse a national's claim before the ICJ.[117] The second is the uncertainty of whether the challenged PMSC conduct can be attributed to its home state as the proper respondent in proceedings before the ICJ. Absent demonstrable attribution of corporate use of force to extort economic rights to the respondent home state, the claimant host state does not have a case. The third is whether the way force is engaged by PMSCs to achieve economic ends will be considered a use of force by the ICJ in the way that Article 2(4) of the UN Charter has been traditionally understood and interpreted. While there appears to be some inclination towards the evolutionary interpretation of treaties among international tribunals,[118] which may

[115] ICJ Statute (n 99) art 36(2)(c).

[116] ibid art 36(2)(d).

[117] Kate Parlett, 'Diplomatic Protection and the International Court of Justice' in Christian J Tams and James Sloan (eds), *The Development of International Law by the International Court of Justice* (OUP 2013) 94–96, relying on *Barcelona Traction, Light, and Power Company, Limited (Belgium v Spain)* (Second Phase) (Merits) [1970] ICJ Rep 3, para 50.

[118] Eirik Bjorge, *The Evolutionary Interpretation of Treaties* (OUP 2014) 63–76, 118–25, 189–91; Christian Djeffal, *Static and Evolutionary Treaty Interpretation—A Functional Reconstruction* (CUP 2016) 214–343.

update perspectives on the use of force, a claim against a PMSC's home state for the PMSC's engagement of force to interfere with new property is unprecedented at the ICJ. Test cases play an important role in clarifying, consolidating, or even modifying international law, but experimental claims carry a significant risk of failure, which may deter some claimants from stepping forward.

Investment arbitration tribunals. The expansive jurisdictional mandate of the ICJ, notwithstanding the strings attached to its invocation, can overlap with the narrower jurisdictional mandate of treaty-based investment arbitration tribunals. To the extent that foreign PMSCs are also mining concessionaires in their client states, they may be considered investors in an investment treaty concluded between their home and host states. Investment treaties contain obligations borne by contracting states vis-à-vis the treatment of qualified investors and their investments. With rising awareness and concern over sustainable development goals, newer generation investment treaties stipulate obligations that investors, and not just host states, have to meet, such as the observance of human rights, environmental protection, and labour laws of the host state.[119] Non-observance of these laws, or acting in relation to the investment that leads to significant damage, personal injuries, or loss of life in the host state, will expose the transgressing investors to penalties in their home state.[120] Newer generation investment treaties also provide for state–state arbitration when there is a dispute concerning the interpretation or application of the treaty.[121] So while an aggrieved host state cannot bring a claim under the treaty directly against an investor, it can bring a claim against the investor's home state if it disputes the way the investor's home state has interpreted or applied the treaty. In the case of a PMSC leveraging on force to monopolize an industry to the calculable detriment of the host state's economic development, and without sanction from its home state which outlaws anti-competitive practices, the host state may initiate a claim in arbitration against the home state for failing to discipline its national for causing significant damage to the host state. Although state–state investment treaty arbitrations are uncommon,[122] they represent a plausible opportunity for host states to strike first without having to attribute investor conduct to the investor's home state, a fact which is obscured by the far greater frequency of investors initiating claims against host states.

[119] See for instance the 2019 Dutch Model BIT art 7(1).
[120] ibid art 7(4).
[121] ibid art 25(1).
[122] Nathalie Bernasconi-Osterwalder, 'State-State Dispute Settlement in Investment Treaties' *International Institute for Sustainable Development* (October 2014) 9–16 <www.iisd.org/system/files/publications/best-practices-state-state-dispute-settlement-investment-treaties.pdf> accessed 30 April 2024.

US courts. When the PMSC interfering with new property is a US national, which the more prominent PMSCs today are,[123] the ICJ's jurisdiction over the PMSC's activities not only overlaps with that of investment arbitration tribunals, but also potentially with the jurisdiction of US courts. This is due in part to the Alien Tort Statute (ATS), which empowers US district courts to assume 'original jurisdiction of any civil action by an alien for a tort only, committed in violation of the law of nations or a treaty of the United States'.[124] As the ATS allows foreign nationals to bring civil actions in US courts alleging violations of international law committed outside the US if their claims 'touch and concern the territory of the United States . . . [and] do so with sufficient force',[125] the likely claimants from Configuration 6 (the modern engagement of force by PMSCs to extract mining concessions) in an ATS litigation are disenfranchised local communities, while the likely respondent is the US-registered PMSC.[126] Additionally, foreign claimants may avail themselves of the Federal Tort Claims Act (FTCA) or the Foreign Claims Act (FCA) if the PMSC engaged in misconduct while operating under a service contract with the US government.[127] Unlike ATS claims, which can be brought directly against the PMSC, FTCA and FCA claims are brought against the US government. The FTCA offers compensation to the victims of negligent or wrongful acts and omissions of US government employees acting within the scope of his or her official duties,[128] while the FCA offers compensation to inhabitants of foreign countries for property damage, personal injury, or death caused by military and civilian members of the US Armed Forces in foreign countries.[129] As promising as these avenues for redress seem, the success rate of launching claims in US courts for PMSC activities hangs in the balance. While there is no precedent on equating PMSCs to US government employees under the FCA to date,[130] the case law on ATS claims continues to evolve,[131]

[123] Michael Picard, 'US Private Military and Security Companies Fuel Corruption and Conflict Risk' *Transparency International UK* (9 August 2022) <www.transparency.org.uk/us-private-military-and-security-companies-fuel-corruption-and-conflict-risk> accessed 30 April 2024.

[124] 28 US Code s 1350.

[125] *Kiobel Et Al. v Royal Dutch Petroleum Co. Et Al.*, 133 US 1660 (2013), 1669.

[126] *Jesner v Arab Bank, PLC*, 584 US 1386 (2018), 1440.

[127] Kuzi Charamba, *Hired Guns and Human Rights—Global Governance and Access to Remedies in the Private Military and Security Industry* (Edward Elgar 2020) 16–17.

[128] 28 US Code Pt VI ch 171; 28 US Code s 1346(b).

[129] 10 US Code s 2734 (842.45).

[130] Kristine A Huskey, 'The American Way: Private Military Contractors & US Law After 9/11—An Update 2010' (2012) PRIV-War Report—The United States of America (National Reports Series 03/10) 1, 33–34.

[131] Although the Supreme Court left open the lingering question of whether the ATS applies to US corporations in *Nestle USA, INC. v Doe Et Al.*, 593 US 1 (2021), a majority of the Justices supported

teasing future watershed rulings on corporate violations of international law.[132]

The challenge of navigating overlapping jurisdictions across different dispute settlement bodies in pursuit of redress for new property interference is twofold. First, as neither the ICJ, nor investment arbitration tribunals, nor the US courts offer established outcomes for the spectrum of new property interference claims as well as their litigants, the choice of one dispute settlement body to proceed in over the others is largely speculative. Until the claim is brought, there is no way of predicting how the claim will be adjudged by the chosen dispute settlement body. Second, to enhance the reception of a test claim, it becomes necessary to present the claim in terms that resonate with the chosen dispute settlement body, which, as far as international courts and tribunals and domestic courts with universal jurisdiction go, is very often a Western-centric institution. The defence of new property, which explicitly rejects the viewing of property exclusively through the Western capitalist lens of private ownership, before Western-centric dispute settlement bodies may end up defeating new property. As bleakly observed by Baars, 'the role of lawyers persuading people to bring cases in (Western) foreign courts is in some way the equivalent of "spreading capitalist law" (as part of the civilising or *capitalising* mission) as done by the corporate colonisers in the nineteenth century . . . Thus, inadvertently, such cause lawyers come to create value for the corporation/corporate capitalism—extracted from those on whom the suffering has been inflicted as well as (often) the natural environment, and barely "compensated" if at all'.[133] New property interference cannot be efficiently redressed in the presence of numerous procedural hurdles, and cannot be effectively redressed in the absence of sufficient and appropriate international law content on property regulation. It is to the systemic shortcoming of content deficiency that the discussion now turns.

Gorsuch J's declaration that '[t]he notion that corporations are immune from suit under the ATS cannot be reconciled with the statutory text and original understanding' (Concurring Opinion, 1).

[132] cf Lucas Roorda and Julian Ku, 'Applying International Law to Corporations: The Limits to the Lessons Offered by the United States Experience with the Alien Tort Statute' in Jean Ho and Mavluda Sattorova (eds), *Investors' International Law* (Hart 2021) 218, where the authors predict that 'the proliferation of ATS lawsuits against corporations has mostly come to an end'.

[133] Grietje Baars, *The Corporation, Law and Capitalism—A Radical Perspective on the Role of Law in the Global Political Economy* (Brill 2019) 370–71.

3.2 Substantive deficiency

Substantive deficiency in international law's content on new property interference is evident from the existing regulatory regimes for cultural property, common property, and, to an arguably lesser degree, contingent property. The regulatory regime for cultural property is a haphazard amalgamation of international cultural heritage law, international criminal law, international investment law, and international trade law,[134] lacking a shared and principled definitional anchor for cultural property and, in turn, a principled approach to cultural property protection.[135] So despite a surfeit of treaties that may purportedly be harnessed to regulate cultural property either directly or indirectly, none of them actually redress cultural property interference via Configurations 1 (private trafficking of art and antiquities) and 2 (public-private trafficking of art and antiquities) with concrete, let alone effective, sanctions meted out through enforcement mechanisms. Similarly to the substantively deficient regime for cultural property, the various regulatory regimes for common property, such as the Antarctic, the Moon and other celestial objects, and the Area, are marked by an elaborate constellation of treaties and regulatory bodies that appear to govern meticulously on paper, but are highly permissive to the extent of being irresolute in practice.[136] The absence of consequences for common property-interfering actions across Antarctica, outer space, and the High Seas is the result of corporate, capitalist capture of the content of common property regulation,[137] which manifests in international law's current inability to redress common property interference via Configurations 3 (overt corporate overfishing in the High Seas) and 4 (covert corporate over-whaling in Antarctica). In contrast to the regulatory regimes for cultural and common property, the verdict of substantive deficiency in the regulatory content of international law for contingent property is more nuanced. While international law appears capable of redressing certain injured 'propertized' economic rights such as when state actors breach or terminate investment contracts, and withhold payment in satisfaction of judgments on legal claims,[138] it lacks the requisite regulatory content to sanction interference with contingent property when corporate actors leverage

[134] See Chapter 2, Section 2.
[135] See Chapter 2, Section 5.
[136] See Chapter 3, Section 3.
[137] See Chapter 3, Section 2.
[138] See Chapter 4, Sections 3.3.1, 3.3.2.

on force to wrest economic rights from states, as seen in Configurations 5 (the historical use of force by trading companies to seize trading concessions) and 6 (the modern engagement of force by PMSCs to extract mining concessions).

Effective redress of sanctionable interferences with new property in international law depends on four cumulative conditions being met: (i) the existence of an adjudicative forum applying international law for redress; (ii) the existence of valid causes of action in international law that can be submitted to that forum; (iii) the option to frame new property interference as a cognizable cause of action in international law before that forum; and (iv) the availability of tangible redress for interference amounting to injury to new property in the eyes of international law. The inability to satisfy any or all of these conditions denotes deficiency in the regulatory content of international law on new property. Configurations 1 (private trafficking of art and antiquities) and 3 (overt corporate overfishing in the High Seas) illustrate the difficulty of satisfying the various conditions for effective redress. The claimants source states in Configuration 1 may have a valid and cognizable cause of action in international law, namely the trafficking of cultural property in violation of Article 3 of the 1970 UNESCO Convention, but lack a forum in which such a cause of action can be brought against individual art smugglers and art dealers as respondents, thereby partially satisfying conditions (ii) and (iii), but not condition (i). Source state claimants can and have pursued redress against individual smugglers and dealers in domestic courts, but precedents reveal the framing of cultural property trafficking as domestic property infractions and the non-application of international law by domestic courts,[139] leading to the non-satisfaction of conditions (i), (ii), and (iii).[140] The claimant corporate fishers in Configuration 3 do not appear to possess a valid and cognizable cause of action in international law against respondent corporate overfishers. While corporate overfishers may be the primary actors in breaching sustainability obligations, such as Article 117 of UNCLOS and Article 28(1) of the BBNJ Agreement, there are no established benchmarks against which the fulfilment or otherwise

[139] *Cyprus v Goldberg 1989* (n 17) 1397–400.

[140] Some may venture that substantive deficiency in international law does not matter if domestic law can step in to fill the redress gap. However, as explained in Section 2.1.1, settling for the downgrading of an international infraction to a domestic infraction and domestic remedies for the sake of expediency trivializes decades worth of effort by states to strengthen, in word or in deed, cultural property protection. Unless these multiple, multilateral international lawmaking episodes are to be written off as meaningless overtures, aspiring towards an international law that is fit for redress purposes is surely preferable to acquiescing in an international law that is not.

of these obligations, which are formally binding only on states parties, can be measured. Moreover, there is no adjudicative forum where corporate fishers can seek redress from other corporate fishers for the unsustainable harvesting of common property, leading to the non-satisfaction of conditions (i), (ii), and (iii).

As existing treaties applicable to Configurations 1 and 3 assign the articulation of redress for art and antiquities trafficking and corporate overfishing in the High Seas to domestic legislators, the availability of tangible redress for new property interference in international law to satisfy condition (iv) must be sought elsewhere. One possible contender is Chapter II of the ASR where Articles 35,[141] 36,[142] and 37 list restitution, compensation, and satisfaction as forms of reparation for injury caused by internationally wrongful acts.[143] Although Chapter II provisions have been employed by some investment arbitration tribunals when determining the redress due from respondent host states to successful investor claimants, the fourth and final Special Rapporteur for the International Law Commission's codification project on state responsibility, which culminated in the ASR, stressed that Chapter II provisions are only applicable to state–state, and not investor–state, disputes.[144] Therefore, as Configurations 1 and 3 do not entail state–state dispute resolution, condition (iv) is not met. The present reality of substantive deficiency and procedural hurdles when redressing new property interference under international law can be alteredif, as some believe, international law is able to redress its own shortcomings. The following and final section of this chapter considers if the prospect of self-correction permits optimism in international law's future ability to better regulate new property.

[141] ASR (n 114) art 35 provides: 'A State responsible for an internationally wrongful act is under an obligation to make restitution, that is, to re-establish the situation which existed before the wrongful act was committed, provided and to the extent that restitution: (a) is not materially impossible; (b) does not involve a burden out of all proportion to the benefit deriving from restitution instead of compensation'.

[142] ASR (n 114) art 36 provides: '1. The State responsible for an internationally wrongful act is under an obligation to compensate for the damage caused thereby, insofar as such damage is not made good by restitution. 2. The compensation shall cover any financially assessable damage including loss of profits insofar as it is established'.

[143] ASR (n 114) art 37 provides: '1. The State responsible for an internationally wrongful act is under an obligation to give satisfaction for the injury caused by that act insofar as it cannot be made good by restitution or compensation. 2. Satisfaction may consist in an acknowledgement of the breach, an expression of regret, a formal apology or another appropriate modality. 3. Satisfaction shall not be out of proportion to the injury and may not take a form humiliating to the responsible State'. See also ASR art 34.

[144] James R Crawford, 'Similarity of Issues in Disputes Arising under the Same or Similarly Drafted Investment Treaties' in Emmanuel Gaillard and Yas Banifatemi (eds), *Precedent in International Arbitration* (Juris Publishing 2008) 99–100.

4. A critique of international law as a complex adaptive system and the outlook for new property regulation

A number of scholars have likened international law to a complex adaptive system (CAS) that 'at a minimum it can detect the disparity between various states that are relevant to its functioning, and identify the cause or nature of a disparity that must be corrected'.[145] Systems theory, in a nutshell, involves the study of different, interactive, component parts that make up a whole.[146] It has been considered a useful lens through which to view international law because it 'provides a top-down vantage point that helps, first, in providing an efficient descriptive model of the international system incorporating minimalist empirical assumptions of state behavior; second, in providing explanatory theories of causation for its set of norms; and third, in predicting generally the system's acceptance or rejection of new putative norms of customary international law'.[147] The descriptive, explanatory, and predictive claims of international law as CAS can be tested against the observation that international law adapts by receiving, processing, and responding to new information with change.[148] And this observation appears to be borne out, to varying degrees, in subfields of international law, such as international environmental law,[149] international human rights law,[150] and international economic law.[151]

The descriptive claim of international law as CAS stands as international environmental law, international human rights law, and international economic law are readily understood as multiple-treaty-based global governance systems for managing environmental phenomena, for upholding human dignity, and for standardizing permissions and prohibitions on cross-border trade and investment activities respectively. The explanatory claim of international law as CAS also stands, as a turn to the abridged history and evolution of each subfield reveals the driving forces behind its current state. International

145 James L Hildebrand, 'Complexity Analysis: A Preliminary Step Toward a General Systems Theory of International Law' (1973) 3 Georgia Journal of International and Comparative Law 271, 306.

146 Ludwig von Bertalanffy, 'The History and Status of General Systems Theory' in George J Klir (ed), *Trends in General Systems Theory* (Wiley-Interscience 1972) 410–11.

147 Anthony D'Amato, 'Groundwork for International Law' (2014) 108(4) American Journal of International Law 650, 651.

148 Hildebrand (n 145) 306.

149 Rakhyun E Kim and Brendan Mackey, 'International Environmental Law as a Complex Adaptive System' (2014) 14(1) International Environmental Agreements: Politics, Law and Economics 5, 15, 17.

150 Steven Wheatley, *The Idea of International Human Rights Law* (OUP 2019) 55.

151 Jean Frédéric Morin and others, 'The Trade Regime as a Complex Adaptive System: Exploration and Exploitation of Environmental Norms in Trade Agreements' (2017) 20(2) (Special Issue) Journal of International Economic Law 365, 368–69; Joost Pauwelyn, 'At the Edge of Chaos? Foreign Investment Law as a Complex Adaptive System, How It Emerged and How It Can Be Reformed' (2014) 29(2) ICSID Review—Foreign Investment Law Journal 372, 376.

environmental law emerged in the 1970s and evolved through a series of multilateral treaties, resolutions, and framework agreements at the initiative of states in response to scientific evidence of environmental degradation and adversity.[152] International human rights law emerged in the aftermath of the atrocities committed against human life and dignity during WWII and evolved through multilateral treaties and enforcing institutions articulating a list of fundamental liberties and rights accruing to every human being.[153] International economic law emerged in the 1940s with the rise of neoliberalism that champions free market competition. This led to the conclusion of multilateral trade agreements to remove barriers to cross-border free trade and the conclusion of bilateral investment treaties to promote and protect foreign investment flows between states.[154]

In contrast, the predictive claim of international law as CAS is debatable. Although legal responses to manage measurable environmental phenomena such as climate change are meant to be evidence-based, stakeholders are more often guided by political rather than scientific considerations when proposing or crafting updates to environmental regulations,[155] prompting the recommendation that '[h]aving the [international environmental law] system to adapt to global environmental changes may require transforming the legal system from merely a reflection of socio-politically agreed standards to something that proactively leads the change in social norms, as informed by science and guided by ethics'.[156] As the system of international environmental law currently stands, 'new putative norms' are only as predictable as the fickle winds of political change. Moreover, given how international human rights law was forged in crisis, it has been suggested that '[s]ignificant reshaping of the system is often the result of momentous events in world politics' and 'when international law undergoes significant change and these transformations cannot be foreseen, we must be aware of the irreversible flow of time through international law, which constantly moves from the past, through the present, to the future, as states and non-state actors respond to new information, but in unpredictable ways'.[157] The absence of a world political event as momentous as WWII after WWII may explain the absence of 'new putative norms' in

[152] Philippe Sands and Jacqueline Peele, *Principles of International Environmental Law* (4th edn, CUP 2018) 21–51.
[153] Wheatley (n 150) 56–58.
[154] Muthucumaraswamy Sornarajah, *The International Law on Foreign Investment* (5th edn, CUP 2021) 4–5.
[155] Fitzmaurice (n 54) 546.
[156] Kim and Mackey (n 149) 17.
[157] Wheatley (n 150) 56–58.

international human rights law. But even if such an event were to materialize in an unforeseeable form at an unforeseeable time, the lack of precedent on predicted change renders the content of and reception towards 'new putative norms' equally unforeseeable. Finally, the predictive claim scrabbles for purchase in international economic law. Few predicted the demise of the Appellate Body, the apex adjudicatory institution of the WTO, as a result of the US blocking appointments to the Appellate Body as members' terms expired. This 'surprise' move,[158] which threatened to throw the entire international trade dispute settlement mechanism into jeopardy, did not lead to the generation of any 'new putative norms' to fill the void and states appear to have settled for a dispute settlement mechanism without appeal. Similarly, few predicted that the substantive *and* procedural 'backlash' against investor overprotection and parallel proceedings in investment arbitration[159] would trigger ongoing multilateral efforts at *only* procedural reform of investment dispute settlement.[160]

An arguably weak predictive claim of international law as CAS does not discredit the use of systems theory to extrapolate international law's capacity to address emerging concerns. It does however imply limits on expectations regarding international law's ability to self-correct, and the extent of such self-correction, in every problematic situation. The occurrence and adequacy of self-correction may be influenced by two factors. The first is path dependence where past solutions to old problems bind present attempts to solve new problems, so much so that 'alternative approaches to existing rules become unthinkable, or even unimagined, as legal paradigms become locked-in'.[161] The second is a preference, grounded in systems theory, for norms that promote stability in international relations, which manifests in how 'international courts and tribunals will tend to be more receptive to a party's arguments if the norms it cites and the principles it relies upon are those that are likely to increase international stability and reduce future friction and controversies'.[162] Both factors are at play in the development of international economic law, where states continue to adhere to investment treaties as the key regulatory

[158] Simon Lester, 'Ending the WTO Dispute Settlement Crisis: Where to from Here?' *International Institute for Sustainable Development* (2 March 2022) <www.iisd.org/articles/united-states-must-propose-solutions-end-wto-dispute-settlement-crisis> accessed 30 April 2024.

[159] See generally Michael Waibel and others (eds), *The Backlash Against Investment Arbitration* (Kluwer Law International 2010).

[160] A glance through the United Nations Commission on International Trade Law Working Group III's agendas on Investor-State Dispute Settlement Reform from 2018 shows that delegates have chosen to focus on procedural reform, see UNCITRAL, 'Working Group III: Investor-State Dispute Settlement Reform' <https://uncitral.un.org/en/working_groups/3/investor-state> accessed 30 April 2024.

[161] Wheatley (n 150) 56.

[162] D'Amato (n 147) 655.

tools for foreign investment activity despite investment treaties being unsuited to the attainment of contemporary objectives such as responsible investor conduct.[163] As investment treaties are concluded between states for the protection of qualified investors and their qualifying investments, treaty treatment obligations are only binding on states. Investors, not being parties to investment treaties, can invoke treaty protection against states, but cannot be bound by the treaty to act in a certain way. And yet, states prefer to retain investment treaties as their primary vehicle for foreign investment regulation, inserting hortatory provisions on investor obligations in newer generation investment treaties,[164] over designing a better vehicle in pursuit of responsible investor conduct. As starting from scratch may entail abandonment of investment treaties and the potential disruption of bilateral relations, states appear to prioritize path dependence and a preference for stability by persisting with investment treaties as an ineffectual solution to the problem of errant investors. From the foregoing, international law as a whole possesses adaptive capacity, and can therefore be considered a CAS.[165] That said, the extent and nature of self-correction may not necessarily be sufficient or fitting, leaving the possibility that some problems may remain knowingly unresolved.

Despite observable displays of international law's adaptive capacity, mainly in the form of treaty signings and updates, in international environmental law, international human rights law, and international economic law, the outlook for new property regulation is mixed. While cultural property regulation will benefit most from the definitional alignment of illustrative cultural property and cultural heritage as new property to foster the development of a coherent body of international law,[166] its main regulating body of international cultural heritage law has been largely non-adaptive, remaining stagnant in content,[167]

[163] The point I make here does not contradict my earlier suggestion in Section 3.1.2 that host states may point to investor obligation provisions in investment treaties when bringing an arbitration claim against the misbehaving investor's home state for misinterpreting the treaty by failing to discipline its national. Resorting to state–state arbitration to drive home the importance of responsible investor conduct is one potential avenue for redressing new property interference by PMSCs, but it does not simultaneously endorse treaty tweaking as the best way forward for closing the investor accountability gap. For alternative means to secure investor accountability in general, see Jean Ho, 'International Law's Opportunities for Investor Accountability' in Jean Ho and Mavluda Sattorova (eds), *Investors' International Law* (Hart 2021) 28–43.

[164] See for instance the appearance of investor obligations provisions in the Reciprocal Investment Promotion and Protection Agreement Between the Government of the Kingdom of Morocco and the Government of the Federal Republic of Nigeria (signed 3 December 2016, not yet in force) arts 14 and 15; and in the Treaty Between the Republic of Belarus and the Republic of India on Investments (signed 24 September 2018, entered into force 5 March 2020) arts 11 and 12.

[165] Kim and Mackey (n 149) 15; Wheatley (n 150) 85–86; Morin and others (n 151) 381; Pauwelyn (n 151) 384–85.

[166] See Chapter 2, Section 4.

[167] See Chapter 2, Section 2.1

and heavily reliant on other specialist fields of international law for enforcement.[168] Resort, if at all, to more treaty signings and updates that purport to improve the existing regulatory regime for cultural property is unlikely to improve matters because part of the reason for the dysfunction is a surfeit, rather than a shortage, of treaties that have done little to advance the understanding of cultural property and the means for its protection. Like cultural property regulation, common property regulation is presently characterized by a surfeit of governing treaties, greatly minimizing the prospect of states and stakeholders advocating a fresh start on a clean slate. The signing of the BBNJ Agreement to address the sustainability deficit in the management of marine biological diversity in the High Seas suggests that treaty signings are still the preferred solution for concerned states plugging perceived content gaps in the existing common property regulatory regime. The rise of sustainability-conscious, or green, consumers may also be a ground-up trigger for international law's overall adaptive tendency to kick in.[169] Whether that begets yet another treaty signing, or the generation of more formally responsive but substantively non-adaptive resolutions and directives,[170] or some other solution to the problem of corporate capture of common property remains to be seen. In contrast, international law's adaptive capacity seems higher when it comes to contingent property, probably because the emergence or eradication of new property is primarily context-driven. As explained in the previous chapter, international law and contingent property appear to enjoy a symbiotic relationship, where the emergence of contingent property can trigger content development in international law, and where international law can adapt to changing contexts and attitudes by retracting the label of contingent property.[171] The generally favourable reception of international tribunals to the framing of contract claims as expropriation claims, entailing the 'propertization' of contract rights and the development of legal content to regulate contract as property,[172] is illustrative of international law's promising adaptive capacity towards certain types of new property.

The mixed outlook for new property regulation is further qualified by the numerous procedural hurdles and substantive deficiencies inherent in international law's institutions and content. As seen in the preceding section, these procedural and substantive obstacles stand in the way of redressing new

168 See Chapter 2, Sections 2.2–2.4.
169 See Chapter 3, Section 4.2.
170 See Chapter 3, Section 2.1.
171 See Chapter 4, Section 4.
172 See Chapter 4, Section 3.3.1.

property interference as they occur in Configurations 1 to 6, because none of these configurations map the two existing routes for property interference redress, namely, an expropriation claim by a foreign investor against a host state before an international tribunal, and a prosecution before the ICC for property destruction by an individual during armed conflict. International law adapted to and developed content to regulate attempts to 'propertize' investment contracts because these attempts were made in the form of investor claims against states in investment arbitration, and could be accommodated by one of the two existing routes for redressing property interference. The extent to which international law adapts to different configurations of new property interference thus depends on how strongly a particular configuration confronts international law's procedural hurdles and substantive deficiencies. The more procedural hurdles and substantive deficiencies a configuration of new property interference needs to overcome, the more remote the possibility of international law adapting to regulate and redress that configuration of new property interference.

5. Conclusion

This survey of how international law struggles to regulate six configurations of new property interference is an indictment of international law. The protagonists of this struggle are two categories of actors whose actions with regard to new property interference and redress reveal how far international law has fallen short of efficient new property regulation. The first category of actors are corporations which exhibit near omnipotence by repeatedly violating international law without earning sanction from international law. Corporate actors are responsible for the bulk of new property interferences as they feature as potential respondents in four out of six new property interference configurations, namely 3 (overt corporate overfishing in the High Seas), 4 (covert corporate over-whaling in Antarctica), 5 (the historical use of force by trading companies to seize trading concessions), and 6 (the modern engagement of force by PMSCs to extract mining concessions). The absence of established adjudicative forums to hear international claims against corporations, the absence of established causes of action in international law against corporations for new property interference, and the absence of redress options specific to corporate offenders explain apparent corporate immunity from international legal sanction.

These absences are the doing of the second category of actors—states—who feature as potential respondents in only one out of six new property interference configurations, namely Configuration 2 (public-private trafficking of art and antiquities), but who have by consensus or acquiescence maintained regulatory regimes that simply fail to hold corporations accountable for sanctionable new property interferences. To date, the treaty-based regulatory regimes for cultural property, common property, and contingent property impose obligations towards new property only on states, even though these obligations can be and have been violated by corporations. When treaties delegate corporate accountability for *international* wrongs to home states applying *domestic* law, it not only, inadvertently, creates an accountability gap for corporations in international law, it also undermines multilateral efforts at new property protection or preservation when home states fail to discipline their corporate nationals. Furthermore, the path-dependent and stability-oriented inclination of states towards treaty signings and updates to plug or correct substantive gaps in international law entrenches corporate unaccountability for new property interference because treaties will only impose binding, enforceable obligations on states, and not on corporations.

Together, aggressive corporate actors and accommodating state actors limit the capacity of international law to adapt fully to and effectively redress the spectrum of configurations of new property interference. The status of international law as CAS has been earned through treaty tweaks that supposedly target and resolve a given concern. However, if treaties are not a suitable vehicle for addressing a concern to begin with, treaty tweaks are at best a partial testament to international law's adaptive capacity. As the practice of concluding treaties upon treaties has not led to the satisfactory regulation of cultural, common, or contingent property, treaty tweaks are unlikely to bring about significant improvement to these flawed regulatory regimes. The removal of the procedural hurdles of conditional dispute settlement and overlapping jurisdictions, as well as the repair of substantive deficiency in the regulation and redress of new property interference, can only be secured through a revisionist approach to international law that goes beyond inobtrusive and ineffectual treaty tweaks. A functional international law that is finally fit for the purpose of new property regulation is surely a worthy destination for the more selfless stakeholders of international law.

Concluding Remarks

New property pushes international law to a regulatory breaking point. When treaties as stalwart sources of international law prescribe obligations without properly identifying and penalizing the violators of those obligations, regulatory regimes built on treaties, such as the ones currently applicable to cultural, common, and contingent property, resemble a mirage. They offer victims shimmering hope and reprieve from a distance but vanish when the victim gets close enough to contemplate and formulate redress for the wrong suffered. The story of international law constantly falling short of delivering what it promises to is the story of new property in international law.

The likeliest reason for the rift in international law between word and deed is the predominance of corporate, capitalist actors using and interfering with new property, preserved by the corporate, capitalist capture of the regulatory content and practices of international law. The capture began when mighty European trading companies managed to invoke international law to justify their blatant use of force to dominate trading routes and concessions in Asia. While the use of force was generally prohibited, it was conveniently permitted when corporate, capitalist interests were threatened or deemed to be at stake. The exceptional status accorded to Western capitalism took root and underscored extended acquiescence in or indifference to a capitalist depiction of property in international law that is grounded in the protection of private property ownership. Fixation on private ownership fostered neglect in other forms of property ownership and, in time, the seeming inability or unwillingness of international law's makers to recognize the different manifestations of imputable ownership in new property. The corporate, capitalist orientation of international law is evident from the complete absence of provisions in international instruments that are enforceable against corporations and individuals illegally trading cultural property (such as art and antiquities) for profit, from the complete absence of provisions in international instruments that are enforceable against corporations and individuals over-harvesting common property (such as whales in the Antarctic and fish in the High Seas) for profit, and from the complete absence of provisions in international instruments

New Property in International Law. Jean Ho, Oxford University Press. © Jean Ho 2024.
DOI: 10.1093/9780191976117.003.0007

that are enforceable against corporations and individuals extorting contingent property (such as mining and other extractive industry concessions) for profit. Once corporate, capitalist actors can use and interfere with others' use of new property with apparent impunity, their capture of international law is complete.

Can international law ever emerge from its current state of new property dysregulation to one day become fit for the purpose of new property regulation? The advocates of international law as a complex adaptive system will answer in the affirmative. But new property regulation is unlike, for instance, the flagging of auxiliary concerns in an ongoing dialogue over an object of regulation that is already well-defined. Treaty tweaks and updates arguably suffice for international environmental law to adapt to new scientific data on prevailing and projected environmental conditions, and for international economic law to adapt to sustainability concerns in the promotion of free trade and foreign investment protection, because the environment, free trade, and foreign investment possess their own widely accepted definitional markers. New property, in contrast, as this monograph has attempted to supply, is missing a definitional anchor. If property has to be reconceptualized with a different set of core attributes than before, the treaties crafted for old property are unlikely to be optimal vessels for change and adaptation when it comes to new property. Eschewing the negotiation of new treaties as the default solution to fill regulatory content gaps or fix regulatory content failings in international law, I believe that the future of new property regulation may lie in less institutionalized, less centralized forms of regulation.

Cultural property is currently regulated by an inchoate patchwork of regimes, some of which were not even established with cultural property governance or protection in mind. The splintering of cultural property into intangible cultural heritage and underwater cultural heritage and its assimilation to other non-proprietary objects of regulation has robbed property of its distinctive identity, and in turn, the impetus for its improved regulation in the form of developing more effective redress against its interference. Cultural property as new property loosens the corporate, capitalist grip on cultural property regulation in two ways. First, by diverting attention away from the protection of private ownership of property to the protection of imputable ownership of property, which can refer to state or public ownership, thereby discouraging continued viewing of property through a capitalist lens. Second, by offering a depiction of cultural property to fill the definitional gap across different regulatory regimes, thereby deflecting the risk of a tightening corporate grip on cultural property regulation inherent in opportunities to capitalize on a definitional void. Cultural property as new property will not completely overhaul the current fragmented regulation of cultural property. But it is poised to ensure that the different fragments are linked by a common thread, and that these fragments may eventually cohere and streamline cultural property regulation.

Common property is possibly the biggest casualty of the corporate, capitalist capture of international law. The leading actors in the exploitation of common property in the Antarctic, in outer space, and in the High Seas are private corporations, often doing so with the blessing (and in some cases, subsidies) from their respective home states. This may explain why existing treaties purporting to regulate the sustainable use of common property fail to offer complementary and enforceable redress of the unsustainable use of common property undertaken for the end of corporate profit-maximization. Common property as new property calls out the institutionalized hypocrisy of treating common property like private property and challenges the prevailing state practice of turning to centralized treaties to indirectly foster sustainable corporate practices. As common property belongs to all, a regulatory blueprint that reflects shared ownership and management of common resources for the benefit of all is preferable to the status quo where private, profit-oriented interests for the benefit of some hold sway. A better way to influence corporate behaviour may be through ground-up volition conditioning where sustainability-conscious consumers redirect their purchasing power towards sustainably sourced and sustainably produced merchandise. The dawn of voluntary corporate compliance with international sustainability pledges or obligations heralds the optimization of common property regulation in international law, and its approximation to successful models of common resource management.

Contingent property takes the corporate, capitalist capture of international law to the next level. While international law resolutely sanctions state interference with contingent property owned by corporate entities via unlawful expropriation claims, it is resolutely silent when corporate entities acquire contingent property from states through the use of force and in clear violation of international law. Contingent property performs a corrective function when the assimilation of a person, a thing, or a right, to property begets a preferential outcome for the claimant seeking redress for interference with his or her person, thing, or right. However, existing dispute settlement fora acknowledge this corrective function when a corporate entity seeks redress for contingent property interference by a state, but not vice versa. Contingent property may very well be the category of new property for which the articulation of pointers for better regulation proves elusive. When the existence of contingent property ebbs and flows with changing contexts, revisions to existing regulatory regimes must constantly keep up with newer circumstances. Any change is therefore more likely to be found in the adaptation or informal supplementation of existing rules through the practice of international law. Ad hoc adjustments will not free international law from its corporate, capitalist shackles, but they serve as important, if sporadic, reminders that an international law for the advancement of all humankind is still very much a work-in-progress.

A story of new property in international law that begins with a charge of dissonance between its parameters and its penalties, and ends with its capture by corporate, capitalist forces makes for decidedly grim reading. But even the darkest night eventually gives way to daylight. The glimmers of hope that punctuate this story illuminate a path towards a more profound, more progressive discourse between the stakeholders of international law on what property is and how it can be better regulated. This monograph has taken the first step in that direction.

Bibliography

Books

Ackerman B, *Private Property and the Constitution* (Yale University Press 1977).

Baars G, *The Corporation, Law and Capitalism—A Radical Perspective on the Role of Law in the Global Political Economy* (Brill 2019).

Baslar K, *The Concept of the Common Heritage of Mankind in International Law* (Martinus Nijhoff 1998).

Bittencourt N d O and others (eds), *Building Blocks for the Development of an International Framework for the Governance of Space Resource Activities—A Commentary* (Eleven 2020).

Bjorge E, *The Evolutionary Interpretation of Treaties* (OUP 2014).

Brand R A and Jablonski S R, *Forum Non Conveniens: History, Global Practice, and Future and the Hague Convention on Choice of Court Agreements* (OUP 2007).

Byers M and Boley A, *Who Owns Outer Space—International Law, Astrophysics, and the Sustainable Development of Space* (CUP 2023).

Charamba K, *Hired Guns and Human Rights—Global Governance and Access to Remedies in the Private Military and Security Industry* (Edward Elgar 2020).

Cheng B, *Studies in International Space Law* (OUP 1997).

Dalrymple W, *The Anarchy—The Relentless Rise of the East India Company* (Bloomsbury 2019).

Dingwall J, *International Law and Corporate Actors in Deep Seabed Mining* (OUP 2021).

Djeffal C, *Static and Evolutionary Treaty Interpretation—A Functional Reconstruction* (CUP 2016).

Douglas Z, *The International Law on Investment Claims* (CUP 2012).

Dromgoole S, *Underwater Cultural Heritage and International Law* (CUP 2013).

Elmahjub E, *An Islamic Vision of Intellectual Property—Theory and Practice* (CUP 2018).

Espinola-Arredondo A and Muñoz-Garcia F, *Common Pool Resources—Strategic Behaviour, Inefficiencies and Incomplete Information* (CUP 2022).

Fabre-Magnan M, *Droit des Obligations 2—Responsabilité civile et quasi-contrats* (5th edn, Presses Universitaires de France 2021).

Fitzhugh G, *Cannibals All! Slaves Without* Masters (Harvard University Press 1966).

Fox D, *Property Rights in Money* (OUP 2008).

Frischmann B M, *Infrastructure—The Social Value of Shared Resources* (OUP 2012).

Gardiner R, *Treaty Interpretation* (OUP 2015).

Georgy K and others (eds), *Legalism: Property and Ownership* (OUP 2017).

Gsovski V, *Soviet Civil Law* (University of Michigan Law School 1949).

Higgins R, *Problems and Process: International Law and How To Use It* (Clarendon Press 1995).

Ho J, *State Responsibility for Breaches of Investment Contracts* (CUP 2018).

Hohfeld W N, *Fundamental Legal Conceptions as Applied in Judicial Reasoning and Other Legal Essays* (Yale University Press 1919).

Ioffe O S, *Soviet Civil Law* (Martinus Nijhoff 1988).
van Ittersum M J, *Profit and Principle—Hugo Grotius, Natural Rights Theories and The Rise of Dutch Power in the East Indies (1596–1615)* (Brill 2006).
Jakubowski A, *State Succession in Cultural Property* (OUP 2015).
Jeffers O, *This Moose Belongs to Me* (HarperCollins 2012).
Jones-Rogers S E, *They Were Her Property—White Women as Slave Owners in the American South* (Yale University Press 2019).
Katzarov K, *The Theory of Nationalisation* (Anthony W Bradley tr, Martinus Nijhoff 1964).
Lauterpacht H, *Private Law Sources and Analogies of International Law* (Longmans, Green & Co. 1927).
Lawson F H and Rudden B, *The Law of Property* (2nd edn, OUP 1982).
Lawson F H and Rudden B, *The Law of Property* (3rd edn, OUP 2002).
Lim C L and others, *International Investment Law and Arbitration—Commentary, Awards and other Materials* (2nd edn, CUP 2021).
Lotsal M, *International Cultural Heritage Law in Armed Conflict* (CUP 2017).
Lovejoy P E, *Transformations in Slavery—A History of Slavery in Africa* (3rd edn, CUP 2011).
Marx K and Engels F, *The Communist Manifesto* (Samuel Moore tr, Penguin 2015, first published 1888).
McPherson C B (ed), *Second Treatise of Government* (Hackett Publishing Company 1980).
Munzer S R, *A Theory of Property* (CUP 1990).
Nafziger J A R and Paterson R K (eds), *Handbook on the Law of Cultural Heritage and International Trade* (Edward Elgar 2014).
Newton S, *The Constitutional Systems of the Independent Central Asian States—A Contextual Analysis* (Hart 2017).
Nolan J and Boersma M, *Addressing Modern Slavery* (University of New South Wales Press 2019).
O'Keefe P J, *Shipwrecked Heritage—A Commentary on the UNESCO Convention on Underwater Cultural Heritage* (2nd edn, Institute of Art and Law 2014).
O'Keefe R, *The Protection of Cultural Property in Armed Conflict* (CUP 2006).
Ostrom E, *Governing the Commons—The Evolution of Institutions for Collective Action* (CUP 1990, 2020 reprint).
Paulsson J, *The Unruly Notion of Abuse of Rights* (CUP 2020).
Penner J E, *Property Rights: A Re-Examination* (OUP 2020).
Penner J E, *The Idea of Property in Law* (OUP 1997).
Posner R A, *Economic Analysis of Law* (9th edn, Wolters Kluwer 2014).
Proudhon P-J, *Qu'est-ce que la propriété? Recherche sur le principe du droit et du gouvernement* (La Librarie de Prévot 1841).
Purdy J, *The Meaning of Property—Freedom, Community, and the Legal Imagination* (Yale University Press 2010).
di Robilant A, *The Making of Modern Property* (CUP 2023).
Rostill L, *Possession, Relative Title, and Ownership in Property* (OUP 2021).
Rothbard M N, *Man, Economy, and State with Power and Market* (2nd edn, Ludwig von Mises Institute 2009).
Rousseau J-J, *Du contrat social; ou Principes du droit politique* (Chez Marc-Michel Rey 1762).
Sadikov O N, *Soviet Civil Law* (M.E. Sharpe 1988).
Sands P and others, *Principles of International Environmental Law* (4th edn, CUP 2018).
Sasson M, *Substantive Law in Investment Treaty Arbitration—The Unsettled Relationship between International and Municipal Law* (Kluwer 2010).

Schrijver N, *Sovereignty Over Natural Resources—Balancing Rights and Duties* (CUP 1997).
Shirlow E, *Judging at the Interface—Deference to State Decision-Making Authority in International Adjudication* (CUP 2021).
Sornarajah M, *Resistance and Change in the International Law on Foreign Investment* (CUP 2015).
Sornarajah M, *The International Law on Foreign Investment* (4th edn, CUP 2017).
Sornarajah M, *The International Law on Foreign Investment* (5th edn, CUP 2021).
Sprankling J G, *The International Law of Property* (OUP 2014).
Stahn C, *Confronting Colonial Objects—Histories, Legalities, and Access to Culture* (OUP 2023).
Titi C, *The Parthenon Marbles and International Law* (Springer 2023).
Vadi V, *Cultural Heritage in International Investment Law and Arbitration* (CUP 2014).
Verdery K, *What Was Socialism, And What Comes Next?* (Princeton University Press 1996).
Vogler J, *The Global Commons—A Regime Analysis* (Wiley 1995).
Waibel M and others (eds), *The Backlash Against Investment Arbitration* (Kluwer Law International 2010).
Wang H, *China from Empire to Nation-State* (Michael G Hill tr, Harvard University Press 2014).
Wilentz S, *No Property in Man—Slavery and Antislavery at the Nation's Founding* (Harvard University Press 2019).
Wheatley S, *The Idea of International Human Rights Law* (OUP 2019).

Book Chapters

Bales K, 'Contemporary Coercive Labour Practices—Slavery Today' in Eltis D and others (eds), *The Cambridge World History of Slavery vol. 4 AD 1804–AD 2016* (CUP 2017) 655.
von Bertalanffy L, 'The History and Status of General Systems Theory' in Klir G J (ed), *Trends in General Systems Theory* (Wiley-Interscience 1972) 407.
Bradford A, 'Antitrust Law in Global Markets' in Elhauge E R (ed), *Research Handbook on the Economics of Antitrust Law* (Edward Elgar 2013) 283.
Burri M, 'Cultural Heritage and Intellectual Property' in Francioni F and Vrdoljak A F (eds), *International Cultural Heritage Law* (OUP 2020) 459.
Charney J, 'The Antarctic System and Customary International Law' in Francioni F and Scovazzi T (eds), *International Law for Antarctica* (2nd edn, Kluwer Law International 1996) 51.
Choudhury B, 'The Role of Soft Law Corporate Responsibilities in Defining Investor Obligations in International Investment Agreements' in Ho J and Sattorova M (eds), *Investors' International Law* (Hart 2021) 151.
Cotterrell R, 'The Law of Property and Legal Theory' in Twining W (ed), *Legal Theory and Common Law* (Basil Blackwell 1986) 90.
Crawford J R, 'Similarity of Issues in Disputes Arising under the Same or Similarly Drafted Investment Treaties' in Gaillard E and Banifatemi Y (eds), *Precedent in International Arbitration* (Juris Publishing 2008) 97.
Crossley P, 'Dependency and Coercion in East Asian Labor, 1800–1949' in Eltis D and others (eds), *The Cambridge World History of Slavery vol. 4 AD 1804–AD 2016* (CUP 2017) 540.
Dickinson A, 'Cryptocurrencies and the Conflict of Laws' in Fox D and Green S (eds), *Cryptocurrencies in Public and Private Law* (OUP 2019) 93.

Dinnen S, 'Trading in Security: Private Military Contractors in Papua New Guinea' in Dinnen S and others (eds), *Challenging the State: The Sandline Affair in Papua New Guinea* (The Australian National University 1997) 112.

Dolšak N and Ostrom E, 'The Challenge of the Commons' in Dolšak N and Ostrom E (eds), *The Commons in the New Millennium* (The MIT Press 2003) 3.

Douglas Z, 'Property, Investment and the Scope of Investment Protection Obligations' in Douglas Z and others (eds), *The Foundations of International Investment Law: Bringing Theory into Practice* (OUP 2014) 363.

Dua J, 'A Sea of Profit—Making Property in the Western Indian Ocean' in Kantor G and others (eds), *Legalism: Property and Ownership* (OUP 2017) 182.

Farrell A and Morgan M G, 'Multilateral Emission Trading: Heterogeneity in Domestic and International Common-Pool Resource Management' in Dolšak N and Ostrom E (eds), *The Commons in the New Millennium* (The MIT Press 2003) 169.

Finkleman P, 'Slavery in the United States—Persons or Property?' in Allain J (ed), *The Legal Understanding of Slavery: From the Historical to the Contemporary* (OUP 2012) 106.

Fitzmaurice M, 'Whales' in Jessie Hohmann and Daniel Joyce (eds), *International Law's Objects* (OUP 2018) 539.

Fox D, 'Cryptocurrencies in the Common Law of Property' in Fox D and Green S (eds), *Cryptocurrencies in Public and Private Law* (OUP 2019) 139.

Fuchs A E, 'Searching for Resources, Offering Security. . . Private Military Companies in Sierra Leone' in Jäger T and Kümmel G (eds), *Private Military and Security Companies—Chances, Problems, Pitfalls and Prospects* (VS Verlag 2007) 105.

Ho J, 'International Law's Opportunities for Investor Accountability' in Ho J and Sattorova M (eds), *Investors' International Law* (Hart 2021) 13.

Honoré A M, 'Ownership' in Guest A G (ed), *Oxford Essays in Jurisprudence—A Collaborative Work* (OUP 1961) 107.

van Ittersum M J, 'Hugo Grotius: The Making of a Founding Father of International Law' in Orford A and Hoffmann F (eds), *The Oxford Handbook of the Theory of International Law* (OUP 2016) 82.

Janssen M A and Ostrom E, 'Adoption of a New Regulation for the Governance of Common-Pool Resources by a Heterogenous Population' in Baland J-M and others (eds), *Inequality, Cooperation, and Environmental Sustainability* (Russell Sage Foundation/Princeton University Press 2007) 60.

Kramer D, 'Does History Repeat Itself? A Comparative Analysis of Private Military Entities' in Jäger T and Kümmel G (eds), *Private Military and Security Companies—Chances, Problems, Pitfalls and Prospects* (VS Verlag 2007) 23.

Kriebaum U and Schreuer C, 'The Concept of Property in Human Rights Law and International Investment Law' in Breitenmoser S and others (eds), *Human Rights, Democracy and the Rule of Law: Liber Amicorum Luzius Wildhaber* (Nomos 2007) 1.

Lambert T, 'Jurisdiction as Property in England, 900–1100' in Kantor G and others (eds), *Legalism: Property and Ownership* (OUP 2017) 115.

Parlett K, 'Diplomatic Protection and the International Court of Justice' in Tams C J and Sloan J (eds), *The Development of International Law by the International Court of Justice* (OUP 2013) 87.

Pech K, 'Executive Outcomes—A Corporate Conquest' in Cilliers J and Mason P (eds), *Peace, Profit or Plunder? The Privatisation of Security in War-Torn African Societies* (Institute for Security Studies 1999) 81.

Penner J E, 'Property Rights' in Gilbert M and others (eds), *The Palgrave Handbook on the Philosophy of Rights* (Palgrave MacMillan *forthcoming*).

Prott L V, 'International Standards for Cultural Heritage' in *UNESCO World Culture Report* (UNESCO 1998) 222.

Regan A J and Dinnen S, 'The Sandline Affair: A Chronology of Significant Events' in Dinnen S and others (eds), *Challenging the State: The Sandline Affair in Papua New Guinea* (Australian National University 1997) 9.

di Robilant A and Syed T, 'Property's Building Blocks: Hohfeld in Europe and Beyond' in Balganesh S and others (eds), *Wesley Hohfeld a Century Later—Edited Work, Select Personal Papers, and Original Commentaries* (CUP 2022) 223.

Roorda L and Ku J, 'Applying International Law to Corporations: The Limits to the Lessons Offered by the United States Experience with the Alien Tort Statute' in Ho J and Sattorova M (eds), *Investors' International Law* (Hart 2021) 213.

Sattorova M, 'The Foreign Investor as a Good Citizen: Investor Obligations to do Good' in Ho J and Sattorova M (eds), *Investors' International Law* (Hart 2021) 45.

Sichelman T M, 'Very Tight "Bundles of Sticks": Hohfeld's Complex Jural Relations' in Balganesh S and others (eds), *Wesley Hohfeld a Century Later—Edited Work, Select Personal Papers, and Original Commentaries* (CUP 2022) 345.

Skoda H, 'People as Property in Medieval Dubrovnik' in Kantor G and others (eds), *Legalism: Property and Ownership* (OUP 2017) 235.

Sornarajah M, 'Evolution or Revolution in International Investment Arbitration? The Descent into Normlessness' in Brown C and Miles K (eds), *Evolution in Investment Treaty Law and Arbitration* (CUP 2011) 631.

Sornarajah M, 'Linking State Responsibility for Certain Harms Caused By Corporate Nationals Abroad to Civil Recourse in the Legal Systems of Home States' in Scott C (ed), *Torture As Tort—Comparative Perspectives on the Development of Transnational Human Rights Litigation* (Hart Publishing 2001) 491.

Vadi V, 'Culture, Development and International Law: The Linkage Between Investment Rules and the Protection of Cultural Heritage' in Borelli S and Lenzerini F (eds), *Cultural Heritage, Cultural Rights, Cultural Diversity—New Developments in International Law* (Brill 2012) 413.

Verdery K, 'Fuzzy Property: Rights, Power, and Identity in Transylvania's Decollectivization' in Burawoy M and Verdery K (eds), *Uncertain Transition—Ethnographies of Change in the Postsocialist World* (Rowman & Littlehead Publishers 1999) 53.

Voon T, 'National Treasures at the Intersection Between Cultural Heritage and International Trade Law' in Francioni F and Vrdoljak A F (eds), *International Cultural Heritage Law* (OUP 2020) 507.

Woodward C W, 'George Fitzhugh, *Sui Generis*' in Fitzhugh G, *Cannibals All! Slaves Without Masters* (Harvard University Press 1966) 18.

Journal Articles

Allain J and Hickey R, 'Property and the Definition of Slavery' (2012) 61(4) International and Comparative Law Quarterly 915.

Allain J, 'The Nineteenth Century Law of the Sea and the British Abolition of the Slave Trade' (2007) 78(1) British Yearbook of International Law 342.

Almohamad A, 'The Destruction and Looting of Cultural Heritage Sites by ISIS in Syria: The Case of Manbji and its Countryside' (2021) 28(2) International Journal of Cultural Property 221.

Arewa O, 'Culture as Property: Intellectual Property, Local Norms and Global Rights' (2007) Northwestern Public Law Research Paper No 07-13.

Bindschedler R L, 'La Protection de la Propriété Privée en Droit International Public' (1959) 90 Recueil des Cours 174.
Blake J, 'On Defining the Cultural Heritage' (2000) 49 International & Comparative Law Quarterly 61.
Blake J, 'The Protection of the Underwater Cultural Heritage' (1996) 45(4) International and Comparative Law Quarterly 819.
Brownlie I, 'Causes of Action in the Law of Nations' (1979) 50(1) British Yearbook of International Law 13.
Byers M, 'Abuse of Rights: An Old Principle, A New Age' (2002) 47(2) McGill Law Journal 384.
Cao L, 'Chinese Privatization: Between Plan and Market' (2000) 63(4) Law & Contemporary Problems 13.
Carmine G and others, 'Who is the High Seas Fishing Industry?' (2020) 3 One Earth 730.
Chen W, 'Arbitrage for Property Rights: How Foreign Investors Create Substitutes for Property Institutions in China' (2015) 24(1) Washington International Law Journal 47.
Craven M, '"Other Spaces": Constructing the Legal Architecture of a Cold War Commons and the Scientific-Technical Imaginary of Outer Space' (2019) 30(2) European Journal of International Law 547.
Crawford J, 'Treaty and Contract in Investment Arbitration' (2008) 24(3) Arbitration International 351.
Crawford M J R, 'Contract as Property: Triangles and Tragic Choices' (2023) 82(1) Cambridge Law Journal 83.
D'Amato A, 'Groundwork for International Law' (2014) 108(4) American Journal of International Law 650.
Douglas S, 'The Nature of Conversion' (2009) 68(1) Cambridge Law Journal 198.
Eleftheriadis P, 'The Analysis of Property Rights' (1996) 16(1) Oxford Journal of Legal Studies 31.
Erie M S, 'Property as National Security' (2024) 1 Wisconsin Law Review 255.
Fachiri A, 'International Law and the Property of Aliens' (1929) 10 British Yearbook of International Law 32.
Farer T, 'The Hierarchy of Human Rights' (1992) 8(1) American University International Law Review 115.
Fikfak V, 'Changing State Behaviour: Damages Before the European Court of Human Rights' (2018) 29(4) European Journal of International Law 1091.
Fox D, 'Relativity of Title at Law and in Equity' (2006) 65(2) Cambridge Law Journal 330.
Gevers C, 'Refiguring Slavery Through International Law: The 1926 Slavery Convention, the 'Native Labor Code' and Racial Capitalism' (2022) 25(2) Journal of International Economic Law 312.
Gevers C, 'Slavery and International Law' (2023) 117 American Journal of International Law Unbound 71.
Gray K, 'Property in Thin Air' (1991) 50(2) Cambridge Law Journal 252.
Handl G F and others, 'A Hard Look at Soft Law' (1988) 82 Proceedings of the American Society of International Law 371.
Handler R, 'Cultural Property and Culture Theory' (2003) 3(3) Journal of Social Archaeology 353.
Higgins R, 'The Taking of Property by the State: Recent Developments in International Law' (1982) 176 Collected Courses of the Hague Academy of International Law 1.
Hildebrand J L, 'Complexity Analysis: A Preliminary Step Toward a General Systems Theory of International Law' (1973) 3 Georgia Journal of International and Comparative Law 271.

Ho J and others, 'Investor Responsibility: The Next Frontier in International Investment Law' (2019) 117 American Journal of International Law Unbound 1.
Islam M W, 'Al-Mal: The Concept of Property in Islamic Legal Thought' (1999) 14 Arab Law Quarterly 361.
Israel B L, 'Space Resources in the Evolutionary Course of Space Lawmaking' (2019) 113 American Journal of International Law Unbound 114.
Jamnejad M and Wood M, 'The Principle of Non-Intervention' (2009) 22(2) Leiden Journal of International Law 345.
Kennedy D and Michelman F, 'Are Property and Contract Efficient?' (1980) 8 Hofstra Law Review 711.
Kim R E and Mackey B, 'International Environmental Law as a Complex Adaptive System' (2014) 14(1) International Environmental Agreements: Politics, Law and Economics 5.
Koskenniemi M and Lehto M, 'The Privilege of Universality—International Law, Economic Ideology and Seabed Resources' (1996) 65 Nordic Journal of International Law 533.
Kuhn A K, 'Nationalization of Foreign-Owned Property in Its Impact on International Law' (1951) 45 American Journal of International Law 709.
Lacerda A L D F and others, 'Plastics in Sea Surface Waters around the Antarctic Peninsula' (2019) 9(3977) Nature 1.
Lametti D, 'The Concept of Property: Relations *Through* Objects of Social Wealth' (2003) 53(4) The University of Toronto Law Journal 325.
Lee P-W, 'Inducing Breach of Contract, Conversion and Contract as Property' (2009) 29(3) Oxford Journal of Legal Studies 511.
Low K F K, 'Bitcoins as Property: Welcome Clarity?' (2020) 136(Jul) Law Quarterly Review 345.
Low K F K and Teo E G S, 'Bitcoins and other Cryptocurrencies as Property?' (2017) 9(2) Law, Innovation and Technology 235.
McCorquodale R and Simons P, 'Responsibility Beyond Borders: State Responsibility for Extraterritorial Violations by Corporations of International Human Rights Law' (2007) 70(4) Modern Law Review 598.
Meron T, 'On a Hierarchy of International Human Rights' (1986) 80 American Journal of International Law 1.
Merrill T W, 'The Landscape of Constitutional Property' (2000) 86 Virginia Law Review 885.
Merryman J H, 'Thinking About the Elgin Marbles' (1985) 83(8) Michigan Law Review 1880.
Morin J F and others, 'The Trade Regime as a Complex Adaptive System: Exploration and Exploitation of Environmental Norms in Trade Agreements' (2017) 20(2) (Special Issue) Journal of International Economic Law 365.
Müller F S, 'The Hierarchy of Human Rights and the Transcendental System of Right' (2019) 20(1) Human Rights Review 47.
Münch F, 'Les Effets d'Une Nationalisation à l'Etranger' (1959) 89 Recueil des Cours 411.
Munzer S R and Raustiala K, 'The Uneasy Case for Intellectual Property Rights in Traditional Knowledge' (2009) 27 Cardozo Arts and Entertainment Law Journal 37.
Nelson J W, 'Safety Zones: A Near-Term Legal Issue on the Moon' (2020) 42(2) Journal of Space Law 604.
O'Connell M E, 'Beyond Wealth: Stories of Art, War and Greed' (2008) 59(4) Alabama Law Review 1075.
O'Keefe P J and Nafziger J A R, 'The Draft Convention on the Protection of the Underwater Cultural Heritage' (1994) 25(4) Ocean Development and International Law 391.
Ostroukh A, 'Russian Society and its Civil Codes: A Long Way to Civilian Civil Law' (2013) 6(1) Journal of Civil Law Studies 374.

Pan J, 'Chinese Philosophy and International Law' (2011) 1(2) Asian Journal of International Law 233.
Pardo A, 'The Origins of the 1967 Malta Initiative' (1993) 9 International Insights 65.
Pauwelyn J, 'At the Edge of Chaos? Foreign Investment Law as a Complex Adaptive System, How It Emerged and How It Can Be Reformed' (2014) 29(2) ICSID Review—Foreign Investment Law Journal 372.
Pearlstein W G, 'Claims for the Repatriation of Cultural Property: Prospects for a Managed Antiquities Market' (1996) 28(1) Law and Policy in International Business 123.
Pekkanen S M, 'Governing the New Space Race' (2019) 113 American Journal of International Law Unbound 92.
Penner J E, 'The "Bundle of Rights" Picture of Property' (1996) 43 UCLA Law Review 711.
Posner E, 'The International Protection of Cultural Property: Some Skeptical Observations' (2007) 8 Chicago Journal of International Law 213.
Prott L V and O'Keefe P J, '"Cultural Heritage" or "Cultural Property"?' (1992) 1(2) International Journal of Cultural Property 307.
Purdy J, 'People as Resources: Recruitment and Reciprocity in the Freedom-Promoting Approach to Property' (2007) 55(4) Duke Law Journal 1047.
Ranganathan S, 'Global Commons' (2016) 27(3) European Journal of International Law 693.
Reddy S, 'Making Heritage Legible: Who Owns Traditional Medical Knowledge?' (2006) 13(2) International Journal of Cultural Property 161.
Ross M and others, 'Potential Climate Impact of Black Carbon Emitted by Rockets' (2010) 37(24) Geophysical Research Letters L24810.
Sanchez J A and others, 'Physical Characterization of Metal-rich Neat-Earth Asteroids 6178 (1987 DA) and 2016 ED85' (2021) 2(5) The Planetary Science Journal 205.
Schrijver N, 'Managing the Global Commons: Common Good or Common Sink?' (2016) 37(7) Third World Quarterly 1252.
Shapreau C J, 'Extension of Express Abandonment Standard for Sovereign Shipwrecks in Sea Hunt, Inc. et al., Raises Troublesome Issues Regarding Protection of Underwater Cultural Property' (2001) 10(2) International Journal of Cultural Property 276.
Simanovic I, 'The Role of the ICTY in the Development of International Criminal Adjudication' (1999) 23(2) Fordham International Law Journal 440.
Stevens R, 'Crypto is Not Property' (2023) 139(Oct) Law Quarterly Review 615.
Sumaila R U and others, 'Winners and Losers in a World Where the High Seas is Closed to Fishing' (2015) 5(8481) Nature 1.
Sunder M, 'The Invention of Traditional Knowledge' (2007) 70 Law and Contemporary Problems 97.
Sunstein C R, 'On Property and Constitutionalism' (1993) 14 Cardozo Law Review 907.
Timmermans K, 'Intellectual Property Rights and Traditional Medicine: Policy Dilemmas at the Interface' (2003) 57(4) Social Science & Medicine 745.
Vandevelde K J, 'A Brief History of International Investment Agreements' (2005) 12(1) UC Davis Journal of International Law & Policy 157.
van de Veer D, 'Are Human Rights Alienable?' (1980) 37(2) Philosophical Studies: An International Journal for Philosophy in the Analytic Tradition 165.
Veseth M, 'The Economics of Property Rights and Human Rights' (1982) 41(2) American Journal of Economics and Sociology 169.
Volokh A, 'Property Rights and Contract Form in Medieval Europe' (2009) 11(2) American Law and Economics Review 399.
Wälde T and Kolo A, 'Environmental Regulation, Investment Protection and 'Regulatory Taking' in International Law' (2001) 50 International and Comparative Law Quarterly 811.

Wang L, 'The Modernization of Chinese Civil Law Over Four Decades' (2019) 14(1) Frontiers of Law in China 39.
Webb P and others, 'Culture at the Frontline: Addressing Attacks on Cultural Heritage' (2016) 14 Journal of International Criminal Justice 1139.
Weston B H, '"Constructive Takings" Under International Law: A Modest Foray into the Problem of "Creeping Expropriation"' (1975– 1976) 16 Vanderbilt Journal of International Law 103.
Williams J F, 'International Law and the Property of Aliens' (1928) 9 British Yearbook of International Law 1.
Witting C, 'Distinguishing Between Property Damage and Pure Economic Loss in Negligence: A Personality Thesis' (2001) 21(3) Legal Studies 481.
Wolff L-C, 'The Relationship Between Contract Law and Property Law' (2020) 49(1) Common Law World Review 31.
Wu M, 'The "China, Inc." Challenge to Global Trade Governance' (2016) 57(2) Harvard International Law Journal 261.

Newspaper and Magazine Articles, Press Releases, and Blog Posts

'China Plans More Moon Missions After Finding New Lunar Mineral' *Bloomberg News* (10 September 2022).
'China Rejects NASA Accusation it will Take over the Moon' *Reuters* (4 July 2022).
'Japan to Resume Whaling in Antarctic Despite Court Ruling' *BBC News* (28 November 2015).
'Rokke to be Released from Jail' *IntraFish* (25 September 2007).
'Vard to Build New Krill Fishing Vessel for Aker Biomarine' *Ship Technology* (15 February 2017).
Aikins M, 'How One Looted Artifact Tells the Story of Modern Afghanistan' *The New York Times Magazine* (8 March 2021).
Bailey M and Gerlis M, 'Guilty Plea over Antiquities' *The Art Newspaper* (5 September 2013).
Bailey S, 'Why Africa is Sending More Satellites into Space' *CNN* (6 October 2021).
Bernasconi-Osterwalder N, 'State-State Dispute Settlement in Investment Treaties' *International Institute for Sustainable Development* (October 2014) <www.iisd.org/system/files/publications/best-practices-state-state-dispute-settlement-investment-treaties.pdf>.
Birkhold M, 'The Iceberg Cowboys Who Wrangle the Purest Water on Earth' *Geoscience* (27 January 2023).
Birkold M, '$166 Water Could Dictate International Iceberg Law' *The Atlantic* (31 October 2019).
Bremmer I, 'China's Ambitious Plans in Antarctica have Raised New Suspicions' *Times* (28 April 2023).
Brodie N, 'Egyptian Objects Sold at Bonhams and Christie's London in 2013' (6 November 2015) <traffickingculture.org/encyclopedia/case-studies/Egyptian-objects-sold-at-bonhams-and-christies-london-in-2013/>.
Carrington D, 'Japan Killed 50 Whales in Antarctic Protected Area, Data Shows' *The Guardian* (4 September 2018).
Carter J, 'NASA Heads for "Psyche", A Mysterious Metallic Asteroid That Could Be The Heart Of A Dead Planet' *Forbes* (12 June 2019).
Cascone S, 'The Met Museum Returns More Looted Art to Greece and Turkey, Including 15 Antiquities Seized From Disgraced Dealer Subhash Kapoo' *Artnet* (3 April 2023).
Chestney N, 'Trawling Could Harm Oceans Like Ploughing Land' *Reuters* (6 September 2012).

Chow D, 'High Risk, High Reward: Startups Are Still Eager to Mine Space Rocks' *NBC News* (9 April 2023).

Coughlan S, 'Harvard Abolishes "Master" in Titles in Slavery Row' *BBC News* (25 February 2016).

Esau I, 'Africa Awaits: Mercenary Outfit Executive Outcomes is Reborn' *Upstream* (8 December 2020).

Feltman R, 'A Japanese Vessel is Set to Kill 333 Whales for "Research"—but is Science Really Behind the Hunt?' *The Washington Post* (30 November 2015).

Foust J, 'European Space Agency (ESA) Awards Contracts for Moon and Mars Exploration' *SpaceNews* (15 October 2020).

Gibbens S, 'Can the Ocean Feed a Growing World?' *National Geographic* (15 August 2018).

Gibbens S, 'High Seas Fishing Isn't Just Destructive—It's Unprofitable' *National Geographic* (7 June 2018).

Guerrero M, 'Opposition Grows Among Countries as Seabed-Mining Efforts Push Ahead' *PassBlue* (1 January 2023).

Harding L, 'The Space Race is Back On—But Who Will Win?' *The Guardian* (16 July 2021).

Harris G, 'What Happened to France's Grand Plans to Return African Heritage?' *The Art Newspaper* (1 June 2022).

Hart R, 'Meet the Billionaires Helping NASA Return to the Moon' *Forbes* (14 February 2024).

Hooper C, 'New Polar Strategy Must Focus on China's Long March to Antarctica' *Forbes* (10 January 2021).

Howcroft E, 'Insight: Crypto and Gaming Collide in High-Risk "Play-to-Earn" Economies' *Reuters* (9 April 2022).

International Seabed Authority, 'ISA Secretariat Holds the First 2023 Meeting of National Focus Points for Capacity Development' (19 May 2023) < www.isa.org.jm/news/isa-secretariat-holds-the-first-2023-meeting-of-national-focal-points-for-capacity-development/>.

International Telecommunication Union, 'About International Telecommunication Union (ITU)' <www.itu.int/en/about/Pages/default.aspx>.

Komiya K and Roulette J, 'Japan's ispace says Moon Lander Unexpectedly Accelerated and Likely Crashed' *Reuters* (26 April 2023).

Leins T, 'Out of this World: The International Satellite Broadband Battle Intensifies' (25 October 2021) <blog.telegeography.com/out-of-this-world-the-international-satellite-broadband-battle-intensifies>.

Lester S, 'Ending the WTO Dispute Settlement Crisis: Where to from Here?' *International Institute for Sustainable Development* (2 March 2022) <www.iisd.org/articles/united-states-must-propose-solutions-end-wto-dispute-settlement-crisis>.

Lies E, 'Outlook Uncertain for Japan's Whaling Industry Despite Commercial Restart' *Reuters* (24 June 2019).

Ling X, 'China's Moon Ambitions Take Shape with Construction Road Map for Research Station', *South China Morning Post* (25 April 2023).

Lipton E, 'Leader of International Seabed Mining Agency Admonished by Diplomats' *The New York Times* (19 March 2023).

Lipton E, 'Secret Data, Tiny Islands and a Quest for Treasures on the Ocean Floor' *The New York Times* (29 August 2022).

MAD Paris, '1980s. Fashion, Design and Graphics in France' <madparis.fr/ExpoAnnees80>.

Marelli C, 'Louis Ghost, The World's Best Selling Design Chair' *Elle Décor* (16 January 2023) <www.elledecor.com/it/best-of/a42673157/louis-ghost-design-chair-best-seller>.

McClanahan P, 'Tourism in Antarctica: Edging Toward the (Risky) Mainstream' *The New York Times* (26 February 2020).

McVeigh K, 'High Seas Treaty: Historic Deal to Protect International Waters Finally Reached at UN' *The Guardian* (5 March 2023).

McVeigh K, 'Row Erupts Over Deep-Sea Mining as World Races to Finalise Vital Regulations' *The Guardian* (21 March 2023).

Miller J and Kinzer S, 'Greek Orthodox Church Icons Ravaged in the Turkish Part of Cyprus' *The New York Times* (1 April 1998).

Miriri D, 'Hundreds of Millions of Dollars Pledged for African Carbon Credits at Climate Summit' *Reuters* (6 September 2023).

Mohdin A and Storer R, 'Tributes to Slave Traders and Colonialists Removed across UK' *The Guardian* (29 January 2021).

Nakamoto S, 'Bitcoin: A Peer-to-Peer Electronic Cash System' <bitcoin.org/bitcoin.pdf>.

NASA, 'Latest Contract Releases' <www.nasa.gov/office/procurement/latest-contract-releases>.

NASA, 'NASA Awards SpaceX Second Contract Option for Artemis Moon Landing' (16 November 2022).

NASA, 'NASA Selects Blue Origin as Second Artemis Lunar Lander Provider' (19 May 2023).

Picard M, 'US Private Military and Security Companies Fuel Corruption and Conflict Risk' *Transparency International UK* <www.transparency.org.uk/us-private-military-and-security-companies-fuel-corruption-and-conflict-risk> (9 August 2022).

Rachwani M, 'Japan's New Whaling "Mother Ship" Being Built to Travel as Far as Antarctica' *The Guardian* (16 February 2023).

Radford A, 'Vatican Returns Parthenon Sculptures to Greece' *BBC News* (25 March 2023).

Reuhl M, 'Singapore Bondholders Prepare to Sue Switzerland over Credit Suisse' *Financial Times* (20 April 2023).

Riordan P and Croft J, 'UK Chambers Removes Xinjiang Genocide Opinion Reference After China Sanctions' *Financial Times* (28 March 2021).

Roeloffs M W, 'Modern Space Race: Japan Pledges $6.6 Billion for Developing Space Sector as U.S. and China Plan Historic Missions' *Forbes* (21 November 2023).

Rubin E, 'Saving Sierra Leone, at a Price' *The New York Times* (4 February 1999).

Ryall J, 'How a Dispute over Whaling could Spur Japan's Exit from US Indo-Pacific Trade Pact: "Kishida has Zero Leeway"' *South China Morning Post* (15 August 2023).

Schachter O, 'Who Owns the Universe?' *Collier's Weekly* (22 March 1952) 71.

Seymour T, 'Is Ukrainian Cultural Heritage under Coordinated Attack?' *The Art Newspaper* (10 June 2022).

Stoilas H, 'Ten Most Wanted Antiquities: Have You Seen These Missing Artefacts?' *The Art Newspaper* (30 October 2020).

Syal R, 'Krilling for Oil' (6 September 2021) <www.oceansinc.earth/krilling-for-oil>.

Syal R, 'Licence to Krill: The Destructive Demand for a "Better" Fish Oil' *The Guardian* (7 September 2021).

Tan J, 'Chefs Explain: Why the Elusive Turbot Fish is Worth its Hefty Price Tag' *Lifestyle Asia* (10 November 2021).

Tsachevsky V, 'Konstatin Katzarov: A Life Devoted to the Sciences and Bulgaria' (17 April 2016) <philosophyclub.bg/konstantin-katzarov-a-life-devoted-to-the-science-and-bulgaria/>.

UNESCO, 'International Day against Illicit Trafficking in Cultural Property' <www.unesco.org/en/days/against-illicit-trafficking?TSPD_101_R0=080713870fab20009695cee851ae9e0f1ed769a940a3239dd2903b816f0c8fd3ea5f0c4fc81a6fe608e90245b8143000324a17ce2e2cb6a59320a88252934f7d498e005cb54e57273b92605511dbae687b5d0935bc3103717a463d14b377efd9>.

Weale S, 'Cambridge College Seeks to Remove Memorial to Patron with Links to Slave Trade' *The Guardian* (15 November 2021).

Weinzierl M and Sarang M, 'The Commercial Space Age is Here' *Harvard Business Review* (12 February 2021).

Wong A, 'Space Mining Could Become a Real Thing—and It Could be Worth Trillions' *CNBC* (15 May 2018).

Yamaguchi M, 'Japan Says It Has "Achieved Its Plan" by Killing 333 Antarctic Whales' *The Independent* (1 April 2017).

Young J, 'Balliol College Oxford Apologies for 300 Years of Taking Slavery Cash' *The Times* (21 March 2021).

Zielinski L Y, 'Disputes over Space Mining on the Horizon?' (18 January 2023) <www.ibanet.org/disputes-over-space-mining-on-the-horizon>.

Official Documents

Ballesteros E B (Special Rapporteur), 'Final Report on the Use of Mercenaries as a Means of Violating Human Rights and Impeding the Exercise of the Right of Peoples to Self-Determination' United Nations Economic and Social Council (24 December 2003) E/CN.4/2004/15.

CCAMLR, 'Illegal, Unreported and Unregulated (IIU) Fishing' <www.ccamlr.org/en/compliance/illegal-unreported-and-unregulated-iuu-fishing>.

CCAMLR, 'Krill Fisheries and Sustainability' <www.ccamlr.org/en/fisheries/krill-fisheries-and-sustainability>.

CCAMLR, 'Schedule of Conservation Measures' <www.ccamlr.org/en/system/files/e-schedule2022-23.pdf>.

Executive Order 13914, 'Encouraging International Support for the Recovery and Use of Space Resources' (6 April 2020).

House of Commons, 'Chapter 2—The Private Military Companies Perspective' (1 August 2002) <publications.parliament.uk/pa/cm200102/cmselect/cmfaff/922/2061322.htm>.

Huskey K A, 'The American Way: Private Military Contractors & US Law After 9/11—An Update 2010' (2012) PRIV-War Report—The United States of America (National Reports Series 03/10).

International Whaling Commission, 'Statement of Government of Japan Withdrawal from IWC' (14 January 2019) <iwc.int/resources/media-resources/news/statement-on-government-of-japan-withdrawal>.

INTERPOL, 'Fighting the Illicit Trafficking of Cultural Property' (2018) <www.interpol.int/content/download/8553/file/UNESCO%20Toolkit%20to%20fight%20the%20illicit%20trafficking%20of%20cultural%20property_web....pdf>.

Koskenniemi M, 'Fragmentation of International Law: Difficulties Arising from the Diversification and Expansion of International Law' Report of the Study Group of the International Law Commission (13 April 2006) UN Doc A/CN.4/L.682.

NASA, 'Artemis Accords' <www.nasa.gov/specials/artemis-accords/img/Artemis-Accords-signed-13Oct2020.pdf>.

Secretariat of the Antarctic Treaty, 'ATCM and Other Meetings' <www.ats.aq/e/atcm.html>.

Secretariat of the Antarctic Treaty, 'Final Report of the Fifteenth Antarctic Treaty Consultative Meeting' (9–20 October 1989, Paris, France) <www.ats.aq/devAS/Meetings/DocDatabase?lang=e>.

Secretariat of the Antarctic Treaty, 'Final Report of the Eighteenth Antarctic Treaty Consultative Meeting' (11–22 April 1994, Kyoto, Japan) <www.ats.aq/devAS/Meetings/DocDatabase?lang=e>.

Secretariat of the Antarctic Treaty, 'Final Report of the Twenty-Seventh Antarctic Treaty Consultative Meeting' (24 May–4 June 2004, Cape Town, South Africa) <www.ats.aq/devAS/Meetings/DocDatabase?lang=e>.

Secretariat of the Antarctic Treaty, 'Final Report of the Thirty-Seventh Antarctic Treaty Consultative Meeting' (28 April–7 May 2014, Brasília, Brazil) <www.ats.aq/devAS/Meetings/DocDatabase?lang=e>.

Secretariat of the Antarctic Treaty, 'Final Report of the Forty-Third Antarctic Treaty Consultative Meeting' (14–24 June 2021, Paris, France) <www.ats.aq/devAS/Meetings/DocDatabase?lang=e>.

UK Law Commission, 'Digital Assets: Final Report' (Law Com No 412, 2023) <www.lawcom.gov.uk/project/digital-assets/>.

UN General Assembly, 'Declaration on the Rights of Indigenous Peoples' (13 September 2007) A/Res/61/295.

UN Press Release SEA/1619 (16 July 1999).

UNCITRAL, 'Working Group III: Investor-State Dispute Settlement Reform' <uncitral.un.org/en/working_groups/3/investor-state>.

UNESCO, 'Convention for the Protection of Cultural Property in the Event of Armed Conflict with Regulations for the Execution of the Convention' <en.unesco.org/node/297944/#edit-sort-by>.

UNESCO, 'Convention on the Means of Prohibiting and Preventing the Illicit Import, Export and Transfer of Ownership of Cultural Property' <en.unesco.org/about-us/legal-affairs/convention-means-prohibiting-and-preventing-illicit-import-export-and>.

UNESCO, 'Fight Illicit Trafficking (1970 Convention)' <en.unesco.org/fighttrafficking/1970>.

UNESCO, 'Fund of the Convention' <en.unesco.org/fighttrafficking/funds>.

UNESCO, 'The Operational Guidelines for the Implementation of the World Heritage Convention' <whc.unesco.org/en/guidelines/>.

UNESCO, 'Training' <en.unesco.org/fighttrafficking/training>.

United Nations Office on Drugs and Crime, 'Signature and Ratification Status' <www.unodc.org/unodc/en/corruption/ratification-status.html>.

United Nations Security Council, 'Final Report of the Panel of Experts on the Illegal Exploitation of Natural Resources and Other Forms of Wealth of the Democratic Republic of the Congo' (S/2002/1146).

United Nations, 'Guiding Principles on Business and Human Rights' <www.ohchr.org/sites/default/files/documents/publications/guidingprinciplesbusinesshr_en.pdf>.

WIPO, 'Traditional Knowledge and Intellectual Property—Background Brief' <www.wipo.int/pressroom/en/briefs/tk_ip.html>.

Yoshikawa M, 'Declarations Recognizing the Jurisdiction of the Court as Compulsory' (6 October 2015) <www.icj-cij.org/declarations/jp>.

Websites

'Aker Biomarine' <www.akerbiomarine.com>.

Coinranking, 'Cryptocurrencies Prices and Signals' <coinranking.com>.

Global Fishing Watch <globalfishingwatch.org/map/?latitude=21.3427880283446&longitude=-21.703099042749272&zoom=0.6977892660286947&start=2023-02-25T00%3A00%3A00.000Z&end=2023-05-25T00%3A00%3A00.000Z&dvIn[0][id]=context-layer-graticules&dvIn[0][cfg][vis]=false&dvIn[1][id]=context-layer-high-seas&dvIn[1][cfg][vis]=true&sidebarOpen=false>.

NASA, 'About Glaciers' <climate.nasa.gov/giv-about-glaciers/#:~:text=Glaciers%20have%20white%20surfaces%20that,This%20raises%20temperatures%20even%20more>.

NASA, 'What is an Orbit?' <www.nasa.gov/audience/forstudents/k-4/stories/nasa-knows/what-is-orbit-k4.html>.

Parlevliet & van der Plas, 'Our Mission' <www.pp-group.nl/en-us/home/id/2>.

Polewater, 'Solution' <www.polewater.com/en/solution/>.

Powell F, '10 Best Crypto Apps & Exchanges of 2023' <web.archive.org/web/20231029201503/https://www.forbes.com/advisor/investing/cryptocurrency/best-crypto-exchanges/>.

Pultarova T, 'How many satellites can we safely fit in Earth orbit?' (27 February 2023) <www.space.com/how-many-satellites-fit-safely-earth-orbit>.

Svalbarði <svalbardi.com>.

UNICEF, 'What Are Human Rights?' <www.unicef.org/child-rights-convention/what-are-human-rights#:~:text=Whether%20civil%2C%20political%2C%20economic%2C,no%20hierarchy%20of%20human%20rights>.

World Sustainability Organisation, 'Friend of the Sea—Certification for Sustainable Seafood, Fisheries and Aquaculture Products' <friendofthesea.org/friend-of-the-sea/>.

Index

For the benefit of digital users, indexed terms that span two pages (e.g., 52–53) may, on occasion, appear on only one of those pages.